DICKENS and the SOCIAL ORDER

DICKENS
and the
SOCIAL ORDER

Myron Magnet

ISI Books
Wilmington, Delaware
2004

This work was funded in part by the National Endowment for the Humanities
Publications Program.

Magnet, Myron.

Dickens and the social order / Myron Magnet. — 2nd ed. — Wilmington, Del. :
ISI Books, 2004.

       p. ; cm.

       First ed. published: Philadelphia : University of Pennsylvania Press, 1985.
       Includes index.
       ISBN: 1932236376

       1. Dickens, Charles, 1812–1870—Political and social views. 2. Literature
       and society—England—History—19th century. 3. Social problems in
       literature. 4. Social control in literature. I. Title.

PR4592.S58 M34 2004   2004102728
823.8—dc22   CIP

Published in the United States by:

       ISI Books
       Post Office Box 4431
       Wilmington, Delaware 19807
       www.isibooks.org

ISI Books is the imprint of the Intercollegiate Studies Institute

Cover design by Sam Torode

Manufactured in the United States of America

To Barbara Crehan

Contents

Acknowledgments

This book has been long in the making, and it has benefited at every stage of its evolution from the generous advice of discerning readers. I am deeply grateful for the learned, careful, and encouraging reading Professors Quentin Anderson and Carl R. Woodring gave its first version, and also for the spiritedly challenging one it received from Professor Steven Marcus. To Professor Robert Newsom I owe a heavy debt for his extensive commentary on a later version, lavish alike in its scholarship and its friendliness. Professors Richard D. Altick, Gertrude Himmelfarb, and Robert L. Patten read the manuscript in time for me to incorporate their unfailingly wise suggestions; I thank them heartily. I acknowledge the support afforded me by the Andrew W. Mellon Foundation when I worked on this book as a member of the Society of Fellows in the Humanities at Columbia University, and I am grateful to the National Endowment for the Humanities for supporting the publication of this volume. My greatest debt is to my wife and closest colleague, Dr. Barbara Crehan. Her invaluable, judicious help and collaboration at every stage and in every day formed the pleasure of writing this book.

Preface to the ISI Edition

Aristotle perhaps didn't go far enough when he said that tragedy was more philosophic than history, concentrating as it does on what *might be* rather than merely on what had been. He might have gone on to say that tragedy— or, more broadly, literature—is more philosophic even than philosophy. It is, after all, a form of knowledge that draws on all our ways of knowing, rather than on ratiocination alone. And it is a more intense, as well as a broader, form of knowledge, since, unlike philosophy, it isn't constantly taking its own pulse, or checking its instruments, anxiously asking itself how it can know this or that. As Dickens would say, it just goes and knows it.

When I began to write *Dickens and the Social Order* over two decades ago, the belief that literature was a repository of knowledge—and important knowledge—was usual enough for critics to take it for granted. At the very least, everybody understood that literature was a treasure trove of documentary knowledge. We could learn about how others lived—the Greeks, the men of the Middle Ages, our own contemporaries: how they judged one another, what they considered good manners, how they fell in love, what their family life was like, how they structured their society, when they dined, how they grew up and took their place in the world of adults.

But that was only the beginning. Literature also teaches us more about psychology than the psychologists can. The inner life—and its relation to the outer appearance, from which it is often (and proverbially) very different—is literature's special subject. It is a particularly complex subject, with its interweaving of motives and impulses, as appetites grapple with ideals, as consciousness both registers and distorts external reality, as natural promptings intersect with social ambitions, and the universal in our nature takes on the fashion and the garb of a particular age.

Here literature's weakness—that, unlike philosophy, it is unsystematic—becomes its great strength. It draws on all our ways of knowing at once: not just the analysis of the outer world, but introspection and intuition as well. We can understand what is going on in the hearts of others because we know what stirs our own hearts, and what *could* stir them. When a writer imagines his characters' inner drama, his description rings true to us because we have felt similar impulses or imagined analogous situations, and, further, can identify sympathetically with something beyond our ken. We grasp intuitively the complex internal mix: the simultaneous interplay of feelings, thoughts, beliefs, and hopes, of conscious and subliminal impulses—as pity combines with social anxiety, say, or eros or vanity or sudden insight to impel a character to behave as he behaves. Literature is the great school of motivation: it teaches us how, out of the complex welter of impulses churning within us, we make the choices that define us and seal our fate.

And it dramatizes for us the consequences of those choices. Do they lead to happiness or misery, decency or not—and for whom? What does the high-handedness of Agamemnon and the anger of Achilles produce? What dire offense from am'rous causes springs? What results from the choices of Emma Bovary and Anna Karenina? What happens to the soul of a man who kills a "useless" old pawnbroker—or, at the urging of his wife, the king of Scotland?

These choices have ramifications not just for individuals but, often, for the whole social order. On many levels, therefore, literature is asking: How should we live? What is the right life for man? And to ask such questions it must ask the further question: What is human nature, and what guideposts and constraints does it set for the kind of life we can choose? How do we realize to the fullest the potentialities for excellence and happiness with which nature endows us? Therefore (to make matters even more richly complex), even while literature is mobilizing all our ways of knowing at once, it often is also taking two simultaneous perspectives, the personal and the social—and examining (at least implicitly) the ways in which the two realms intersect with and affect each other. Like a great polyphonic musical work, many different voices interweave to create one larger harmony, transcending the sum of its parts.

Literature is a conversation across the ages about our experience and our nature, a conversation in which, while there isn't unanimity, there is a surprising breadth of agreement. Literature amounts, in these matters, to the accumulated wisdom of the race, the sum of our reflections on our own existence. It begins (especially in novels like those I discuss here) with observation, with reporting, rendering the facts of our inner and outer reality with acuity sharpened by imagination. At its greatest, it goes on to show how these facts have coherence and, finally, meaning. As it dramatizes what actually happens to concrete individuals trying to shape their lives at the confluence of such a multiplicity of imperatives, it presents us with concrete and particular manifestations of universal truths. For as the greatest authors know, the universal has be embodied in the particular—where, as it is enmeshed in the complexity and contradictoriness of real experience, it loses the clarity and lucidity that only abstractions can possess.

Well, you may object, if this is what literature's insights amount to, then it is a realm of opinion, not knowledge. And in fact just such doubts were eating away at the confidence of literary critics, with growing force, over the years that I wrote *Dickens and the Social Order*. In the face of science, with its spectacular practical achievements and its unequivocal experimental truths, what claim had literature to a kind of truth? In what way could literature constitute knowledge? Wasn't it just fantasy—interesting perhaps, but ultimately ephemeral and useless? And if anyone wanted to know about the world that literature supposedly elucidated, did we not have the "human sciences"—studies like sociology and psychology and anthropology, which brought the rigor and authority of science (or so their practitioners claimed, at least) to what literature handled in so amateur a fashion?

In the decades I happily spent in journalism after writing this book, I couldn't help but develop an almost automatic skepticism about the claims of the human sciences, even sometimes about the claims of the harder sciences. How many "studies" and "reports," with tables of data in small print appended, purported to reveal truths about welfare or policing or sex education but in fact revealed nothing but the initial prejudices of the "investigators"? My epiphany came when I interviewed the nation's leading climatologists for a magazine article on acid rain and discovered mostly ideology, not knowledge. When I also learned years ago that academic paleontologists at that time couldn't hope to get tenure if they questioned the theory that a giant meteor explosion had caused the extinction of the dinosaurs—thus providing a model of what a so-called "nuclear winter" would produce—my skepticism took on a certain wryness.

The social scientists have a mantra: "The plural of anecdote is not data." I beg to differ. An accumulation of accurate stories about how the human world works, stories that provide an account wrapped in an interpretation, add up to knowledge, better knowledge than we can get elsewhere. Data are meaningless until we can articulate a story that makes sense out of them, after all, and literature makes sense out of the data of human experience.

Can anyone think that there is more understanding to be gained about the human heart from Freud than from Shakespeare—that the studies of Dora or the Wolf Man approach anywhere near to the profundity of understanding embodied in *Macbeth* or *Lear*, with their unflinching elucidation of man's (and woman's) capacity for evil? Can anyone think that the studies of Margaret Mead or Alfred Kinsey tell us anything nearly as true as Virgil or Ovid? Does the sociobiology of E. O. Wilson or Richard

Dawkins tell us any more than we learn from Homer or Yeats?

An exquisite little poem of Tennyson's, called *1865–66*, sums up this point infinitely better than I could do:

> I stood on a tower in the wet,
> And New Year and Old Year met,
> And winds were roaring and blowing;
> And I said, 'O years, that meet in tears,
> Have ye aught that is worth the knowing?
> Science enough and exploring,
> Wanderers coming and going,
> Matter enough for deploring,
> But aught that is worth the knowing?'
> Seas at my feet were flowing,
> Waves on the shingle pouring,
> Old Year roaring and blowing,
> And New Year blowing and roaring.

What's wanted is wisdom: the ability to see into the heart of things. This is the kind of knowledge that Plato describes so poetically in that most literary of all philosophical passages, the allegory of the cave. It is the knowledge that sees through the world of appearances to the Truth, of which the appearances are but an emanation—a knowledge that requires a lifetime of reason and study to attain but that comes finally in a flash of intuition, because the Truth is in us, in an inner nature we can glimpse by introspection and intuition, as well as in the world. And this is the knowledge that great literature embodies.

It is a knowledge that has its practical uses, too, no less than scientific knowledge, for if it doesn't build computers or space shuttles, it builds civilizations. It defines what it means to be human, dramatizing the values and ideals, the web of culture, that differentiate us from the beasts.

Consider three very brief examples. Start with Sophocles, since *Oedipus Rex* really does stand at the beginning of our tradition. Here is a work in which the author stacks the deck just as much as you can possibly stack it. A man commits two terrible crimes—universally terrible, not just bad by the standards of this or that society. But he didn't know that he was committing them; he didn't know that the man he killed was his father or the queen he married was his mother. Not knowing what he was doing, he certainly didn't *intend* to commit these crimes. Furthermore, he was *fated* to do these terrible things, as oracles plainly stated at his birth. So with every kind of extenuating circumstance surrounding his actions, was he responsible?

Sophocles answers with a resounding Yes. What it means to be human, he shows us, is to take responsibility for one's actions. In a world of uncertainty and chance, where so much is out of our control, this is the only way we can assert that we are moral creatures with free will, whose doings have meaning, rather than beings who are simply part of the mere flux and confusion of brute creation. This is a hard doctrine, but one that has undiminished resonance in an era when our search for extenuation and victimization diminishes rather than ennobles all it touches. And it is this acceptance of responsibility that makes Oedipus truly a tragic hero, with equal emphasis on both those words.

Now flash forward two millennia to a dramatic world that seems like it belongs on another planet, the world of Mozart's magical comic opera *Così Fan Tutte*—"They *All* Do It." Its libretto, written by Lorenzo da Ponte, who also wrote the libretti to *Don Giovanni* and *The Marriage of Figaro* before ending up in New York as Columbia's first professor of Italian, tells the wonderfully silly story of a bet two handsome young men make with their cynical older friend. Your two girlfriends, the older man says, whom you claim to be paragons of faithfulness, will not stay true to you if put to the test. Pretend to be called off to war, then come back disguised as noble Albanians, woo *each other's* girls, and you'll see.

Well, you know the result. But when the boys pretend to go off to war, the girls sing such a piercingly sweet lament of loss and farewell (for we are in a realm of literature *plus*) that you know their love is real, even though they later fall for the supposed Albanians and so prove—temporarily—unfaithful. And the opera's point is that, yes, from one point of view, one good-looking boy is much like another. But from another point of view, the person we choose is unique and special and the only one for us. We *are* creatures of animal instinct; but as we marshal that indiscriminate instinct into an act of discriminating and binding choice, we transform the natural into the human and create a new realm of feeling and meaning in the process.

Così gets performed somewhere every year, and Jane Austen's *Emma*, published a quarter century later, is just as perennial: Gwyneth Paltrow stars in the recent movie version, and Alicia Silverstone played the same character in the modern adaptation, *Clueless*. No wonder this story has lasted: its title character is adorable—irresistible despite her invincible self-satisfaction and self-delusion, perhaps excusable in one so very young and pretty and, as it happens, upscale. The story's key event is an act of bad manners: Emma insults a family friend, Miss Bates, and wounds her feelings. True, Miss Bates is the kind of boring old maid whose endless chatter about trivialities makes you cringe when you see her coming, but she is a harmless and kindly person. True, too, Emma's rudeness doesn't approach what you can now hear on TV every hour of the day; it is only a sarcastic crack about Miss Bates's talkiness. But the man Emma loves calls her on the carpet her for her behavior: she's at the top of the social heap in her little town, he says, and if she treats Miss Bates with contempt, others will follow suit, causing injury to a poor and dependent but good-hearted person. Manners are not trivial, a matter of which fork to use; they are a department of morals, part of the code—that web of culture, again—by which we succeed in living in harmony with each other. Manners are another key part of the humanizing project, through which we convert eating into dining, sex into romance and courtship, and our everyday interactions into occasions for cooperation rather than conflict.

The four great but relatively neglected works I discuss in *Dickens and the Social Order* are very much part of this project. They add up to what for another writer would constitute a magnificent life's work in itself, a tour de force that is like a university education in psychology, political theory, comparative political science, cultural anthropology, sociology, history, philosophy, and more—all transfigured and illuminated by the genius of the writer rightly said to be Inimitable, so that the reader can hardly believe that anything so full of pleasure can also be so full of wisdom. But reading these works, and thinking about them, will enlarge and deepen your understanding of our nature and what it is that makes us human.

One final point. By the time *Dickens and the Social Order* appeared in print, the era that confidently viewed literature in the way I have described was over; and the book, however kind the reviews that greeted it, seemed to belong to a past not only obsolete but malign. A newly emergent critical orthodoxy was taking a wrecking bar to literature. Critics no longer saw the literary enterprise as reliably trying to show us the truth of our condition and the possibilities it offers, but instead as trying to hoodwink us into tolerating political and social oppression that we would instantly reject, could we but free our minds from the myths and mystifications with which authors, mere apologists of the established and the powerful, had beguiled us. The critic's job now was not to dive down to the heart of the truth the author had grasped and explain to a new generation of readers how it applied to lived experience; he was to unmask the author's imposture, to reveal how the author, unconscious himself of his actual motives and blind to the reality he purported to illuminate, really was a kind of lackey, devoid of the critic's keen ability to see that the social relations, conventions, and beliefs that the author celebrates as humanizing and civilizing man in reality do exactly the opposite, constraining and diminishing him. To these critics, the truth of literature became its falsehood; the author, however great, became the gullible propagandist of one or another tyranny.

For all that, the literate public kept on reading literature, whose great works will still be there to instruct and inspire mankind long after the works of that angry, arrogant, and obtuse generation of critics have turned to dust.

— *Myron Magnet*
February 2003

Introduction

What are we to make of the *other* Dickens? Not Dickens the liberal reformer, readily recognizable to five generations of readers, but rather the darker Dickens who had (as Humphry House saw) "a strong authoritarian strain in him."[1] What are we to make of the Dickens who had an "almost fanatical devotion to the Metropolitan Police"—who showed, in the words of his younger colleague, G. A. Sala, "a curious and almost morbid partiality for communing with and entertaining police officers," and who not only loved hearing their exploits over brandy and cigars in his *Household Words* office, but who also recounted with gusto the choicest of their Scotland Yard anecdotes in a series of articles in that magazine?[2] What is to be made of the Dickens who, as early as 1843, confided to Lord Brougham his wish to be a police magistrate, and who, in 1846, sounded out "a leading member of the Government to ascertain what chances there might be for his appointment, upon due qualification, to the paid magistracy of London"?[3] How can we square with our usual image of Dickens the picture he paints of himself taking a walk and falling into his habit of "regard[ing] my walk as my beat, and myself as a higher sort of police-constable doing duty on the same"? "There is many a ruffian in the streets whom I mentally collar and clear out of them, who would see mighty little of London . . . if I could deal with him physically."[4]

On occasion, indeed, Dickens *did* interfere physically: as when, for example, he "had the honour of myself giving chase, on Westminster Bridge, to another young Ruffian, who . . . had nearly thrown a modest young woman into a swoon . . . by his shameful manner of attacking her. . . ."⁵ But few Englishmen nowadays, he bitterly complains in an article of 1857, would take the trouble of interfering to prevent or apprehend a law-breaker; only the other day, a brutal murder was committed in a shop in one of London's main streets, while bystanders looked on passively.⁶ Much better, in all such cases, to take action. For instance, when boys throw stones in the streets and no policeman is at hand, let us resolutely appeal to "our own riding-whips and walking-sticks."⁷

What are we to make of a story in a similar vein that Dickens tells about himself in this same article from *All the Year Round*? When his small children were taken regularly by their nurses to play in Regent's Park, he reports, he was shocked by the ostentatious braying of foul language so often met with there. Assuring himself that the Police Act made public swearing a punishable offense, Dickens went out, looking for trouble. This he found, in the shape of a luckless girl of seventeen or so, surrounded by a "suitable attendance" of blackguard youths and boys, in the midst of whom she energetically swore, cursed, sang, and danced—and, passing Dickens in the street, swore at him too. For a mile, the celebrated novelist followed this crew, while they made merry at his expense—until at last a police constable hove into view. As Dickens addressed the policeman, the youths melted away, leaving the maiden to her fate.

Do you know who I am? Dickens asked the constable. Yes, certainly. Then, returned Dickens, please arrest that girl for using bad language in public. But the constable had never heard of such an offense and would take the girl into custody only on being assured that Dickens would take full responsibility. Dickens rushed home to get his copy of the Police Act—he *owned* one—the girl meanwhile being bundled off to the police station, where Dickens appeared to file formal charges.

Next morning, armed with his Police Act, Dickens presented himself before the suburban magistrate to give his evidence. But the magistrate was not pleased to see him, considering him "as a much more objectionable person than the prisoner;—one giving trouble by coming there voluntarily," and coming there to press bloody-mindedly what the magistrate thought a frivolous charge. What was more, the prisoner had gotten herself up to look like "an elder sister of Red Riding Hood," and Dickens, insistent that she be prosecuted, was (he felt) being regarded as the Wolf. Surely Mr. Dickens, said the magistrate, surely you don't want this girl to be sent to jail on such a charge. Yes I do, said Dickens "grimly"; otherwise I wouldn't have come. Here's the law in the Police

Act in black and white: do your duty. Whereupon Dickens was sworn, gave his evidence, and was satisfied to see the girl sentenced to ten shillings or ten days. Nor was this the only time Dickens appeared at a police station to lodge a complaint: in 1844, he tried to prosecute a begging-letter writer who had defrauded him, only to have the magistrate discharge the culprit with compliments and to feel himself "universally regarded as a sort of monster."[8]

How is our image of Dickens to accommodate his characteristically stern—even truculent—views about dealing with criminals both in and out of jail? The law regularly fails to punish sufficiently those who break it, Dickens complains. An "intolerable brute," a "wild beast in a man's form," can beat a policeman savagely and cripple him for life, and he receives a prison sentence not of years but of months.[9] Indeed, so soft-heartedly and soft-headedly solicitous are the courts toward criminals that it usually seems they believe "that the real offender is the Murdered Person; but for whose obstinate persistency in being murdered, the interesting fellow-creature to be tried could not have got into trouble."[10] One wonders if the courts are "saving up" and "preserving" criminals—like Partridges! In any event, the streets are swarming with "Ruffians," and so one clearly has to conclude that the Government is not succeeding "in the discharge of any Government's most simple elementary duty." The thing to do with this whole class of Ruffians is to lock them up and throw away the key; and if the Government does not want to use perpetual preventative detention to clear the streets of such a pestiferous nuisance, then it has no business coming round to citizens and trying to collect taxes. Ruffians ought to be whipped, their backs "scarified often and deep" by the authorities. For the Ruffian is "the common enemy to be punished and exterminated."[11]

On penology Dickens was often no less harsh. "[T]hroughout his career," Philip Collins concludes, "he approved of severe penal measures, and inclined more towards a deterrent than a curative policy." This inclination "became stronger, and was more vehemently expressed, the older he grew."[12] Thus, on the question of what kind of work prisoners ought to do in jail (to take a representative example), Dickens recommended that we ought "to discover what kind of work [prisoners] like least, and to give them that work to do in preference to any other." There should be, "for all such characters, a kind of work in gaols, badged and degraded as belonging to gaols only, and never done elsewhere."[13]

Turning from domestic to foreign matters, do we expect to find the novelist we value for his generosity ranging himself with Carlyle in support of Governor Eyre's notoriously brutal suppression of the 1864 Negro uprising in Jamaica? Are we not taken aback by his program for dealing with the Indian mutiny, which is, like Mr. Kurtz's, to exterminate all the brutes?[14] And how shall we assimilate the views he expresses with rather wild relish in an 1853 essay on "The Noble Savage"?[15] "I have not the least belief in the Noble Savage," he declares. "I consider him a prodigious nuisance, and an enormous superstition." Savages are *not* noble, and it is a contemptible stupidity to express any "maudlin admiration" for them or to draw "any comparison of advantage between the blemishes of civilisation and the tenor of [their] swinish life." Properly, one should "abhor, detest, abominate, and abjure" the Savage, for he is "cruel, false, thievish, murderous; addicted more or less to grease, entrails, and beastly customs; a wild animal." Indeed, he "has no moral feelings of any kind, sort, or description; and his 'mission' may be summed up as simply diabolical." For example, all his "wars with his fellow savages (and he takes no pleasure in anything else) are wars of extermination." Clearly, therefore, "if we have anything to learn from the Noble Savage, it is what to avoid. His virtues are a fable; his happiness is a delusion; his nobility, nonsense." Emphatically we have no right to be cruel to this "miserable object . . . ; but he passes away before an immeasurably better and higher power than ever ran wild in any earthly woods, and the world will be all the better when his place knows him no more"—when, in other words, he has been "civilised off the face of the earth."

This cluster of attitudes—so many of them by no means shared by present-day Dickens enthusiasts, who find their conservative tendency troubling—nevertheless constitutes a coherent structure of belief and feeling rather than a set of quirky, unexamined prejudices. Such views, moreover, are not extrinsic to Dickens's novelistic achievement but instead are imbedded in the grain of his artistic imagination, and therefore they require not merely notice, such as they have received from House or Collins, but detailed analysis. The present study aims to show that these sentiments, often expressed with disquietingly excessive zeal in the quotations I have chosen, derive from a way of seeing the world which—though its influence is marked in Dickens's late books (and all these quotations come from the last two decades of his life)—nevertheless resolved itself into clear focus early in his novelistic career.

Indeed, four books written between 1838 and 1844 take this world view as a central issue, fully working it out among them in all its complex ramifications and forming, by their concentration on the same essential questions, a discrete phase in Dickens's intellectual and artistic development. Far from being immature or imperfect apprentice versions of *Bleak House* or *Little Dorrit*, the novels of this period have different interests and a different focus. *Barnaby Rudge*, for example, despite being an historical novel centering on a spectacular explosion of mob violence, shares little in common with the specific concerns, either personal or political, of *A Tale of Two Cities*. What these early novels attempt is something other than what the later masterpieces so magnificently achieved, and, though hitherto not much discussed by critics, they are admirable accomplishments in their own right—so much so, I think, that Dickens would be held a major English novelist even had he written no novels after his thirty-third birthday.

What is at issue in the four books this study takes as its subject is nothing less than Dickens's understanding of the nature and function of society itself, of civilization considered as a general condition independent of its manifestation in this or that historical polity. Like the tradition of political philosophy whose English ancestor was Thomas Hobbes, Dickens's first approach to this question was a meditation on human aggression. In *Nicholas Nickleby* (1838–39), he concluded that aggression was an inborn instinct, uninhibited by anything in man's "natural" constitution and continually threatening to make human life into the universal war that Hobbes's myth of the state of nature imagines it originally was. Seizing on this defining feature of human nature, *Nickleby* is a Madame Tussaud's exhibit of the various forms of man's constitutional aggressiveness; and though the novel fails to reach a comprehensive solution to the whole perplexing issue, its consideration of ways in which aggression may be redirected and defused is Dickens's first large step in that direction, providing him with some of the essential terms in which his definitive response to the problem will be formulated in *Barnaby Rudge*.

For in *Barnaby* (1841) Dickens discovers that the great force serving to restrain and neutralize human nature's inherent aggressiveness is civilization, externally embodied in society and internally institutionalized within the mind of every civilized individual. The first part of the novel differentiates civilized man from two representative examples of aggressive, dangerous, not-fully-human "natural" man, suggesting that the civilized man has—and the natural man lacks—an internal faculty of civilization modern readers will see as analogous to Freud's superego. This faculty civilized man develops through his relationship with his father. That relationship, never experienced by the novel's two natural men, has as its content primarily the oppression of the son by the father, which, rendering the son civilized, simultaneously makes him unhappy and unfree.

This price is worth paying, the novel's first part insists, because only in civilization does man attain his full humanity. Part II of *Barnaby* answers the question in another way in its imaginative reconstruction of the Gordon Riots of 1780—which constitute, in Dickens's view, an epidemic breaking-out of those powerful impulses of cruelty and aggression he sees as inherent in human nature. In these riots, London was momentarily reduced to the brutish anarchy of the state of nature, graphically disclosing the Hobbesian truth about man's original condition and revealing how imperatively men *need* civilization, despite its concomitant discontents, to shield them from the terrors of the war of all against all. But Dickens by no means minimizes the cost of the benefits conferred by society, for not only does social life entail upon every individual a quantum of unhappiness which is *caused* by the process of civilization, but also the necessary *public* authority erected by men to guarantee the social contract has an inherent tendency to resolve itself into nothing more than the violence at its disposal. It thus perpetually presents the threat of becoming as savage as the savagery it was instituted to civilize. It is possible to have a society in which, as Edmund Burke cautioned, "at the end of every vista, you see nothing but the gallows." [16]

Shortly after the completion of *Barnaby*, Dickens sailed for America, where he found, with disconcerted surprise, massive confirmation of the political outlook to which he had just finished giving so elaborate a formulation. His report of this experience is to be found in both *American Notes* (1842) and *Martin Chuzzlewit* (1843–44), the two books bringing to a close the stage in his progress as a writer that this book will discuss. But several additional prefatory words are in order before the discussion can get under way in earnest.

First, while I think that an understanding of how Dickens's complex imaginative theory of the nature of society and the civilized condition developed is essential to grasping the shape of his career as a whole, I must emphasize my belief that the books discussed here are valuable and important on their own merits. The relative critical neglect and deprecation they have received reflects, I think, so acute a discomfort with their politics that commentators have more often preferred to accuse them of being about nothing than to confront their uncongenial messages. I do not pretend that a book like *Nicholas Nickleby* approaches the stature of something like *Our Mutual Friend*, but *Nickleby* clearly contains a principle of vitality that in the last couple of years has made an eight-and-a-half-hour dramatization of it the hit of the London and New York theater seasons. *Barnaby Rudge*, by contrast, *is* a great novel—"the turning point," as Angus Wilson rightly judges, "in Dickens's growth from an extraordinary to a great novelist" [17]—and not only does its excellence justify, but also its intellectual complexity requires, the fullness of analysis the present study accords it. *Martin Chuzzlewit's* quality needs fewer words of defense, a sufficiency of critics having recognized it as the comic masterpiece it is, while a discussion of *American Notes* needs no apology, being a pioneer in unexplored territory.

Second, my emendation of the prevailing orthodoxy about Dickens clearly goes beyond championing these early novels and contending that his development is a more complex matter than has hitherto been recognized. For I am undertaking to show that Dickens—in spite of his flow of comic genius, his inveterate taste for the grotesque, his sentimentality, his middle-class philistinism—is nevertheless a novelist who *thinks*. He was not a writer who wrote unreflectingly, automatically, directly out of his unconscious. His method of proceeding, as he himself describes it, was quite different. Of the plotting of *Barnaby*, for example, he writes to his close friend and biographer John Forster: "I didn't stir out yesterday, but sat and *thought* all day; not writing a line; not so much as the cross of a t or the dot of an i. I imagined forth a great deal of *Barnaby* by keeping my mind steadily upon him."[18] More graphic is the glimpse he gives to his banking-heiress friend Miss Coutts of his walking "up and down the house, striking my forehead dejectedly" in the "agonies of plotting and contriving" *Martin Chuzzlewit*: "unless I were to shut myself up, obstinately and sullenly in my own room for a great many days without writing a word, I don't think I should ever make a beginning."[19] And what came out of these agonies was thought of a high order.

True, Dickens had no formal higher education. However, this has never been a barrier to intellectual achievement, and Dickens did spend long hours—"the usefullest to himself he had ever passed"[20]—in the British Museum reading room during the first half of the 1830s, acquainting himself with a wide range of literary, historical, and biographical works.[21] Probably this is when he put himself in touch with the tradition of political philosophy so influential in the books analyzed here, an acquaintance perhaps strengthened by his experience as a Parliamentary reporter during these years. Certainly these ideas were "in the air" at this time, available to any thoughtful man: it is on this tradition that the leading Victorian belief in the "progress of civilization" rests. But what texts exactly transmitted this body of thought to Dickens is hard to specify, except to say that by the time he wrote *Nickleby* he had certainly read Burke, not without effect, as the rhetoric of that novel's MP, Mr. Gregsbury, makes clear:

Whether . . . I behold the peaceful industrious communities of our island home, her rivers covered with steam-boats, her roads with locomotives, her streets with cabs, her skies with balloons of a power and magnitude hitherto unknown in the history of aeronautics in this or any other nation—I say, whether I look merely at home, or stretching my eyes further, contemplate the boundless prospect of conquest and possession—achieved by British perseverance and British valour—which is outspread before me, I clasp my hands, and turning my eyes to the broad expanse above my head, exclaim, "Thank Heaven, I am a Briton!"[22]

What is this but a burlesque of the language of Burke's *Reflections?*—

Indeed, when I consider the face of the kingdom of France, the multitude and opulence of her cities, the useful magnificence of her spacious high roads and bridges, the opportunity of her artificial canals and navigations opening the conveniences of maritime communication through a solid continent of so immense an extent; when I turn my eyes to the stupendous works of her ports and harbors, and to her whole naval apparatus, whether for war or trade; . . . when I reckon the men she has bred for extending her fame in war . . . —I behold in all this something which awes and commands the imagination. . . . I must think such a government well deserved to have its excellences heightened, its faults corrected, and its capacities improved into a British constitution.[23]

And in this widely read and widely influential classic, the whole tradition is summed up and reinvigorated.

One last point. Dickens, and above all in these early novels, is of course a supremely comic writer, and to reconstruct the development of his understanding of the nature of the social order requires one—like some lumbering Caliban—to unpack effervescent jokes, to press rudely through the decorum of urbane, diffident, slightly ambivalent irony in search of meaning, insensitively to take seriously what appears as lighthearted entertainment, offered in a spirit of generous good fellowship. Alas, a critic's lot is not a happy one, doubly doleful for a critic who likes a joke himself. All I can say in mitigation is that Dickens's humor will still be funny when I am done, and his political philosophy—the essentially conservative world view with which his liberal reformism is inextricably intertwined—will be more clearly comprehensible to readers than before. And though this political theory ceased to occupy the center of his attention after *Martin Chuzzlewit*, it by no means disappeared from his imagination, for it constitutes the fundamental ground of implicit assumption in which his subsequent understanding of society is firmly rooted.

Part One

Nicholas Nickleby

All children ought to love [Dickens]. I know two that do, and read his books ten times for once that they peruse the dismal preachments of their father. I know one who, when she is happy, reads Nicholas Nickleby; when she is unhappy, reads Nicholas Nickleby; . . . when she has nothing to do, reads Nicholas Nickleby; and when she has finished the book, reads Nicholas Nickleby over again. This candid young critic, at ten years of age, said, "I like Mr. Dickens's books much better than your books, papa"; and frequently expressed her desire that the latter author should write a book like one of Mr. Dickens's books. Who can?

(W. M. Thackeray, *The English Humourists of the Eighteenth Century*)

1

The Problem of Aggression

Nicholas Nickleby isn't just "about" aggression; it is *obsessed* with it. Some act of violence impends or erupts in virtually every chapter, and hatred is the book's most conspicuous emotion. Ralph Nickleby hates Nicholas Nickleby at first sight (3), as does Mrs. Squeers, and Fanny Squeers, mortified by Nicholas's rejection of her attentions, "hated and detested him with all the narrowness of mind and littleness of purpose worthy a descendant of the house of Squeers." But, like her mother, she comforts herself with the thought that "every hour in every day she could wound his pride and goad him with the infliction of some slight, or insult, or deprivation" (12).

But Fanny is, after all, a virtuoso of hatred.

"I hate everybody," said Miss Squeers, "and I wish that everybody was dead—that I do."

"Dear, dear!" said Miss Price, quite moved by this avowal of misanthropical sentiments. "You are not serious, I am sure."

"Yes, I am," rejoined Miss Squeers, tying tight knots in her pocket-handkerchief and clenching her teeth. "And I wish I was dead too. There." (12)

Like so many characters in *Nickleby*, Fanny is so aggressively self-centered that she does not include herself in "everybody," and Dickens is able to imagine in her an aggression so radical that it not only encompasses self-annihilation but contemplates laying all creation waste. Though not in Fanny's class, another champion hater is Miss Knag, who comes to "detest and hate" the much younger and beautiful Kate Nickleby (18). Similarly, Sir Mulberry Hawk, measuring his dislike of his dupe Lord Frederick Verisopht "by the extent of the injuries he had inflicted upon [him] . . . began to hate him cordially" (50).

A random, spontaneous aggressiveness permeates the novel, leading people—for casual amusement—to pull down outdoor statues (3) and rip knockers off house doors (16). Fistfights break out so often that five of Phiz's illustrations depict them. For example, Nicholas thrashes Squeers at Dotheboys Hall, leaving off only when he has exhausted himself with violence (13), and Newman Noggs later brains that worthy instructor of youth with a pair of bellows (57). Earnest Frank Cheeryble enters the novel in the midst of a fistfight (43). Even the complacent Mr. Lillyvick falls upon Miss Snevellicci's father (30), and mild Miss La Creevy angrily expresses a readiness to insert a fruit knife into Ralph Nickleby (31). Going beyond fiction, the preface to the first edition of the novel reports that one of the several Yorkshire schoolmasters who believe themselves to be Mr. Squeers's original has "meditated a journey to London, for the express purpose of committing an assault and battery upon his traducer."

Even from this handful of examples it seems unlikely that the recurrence of aggression in *Nickleby* is an irrelevant tic on Dickens's part. But the novel is charged with an overwhelming accumulation of such instances, from the description of Mr. Bobster, so "ferocious" that "[h]e'd kill 'em all—box the young lady's ears—he does—often" (40), to the description of the pugnacious (and pugnaciously named) Mr. Pyke, who, escorting Mrs. Nickleby to the theater, threatens "to 'smifligate' a very old man who accidentally stumbled in her way," and "to 'smash' the assistant box-keeper for happening to mistake the number" (27). When even parties turn into orgies of violence—the morning-after debris of Lord Frederick's gathering includes, among the "many other tokens of riot and disorder," a "champagne bottle with a soiled glove twisted round the neck, to allow of its being grasped more surely in the capacity of an offensive weapon" (26)—then clearly the problem of aggression is at the very core of *Nicholas Nickleby*'s imaginary world.

Several further examples will not only illustrate how single-minded is Dickens's concern with this theme from start to finish of the book but will also show that aggression in *Nickleby* usually is not a means (however deplorable) to an end. It is an end in itself, offering its own peculiar satisfactions. Thus Mr. Wackford Squeers, who views his pupils as his "proper and natural enemies" and who accordingly wears a shooting jacket in the schoolroom, to which he goes "armed" with a cane (8), mightily enjoys the flogging central to his pedagogic method. When he prepares to "operate upon" Smike, he "literally feast[s] his eyes" on him and touches him "[w]ith hands trembling with delight" (13). Later, recapturing Smike, Mr. Squeers discovers an indecent refinement of pleasure when he bundles the unfortunate runaway into a cab and beats him with an umbrella. " 'I never threshed a boy in a hackney-coach before,' said Mr. Squeers, when he stopped to rest. 'There's inconveniency in it, but the novelty gives it a sort of relish too!' " (38).

Sexual aggression figures at the center of the novel. Nicholas worries that Ralph may have placed Kate in some situation "where her youth and beauty would prove a far greater curse than ugliness and decrepitude" (8). That is just what happens. First, Victorian readers would grasp at once that Ralph, by sending Kate to work for a dressmaker, puts her virtue at risk. Such girls, Richard Altick writes, were notoriously "exposed to the wiles of men both inside the shop and on the pavements outside as well. . . . Thus, Dickens was able to arouse . . . a concern which he did not need to made explicit,"[1] though the lecherous Mr. Mantalini makes the danger plain enough. Second—overt and much more sinister—is Mulberry Hawk's sexual pursuit of Kate. His "constant and unremitting persecution" (27–28) has as its object "the successful reduction of her pride." Though he leaves uncompleted his vow to "drag that pattern of chastity, that pink of prudery, the delicate sister, through—" (38), it is clear that he is threatening to violate and humilate Kate utterly, perhaps even to the point of rape. And this repulsive ambition, as Dickens presents it, points to the possibility of a sexuality so dedicated to domination as to constitute only another category of aggression.

Sexual violence erupts even into one of Mrs. Nickleby's interminable monologues, this one concerning

a case in the day before yesterday's paper, extracted from one of the French newspapers, about a journeyman shoemaker who was jealous of a young girl . . . and who went and hid himself in a Wood with a sharp-pointed knife, and rushed out as she was passing by with a few friends, and killed himself first, and then all the friends, and then her—no, killed all the friends first, and then herself, and then *him*self—which is quite frightful to think of. Somehow or other . . . they always *are* journeymen shoemakers who do these things in France . . . —something in the leather, I suppose. (37)

It is to justify her fears that her mad neighbor will be driven to despairing violence by her rejection of his advances that Mrs. Nickleby tells this unintentionally funny story. She is curiously right to see so intimate a connection between his amorousness and aggression. Just as Mr. Snevellicci "knew in his cups three distinct stages of intoxication,—the dignified—the quarrelsome—the amorous" (30), so too for the mad gentleman are violence and lubricity but two points on the same spectrum. To say the least, his systematic bombardment of Mrs. Nickleby with cucumbers and vegetable marrows of enormous size does suggest a somewhat overbearing theory of his own sexuality. And indeed, his lechery turns out to be simply a transformed version of his aggression; his keeper says he was, before he went mad,

the cruelest, wickedest, out-and-outerest old flint that ever drawed breath. . . . Broke his poor wife's heart, turned his daughters out of doors, drove his sons into the streets—it was a blessing he went mad at last, through evil tempers, and covetousness, and selfishness, and guzzling, and drinking, or he'd have drove many others so. (41)

This man's marriage is only one of several that *Nickleby* depicts as battlegrounds. Mr. Bray treated his wife with systematic cruelty until she died "broken-spirited from suffering and ill usage" (46). Arthur Gride, whose projected marriage to Madeline Bray Dickens presents as a special case of sexual aggression, plans to "taunt" Madeline with her memory of Nicholas and "break her spirit by this means and have her under my thumb" (53). The fraudulent story Ralph invents to establish Snawley as Smike's father contains, to make it *more convincing*, an invented instance of this kind: Mr. Snawley's first marriage is said to have been simply "a system of annoyance . . . which [husband and wife] seem to have adopted towards each other" (45). It is unhappily whispered that rakish Mr. Snevellicci, too, occasionally beats his wife (30).

As if all this were not enough, violence pervades even the novel's inanimate world. The buildings express aggression: "The very chimneys appear to have grown dismal and melancholy . . . ; and here and there some taller stack than the rest, inclining heavily to one side, and toppling over the roof, seems to meditate taking revenge for half a century's neglect, by crushing the inhabitants of the garrets beneath" (14). And violence is not confined to the city. In a beautiful rural landscape, Nicholas and Smike

walked upon the rim of the Devil's Punch Bowl, and . . . Nicholas read the inscription . . . which tells of a foul and treacherous murder committed there by
night. The grass on which they stood had once been dyed with gore, and the
blood of the murdered man had run down, drop by drop, into the hollow which
gives the place its name. (22)

Nor is this the only time that murder enters the book, for Arthur Gride is
killed by thieves at the novel's end (65), in a murder strangely unacharac-
teristic of Dickens. In contrast to the murder of Tigg in *Martin Chuzzlewit*, for example, or of Nancy in *Oliver Twist*, the murder of Gride—
committed by anonymous strangers—is, like so much of the aggression
in *Nickleby*, random, gratuitous, and oddly impersonal.

Social institutions, too, appear in the novel largely in relation to aggression. The one time we see policemen, for instance, they start pum-
melling innocent bystanders, when, at a farcical meeting of the Metropolitan Hot Muffin Company, the impatient audience begins to hoot and
yell. The policemen, wanting "to quell the disturbance" but unwilling to
fight their way through the crowd to reach those responsible,

immediately began to drag forth by the coat tails and collars all the quiet people
near the door; at the same time dealing out various smart and tingling blows with
their truncheons, after the manner of that ingenious actor, Mr. Punch, whose
brilliant example, both in the fashion of his weapons and their use, this branch of
the executive occasionally follows. (2)

This joke has reference to a stern reality, for in the world of *Nicholas Nickleby* the law itself is no more than an instrument of violence, to which, for
example, Ralph Nickleby resolves to turn as his ultimate weapon against
his nephew. "The protracted and wearing anxiety and expense of the law
in its most oppressive form, its torture from hour to hour, its weary days
and sleepless nights—with these I'll prove you," he growls at Nicholas,
"and break your haughty spirit, strong as you deem it now" (45). And
this is no idle threat, as *Bleak House* makes clear.

The only large social institution that has a palpable presence in *Nickleby*, though mentioned but once, is the embodiment of the law in its
most terrible form, in its incarnation as pure, though legitimate, violence.

There, at the very core of London, in the heart of its business and animation, . . .
stands Newgate; and in that crowded street on which it frowns so darkly . . .
scores of human beings, . . . have been hurried violently and swiftly from the
world, when the scene has been rendered frightful with excess of human life;

when curious eyes have glared from casement, and house-top, and wall and pillar, and when, in the mass of white and upturned faces, the dying wretch, in his all-comprehensive look of agony, has met not one—not one—that bore the impress of pity and compassion. (4)

In this novel about aggression, in other words, social authority appears as merely another engine of violence; in *Nickleby* the heart of the city (in more than a geographical sense) is the gallows.

. . .

But I do not say that aggression is *Nickleby*'s central issue only because the novel is saturated with details like these. More important, the book as a whole makes an extended analysis of aggression in its two most interesting characters, the villains Ralph Nickleby and Wackford Squeers, whose machinations turn the wheels of *Nickleby*'s plot.

Squeers, as proprietor of a Yorkshire school, is associated with what in Dickens's imagination from his childhood onward is the most loathsome depth of human cruelty. These Yorkshire warehouses for unwanted children, Dickens reports in the novel's 1848 preface, had always exemplified to him a degree of sadism and violence almost unimaginable but nevertheless in constant occurrence. To prepare for writing *Nickleby*, he made an expedition to Yorkshire to investigate with his own eyes the truth of his childhood impression. Alas, he confirms, he was not mistaken. And as for *Nickleby*'s representation of such horrors in Dotheboys Hall, he feels obliged to assure the reader,

emphatically and earnestly, that Mr. Squeers and his school are faint and feeble pictures of an existing reality, purposely subdued and kept down lest they should be deemed impossible—that there are upon record trials at law in which damages have been sought as a poor recompense for lasting agonies and disfigurements inflicted upon children by the treatment of the master in these places, involving such offensive and foul details of neglect, cruelty, and disease, as no writer of fiction would have the boldness to imagine.

The reality and the magnitude of human aggression, even against defenseless children, is such that not even Dickens himself, for all the power of his imagination, could dream up such atrocities. You have to see them to believe them—but they are undeniably there to be seen. (It is gratifying to think that *Nicholas Nickleby* served to shame these institutions out of business in short order.)[2]

In Squeers, Dickens presents an aggression that seeks to appropriate all reality, people as well as things, as grist for the mill of the self. His unhappy pupils are only so much raw material for him to turn to account. They are like cattle, literally put out in the fields to "graze" (34) and kept only for the profit they provide. "There's youth to the amount of eight hundred pound a-year at Dotheboys Hall at this present time," says Squeers. "I'd take sixteen hundred pound worth if I could get 'em" (34). From another point of view, the boys are like slaves, as Squeers's explanation of why he wants an assistant makes explicit: "A slave driver in the West Indies is allowed a man under him, to see that his blacks don't run away, or get up a rebellion; and I'll have a man under me to do the same with *our* blacks" (9). It is no metaphor to say that Smike, even lower in status than the other pupils, is indeed Squeers's slave, endlessly toiling without wages and flogged without mercy for trying to escape.

How bad is the dirt, the want, the cold, the flogging, the sadism? Look at the victims—who sometimes die from this treatment—sleeping five to a bed at dawn on a winter's day:

It needed a quick eye to detect from among the huddled mass of sleepers, the form of any given individual. As they lay closely packed together, covered, for warmth's sake, with their patched and ragged clothes, little could be distinguished but the sharp outlines of pale faces, over which the sombre light shed the same dull heavy colour, with here and there a gaunt arm thrust forth: its thinness hidden by no covering, but fully exposed to view in all its shrunken ugliness. There were some who, lying on their backs with upturned faces and clenched hands, just visible in the leaden light, bore more the aspect of dead bodies than of living creatures, and there were others coiled up into strange and fantastic postures, such as might have been taken for the uneasy efforts of pain to gain some temporary relief, rather than the freaks of slumber. A few—and these were among the youngest of the children—slept peacefully on with smiles upon their faces, dreaming perhaps of home; but ever and again a deep and heavy sigh, breaking the stillness of the room, announced that some new sleeper had awakened to the misery of another day. (13)

What is Dotheboys Hall, if not a concentration camp for children?

Along with the physical abuse, Squeers subjects these boys to another form of violence, less flagrant but devastating enough in its insidious way. The schoolmaster's zany and pitilessly jeering explanation of his "educational system" calls attention to this further level of brutalization inflicted on the boys by leaving them without an education.

"This is the first class in English spelling and philosophy, Nickleby," said Squeers. . . . "Now, then, where's the first boy?"

"Please, Sir, he's cleaning the back parlour window. . . ."

"So he is, to be sure," rejoined Squeers. "We go upon the practical mode of teaching, Nickleby; the regular education system. C-l-e-a-n, clean, verb active, to make bright, to scour. W-i-n, win, d-e-r, der, winder, a casement. When the boy knows this out of book, he goes and does it. . . . Third boy, what's a horse?"

"A beast, Sir," replied the boy.

"So it is," said Squeers. . . . "A horse is a quadruped, and quadruped's Latin for beast. . . . As you're perfect in that, . . . go and look after *my* horse. . . . The rest of the class go and draw water up till somebody tells you to leave off. . . ."

So saying he dismissed the first class to their experiments in practical philosophy. (8)

The definition of a horse cannot fail to bring to mind Mr. Gradgrind in *Hard Times* examining the pupils trained according to his educational system, and the comparison is worth making.

"Bitzer," said Thomas Gradgrind. "Your definition of a horse."

"Quadruped. Graminivorous. Forty teeth, namely twenty-four grinders, four eye-teeth, and twelve incisive. Sheds coat in the spring; in marshy countries, sheds hoofs, too. Hoofs hard, but requiring to be shod with iron. Age known by marks in mouth." Thus (and much more) Bitzer.

"Now, girl number twenty," said Mr. Gradgrind, "you know what a horse is." (Bk. I, ch. 2)

However much this definition blows into atoms the complicated living reality of a horse, and however meaningless it is to Bitzer, who parrots it by rote, still the observations contained in it are not meaningless. They do describe equine qualities, and they represent the sustained effort of generations to describe the world comprehensively. Bitzer's definition is the sawdust and rubble of what is incontestably a noble project.

Though Gradgrind trivializes, falsifies, and makes oppressive a certain kind of knowledge, he does so because his faith in it is too large rather than otherwise. Misguided though he is, he believes the Coketown pupils are being taught with the success he sincerely wishes. With Squeers the case is different. While Gradgrind, interposing between his pupils and reality a blanket of words, abstract notions, mathematical tables and formulae, crushes the world of actual experience by laying upon it too heavy an explanatory superstructure, Squeers's educational system deprives the Dotheboys pupils of every one of those interpretive categories and beliefs that human culture has devised to make sense out of reality's apparent disorder. (Indeed, the difference between these two educations that Dickens holds up for criticism—the one utterly negligent and the other stifling— perfectly epitomizes the shift in general social outlook distinguishing his later works from his early ones.)

The largely unmediated relation to reality to which Squeers abandons his pupils by sending them to "go and know" the world with their own pathetic resources undeveloped by adequate immersion in culture results in their knowing little and understanding less: human reason needs the warmth and light of culture for its proper unfolding. But in fact every human excellence in these boys is blasted under the influence of Squeers, who so extensively deprives them of that cultural medium whose nourishment is essential that their humanity itself is stunted and withered. This deprivation is part of a vicious cycle, for insofar as the boys really have suffered a diminution of humanity, they are even less capable of kindling compassion and inhibiting the aggression of others. And so they are that much easier for Squeers to abuse.

Curiously, both Squeers and his wife choose for themselves a version of the unmediated relation to reality they force upon their pupils, and this is another facet of their aggressive affirmation of godlike mastery over all reality. Their self-assertion is so absolute that it includes even the claim of independence from language. A "man may call his house an island if he likes," Squeers insists (7), and his wife "always calls things and people by their wrong names," while claiming nevertheless to "see them with right eyes" (9). Just as she has removed all obstacles in the way of the use she wants to make of the boys, she asserts she can also appropriate all reality for herself with equal directness, relating to it with an immediacy of apprehension that obliterates the distinction between herself and the object of her "thought." She does not need language to "go and know" something; for her the abstraction of language, an untrustworthy artifice of civilization, simply takes the edge off her God-given ability to apprehend truth immediately.

. . .

Though Ralph Nickleby's stagey language makes him easy to mistake for a stock melodramatic villain, the power his final drama has to affect and disturb reveals him as a more complex imaginative achievement than that. Through him, in fact, *Nickleby* makes its primary exploration of the psychology of aggression, for though in Squeers Dickens is chiefly interested in how unbounded aggression's scope can be, in Ralph he is more concerned with what kind of psychological makeup is consistent with the aggressive atomism so troubling to him throughout the novel. And this concern with the inner aspect of the problem of aggression, coupled with his meditation on what happens to people who like the Dotheboys pupils are deprived of culture's nurture, leads in *Barnaby Rudge* and *American Notes* to a recognition that the solution to aggression is in large part a psychological matter, as is the problem itself.

Thus, while Ralph is a usurer, his ruling passion is not avarice, as with Arthur Gride. Most unmiserly is this avowal to Squeers: "I spend money to gratify my hatred, and you pocket it, and gratify yours at the same time. You are at least as avaricious as you are revengeful—so am I. Which is best off? You, who win money and revenge . . . ; or I, who am only sure of spending money in any case, and can but win bare revenge at last?" (56). Even more unmiser-like is his reflection, in the same chapter, that he can manage to tolerate his huge loss of ten thousand pounds if only he can begin to "retaliate upon" Nicholas. From early on Ralph showed this trait: recounting how Ralph's wife ran away with a younger man years before, Mr. Brooker observes that Ralph "followed the fugitives—some said to make money of his wife's shame, but I believe to take some violent revenge, for that was as much his character as the other—perhaps more" (60). Forced to choose between his greed or his aggression, he always chooses violence. He is capable of elevating "his quiet and stealthy malignity to such a pitch, that there was scarcely anything he would not have hazarded to gratify it" (34). His paramount emotion is hatred, and he loves money because he knows it is the best weapon malice can have. Indeed, in *Nickleby*, money—"whose every coin is rusted with tears, if not red with the blood of ruined men" (53)—is imagined unambiguously as an instrument of power in the service of aggression, a less complex function than Dickens gives it in his later novels. "As a portion of the world affect to despise the power of money," says Ralph, characteristically, "I must try and show them what it is" (34).

So essential to Ralph's identity is his aggression that when it momentarily slackens he feels he does not exist. Late in the novel, sleepless and anxious, he worries that he is losing control both of the situation and of himself. As his sense of identity relentlessly disintegrates, Charles Cheeryble, whom he detests, comes to call, with "beneficial effect." The visit

instantly roused all [Ralph's] dormant energies, rekindled in his breast the passions that for many years had found an improving home there, called up all his wrath, hatred, and malice; restored the sneer to his lip, and the scowl to his brow, and made him again in all outward appearance the same Ralph Nickleby that so many had bitter cause to remember.

His hatred and malice make him "a man again" (59).[3]

To gratify this malice there is finally nothing he will not hazard. Remembering how he once sat on a coroner's jury investigating a suicide, he recalls the draped, marmoreal figure of the dead man and also

the pale and trembling relatives who had told their tale upon the inquest—the shrieks of women—the silent dread of men—the consternation and disquiet—the victory achieved by that heap of clay which with one motion of its hand had let out the life and made this stir among them—— (62)

Strange to judge this a victory: but so Ralph understands the dead man's success in horrifying those around him by his uncompromising power of violence. With just that intention does Ralph choose suicide as an act of aggression against nothing less than the entire cosmos. Shaking "his clenched hand at the sky above him" (62), he dies defying the universe, making his self-annihilation his ultimate act of cosmic self-assertion. It really is, as Arthur Gride had seen earlier, a case of "Mr. Nickleby against all the world" (47).[4]

Dickens fills out with Ralph the notion, very quickly sketched with Mrs. Squeers, of implacable aggression associated with the assertion of a special relation to truth. Ralph goes Mrs. Squeers one better by claiming to see not only the world but also himself with "right eyes."

When men are about to commit . . . some injustice, it is not uncommon for them to express pity for the object either of that or some parallel proceeding, and to feel themselves at the time quite virtuous and moral, and immensely superior to those who express no pity at all. This is a kind of upholding of faith above works, and is very comfortable. To do Ralph Nickleby justice, he seldom practised this sort of dissimulation; but he understood those who did. (54)

This pretension to absolute authenticity, without artifice or illusion, confers in Ralph's view a license to despise all others:

Affecting to consider himself but a type of all humanity, he was at little pains to conceal his true character from the world in general. . . . The only scriptural admonition that Ralph Nickleby heeded, in the letter, was "know thyself." He knew himself well, and choosing to imagine that all mankind were cast in the same mould, hated them. (44)

Both his hatred of others and his assertion of untainted authenticity generate his characteristic contempt for man's life in society, as his speech lamenting a huge speculative loss late in the novel suggests.

—Ten thousand pounds! How many proud painted dames would have fawned and smiled, and how many spendthrift blockheads done me lip-service to my face and cursed me in their hearts, while I turned that ten thousand pounds into twenty! While I ground, and pinched, and used these needy borrowers for my pleasure and profit, what smooth-tongued speeches, and courteous looks, and civil letters they would have given me! The cant of the lying world is, that men like me compass our riches by dissimulation and treachery, by fawning, cringing, and stooping. Why, how many lies, what mean and abject evasions, what humbled behaviour from upstarts who, but for my money, would spurn me aside as they do their betters every day, would that ten thousand pounds have brought me in! (56)

This passage, despite its stilted language, is true; and out of such materials any number of French realistic novels have been constructed. Balzac or Flaubert, for example, would have said, yes, this is indeed the human condition: men in society do lie and flatter and deceive and humiliate themselves—especially when money is to be got by it—and they do need money to live, however much they affect disdain for it. That Ralph has perspicacity and intelligence enough to see this gives Dickens more than a flicker of sympathy for him, and he finds something admirable in the stringency of Ralph's judgment, however incomplete, of himself and others. But for all his penetration, Ralph lacks an essential understanding. A Balzac or a Flaubert would, like Dickens, have the insight to say further, as Ralph would not, that society is where men have to live, like it or not. No one escapes.

When Ralph says that "births, deaths, marriages, and every event which is of interest to most men, had . . . no interest for me" (56), what he is of course rejecting is not human life in general but social life in particular. And the last words he utters—answering the sound of a distant bell in whose tolling he hears the voice of society itself—provide the fundamental terms in which his rejection of man's collective life is couched:

Lie on! . . . with your iron tongue; ring merrily for births that makes expectants writhe, and marriages that are made in hell, and toll ruefully for the dead whose shoes are worn already. Call men to prayers who are godly because not found out, and ring chimes for the coming in of every year that brings this cursed world nearer to its end. (62)

Ralph abhors society because it is a tissue of falsehood which renders in-authentic all who participate in it: it requires us to dissimulate, to perform roles of our own and other people's invention, to speak in euphemisms with which ultimately we delude even ourselves. Ralph cannot tolerate the thought that society is decisively involved in his sense of himself and therefore in his very identity. To be thus tainted—to be inescapably incorporated with others—would be to have one's reality grow insubstantial and to cease to be the exclusive source of one's own validation.

The ideal of authenticity to which Ralph aspires is an ideal of radical freedom and absolute self-assertion. Locating all authority in the self, this ideal is bound, in addition, to conceive of the self in a peculiarly simple way, identifying it at last with nothing more than the material processes of life and the primitive instincts. Thus for Ralph—who habitually calls people "dogs" and who "growls" more than he speaks—the most animalistic behavior is the most real. Dickens economically formulates the problem while burlesquing it when Mrs. Kenwigs, overcome with emotion, weepily falls into a faint. Mr. Kenwigs waves a smelling-bottle under her nose so assiduously that "it became a matter of some doubt whether the tears which coursed down her face, were the result of feelings or *sal volatile*" (15). Ralph would have said *sal volatile*—it can all be explained mechanically: "The spirit does but mean the breath." By the same token Ralph does not believe in love, remarking that "All love—bah! that I should use the cant of boys and girls—is fleeting enough" (34). It is only, he would say, a fever in the blood, and whatever poetry has been attached to it is only there to paper over the degrading biological reality.

Ralph is willing to accept so reduced a conception of personal identity so long as the residue remaining after everything else has been boiled away is absolute. But what is left? As Dickens presents it, the ideal of pure authenticity, insisting on one's perfectly self-subsistent integrity, un-breached by the pressure of other lives, must come to identify the self with its own aggression, because this is the instinct that most uncompromisingly holds the self in opposition to others. Authenticity of this militant purity involves a universal aggression that at last turns against life itself. "I am not a man to be moved by a pretty face," says Ralph. "There's a grinning skull beneath it, and men like me who look and work below the surface see that, and not its delicate covering" (31). Thus to be dead is to have achieved unqualified authenticity; and Ralph embraces his own death as the ultimate assertion of his self-generating reality.

A glance at *A Christmas Carol* will suggest the sources of Ralph's will to authenticity, for Ebenezer Scrooge is a more fully developed version of the conception embodied in Ralph Nickleby. I say this not just because both characters are avaricious money-lenders but, more important, because they both reject as humbug the fully socialized life of man, whose apotheosis is a Dickens Christmas.

Scrooge has come to be the man he is at the beginning of the story by following the same road Ralph trod. As Scrooge's fiancée tells him when ending their engagement: "You fear the world too much. . . . All your other hopes have merged into the hope of being beyond the chance of its sordid reproach. I have seen your nobler aspirations fall off one by one, until the master-passion, Gain, engrosses you" (Stave 2). Thus, while Scrooge, like Ralph, is single-mindedly concerned to preserve his sense of himself untainted by the opinions held of him by others, he too once had "nobler aspirations," just as Ralph feels he might have been a better, happier man had his marriage succeeded, or had Kate come to live in his house, or had his son remained with him and "been a comfort to him and they two happy together" (62).

One reason Ralph hates Nicholas so bitterly from their first meeting is that Nicholas reminds Ralph of his brother:

When my brother was such as he, . . . the first comparisons were drawn between us—always in my disfavour. *He* was open, liberal, gallant, gay; *I* a crafty hunks of cold and stagnant blood, with no passion but love of saving, and no spirit beyond a thirst for gain. . . . Recollections like these . . . flock upon me—when I resign myself to them—in crowds, and from countless quarters. (34)

This train of thought, not followed far in *Nickleby*, is pursued at length in *A Christmas Carol*, which consequently offers a closer view of the impulse toward authentic selfhood in men devoted to exercising aggressively "the power of money." What Ralph and Scrooge have been trying to do is avoid the whole range of "recollections like these." At Marley's first supernatural appearance, Scrooge's blood becomes "conscious of a terrible sensation to which it had been a stranger from infancy . . . ," and the large implication of Stave 1 as a whole is that his entire life has become an effort to deny that "terrible sensation" associated with his earliest years. His reclamation begins with his being forcibly confronted again with all that childhood pain and coming at last to look on his younger self with a compassion hitherto frozen by the shame and humiliation that overshadowed his childhood. The wish to obliterate their childhoods is what leads Scrooge and Ralph to shrink to such mean and penurious limits the compass of the self, in the name of making absolute its autonomy.

Characters like these point to one of the possible fates that lie in wait for men. Under the pressure of their distorting experience, people really do make such choices, which distort them still more. And to figures such as these, no less complex than interesting in their peculiar and extreme relation to money, such incantatory explanations as "the anal organization of character" or "the folkloric motif of the demon miser" do no justice. But even a character like Arthur Gride, to whom such stock formulae are more appropriate, is not sufficiently explained by them. He too has come—how, we are not told—to pique himself on the special authenticity of his life as a usurer. Observe him poring over his ledger:

Well-a-day now, this is all my library, but it's one of the most entertaining books that were ever written; it's a delightful book, and all true and real—that's the best of it—true as the Bank of England, and real as its gold and silver. Written by Arthur Gride—he, he, he! None of your story-book writers will ever make as good a book as this, I warrant me. It's composed for private circulation—for my own particular reading, and nobody else's. He, he! (53)

All the familiar threads are here—absolute truth, absolute self, and the rejection of the factitious "story-book" life of the spirit in culture. But without the intelligence of Scrooge or Ralph Nickleby, which allows them (at least in part) to choose such a fate with their eyes open and to offer it as a mistaken but nonetheless understandable judgment on the world, a destiny like this excites no sympathy to qualify our repugnance.

Such a strategy for insuring authentic selfhood as Ralph Nickleby adopts is riddled with ironies, two of which need mentioning here. First, claiming immunity from the duplicity and self-deception that social life imposes, Ralph asserts that he has no secrets and that therefore it is not possible to blackmail him. "To be plain with you," he confidently advises Brooker, "I am a careful man, and know my affairs thoroughly. I know the world, and the world knows me" (44). The irony is that Ralph does indeed have a secret; what makes it a secret is that he himself doesn't know it. Alas, it is not possible to "know thyself" as absolutely as Ralph claims.

The second irony is deeper. Ralph perceives that allowing the opinions of others to affect his sense of his own being would greatly qualify his authenticity, and thus his choosing to be a villain (like some "heroic" existential *homme revolté*) explicitly signals his rejection of the judgments and interests of others. But of course this choice of authentic selfhood is an ideal only a highly developed self-consciousness could invent, and the doubleness involved in self-consciousness necessarily dilutes the pure authenticity to which Ralph pretends. Jean-Jacques Rousseau's account of the origin of self-consciousness (to take a convenient example) suggests why this must be so: self-consciousness arose, says he, at the moment when, having abandoned their primeval solitude and having newly formed themselves into bands, primitive men began to compare themselves to each other and thus to become for the first time also observers of themselves.[5] Self-consciousness, in this view, is a product of one's relation to others; one's awareness of others is inseparable from one's sense of one's own identity. Absolute authenticity, impervious to the opinion of others and with all the solidity of a fact of nature, is thus the prerogative only of an unreflecting creature like the original natural man of Rousseau's *Discourse on Inequality*; and such a creature avoids experiencing his identity as problematic not because he is exempt in his solitariness from the hypocrisy inherent in social life but rather because he has not yet developed a sense of himself as a self. Thus, although Ralph is quite right to see society as subversive of the kind of authenticity to which he aspires, the problem is nevertheless more radical than he supposes and cannot be solved by such meager contrivances as the antisocial behavior he adopts. This is not an emancipation from society but only another position taken with respect to it. The taint lies not just on the surface but at the heart of our being.

And so Ralph's effort to achieve the authenticity of nature ineluctably leads him to the authenticity of death. This notion, which Tennyson also intermittently held, may be said to be the last stand of the pastoral ideal, as in the opening lines of "Tithonus":

> The woods decay, the woods decay and fall,
> The vapours weep their burthen to the ground,
> Man comes and tills the field and lies beneath,
> And after many a summer dies the swan.

The fact that men (like all living things) die puts them at last in harmony with the vast, majestic movement of the cosmos. Men become elemental in their deaths, as they are

> Rolled round in earth's diurnal course,
> With rocks, and stones, and trees.[6]

Only in death do we become fully a part of that immense and regular force that rolls through all things.

So Ralph returns himself to nature, but in a way that stands the pastoral tradition completely on its head. "No bell or book for me," he cries; "throw me on a dunghill, and let me rot there to infect the air!" (62). He does not so much subside as explode into the energies that animate nature, a nature that here is terrible and corrupt. Its processes are decomposition and disease, and Ralph merges himself into its malignity.

.　.　.

Where is all this aggression coming from? Whether it is an inseparable part of human nature or a by-product of social arrangements is, to be sure, among the most vexed and fundamental of "those problems of human nature, which may be noted down, but not solved" (28). Though Dickens never had a simple view of the question of aggression—his ability to face paradox and contradiction with equanimity was after all one of the elements of his genius—in *Nickleby* he does have a consistent assumption about its source. It appears to him a constitutive element of human nature, universal among men, with virtually the status of an instinct.

The passage in which "oily" Mr. Snawley, seizing Smike in a headlock, fraudulently claims that his "parental instinct" has enabled him to recognize in this unfortunate boy his lost son makes this point brilliantly. What was it, asks Snawley, that made me interested in Smike when I first saw him? What was it "that made me burn all over with a wish to chastise him severely" for escaping from Dotheboys Hall?

> "It was parental instinct, sir," observed Squeers.
>
> "That's what it was, sir," rejoined Snawley; "the elevated feeling . . . of the ancient Romans and Grecians, and of the beasts of the field and birds of the air, with the exception of rabbits and tomcats, which sometimes devour their offspring. My heart yearned towards him. I could have—I don't know what I couldn't have done to him in the anger of a father."
>
> "It only shows what Natur is, sir," said Mr. Squeers. "She's a rum 'un, is Natur."
>
> "She is a holy thing, sir," remarked Snawley.
>
> "I believe you," added Mr. Squeers, with a moral sigh. "I should like to know how we should ever get on without her. . . . Oh what a blessed thing, sir, to be in a state of natur!" (45)

The cannibal cats, the anger of a father, the wish to chastise—at every moment this zany "philosophical discourse" hilariously subverts the venerable idea that beneficent nature, imbued with moral intentions, endows all creatures only with innocent and praiseworthy impulses which should be taken as moral norms, tending as they do only toward harmony, health, and tranquility. On the contrary, as Snawley's travesty of sentimental primitivism insistently reminds us, so endemic is violence in the natural world, so violent are some of the instincts with which nature has endowed living creatures, that some animals devour their babies—an act of shocking and (as we say) unnatural violence that, along with other such shocking occurrences, nevertheless happens often enough in the course of nature.

No wonder Dickens growled when he went to see Edward Stirling's dramatization of Nickleby just after it opened in November 1838. Though he was generally satisfied, he hated the "sundry choice sentiments and rubbish regarding the little robins in the field which have been put in [Smike's] mouth by Mr. Stirling the adaptor." Mrs. Keeley, who played Smike, remarked later, "I shall never forget Dickens's face when he heard me repeating these lines. Turning to the prompter he said, 'Damn the robins; cut them out.'"[7] Such "rubbish" is exactly contrary to the whole spirit of this novel, and perhaps Dickens had Stirling's lines in mind when in the "philosophical discourse" (in the May 1839 number of Nickleby) Snawley waxes lyrical about the "beasts of the field and birds of the air."

Moreover, the whole dramatic situation of Snawley's discourse shows that there is no "parental instinct" that enables a father intuitively to recognize his long-lost son. For, though Snawley is not Smike's father, Ralph Nickleby, presiding over this confrontation and over the whole lethal persecution of Smike, is; and certainly he is without the slightest intimation of any relationship to this unfortunate victim. Nature provides no safeguards to prevent such savage things as fathers killing their children. And finally, any lingering temptation to credit Snawley's and Squeers's vaporings about holy instincts and the blessed state of nature must be utterly extinguished by the Aggression Quotient of this passage, so to speak. How holy can our instincts be if, even while glorifying them, these two work themselves up to so extreme a pitch of malice that they threaten to explode with it, leaving behind only two pairs of smoking boots?

This is not to say that Dickens sees aggression as the only instinct inherent in human nature. Far from it, if his imagination pictures even a Squeers as able to like his wife and foster his children. But the presence of a powerful charge of aggression along with the more genial impulses in every human constitution makes human nature a more problematic quantity than is admitted by the sentimental primitivism Squeers and Snawley burlesque. To be sure, the seeds of what Snawley calls elevated feelings are part of every man's original endowment, but so qualified and mixed with baser feelings that, as Charles Cheeryble explains, they can readily be eradicated:

Natural affections and instincts . . . are the most beautiful of the Almighty's works, but like other beautiful works of His, they must be reared and fostered, or it is as natural that they should be wholly obscured, and that new feelings should usurp their place, as it is that the sweetest productions of the earth, left untended, should be choked with weeds and briars. (46)

Human nature, after all, is a subcategory of nature in general, and it necessarily shares nature's liberal endowment of violence. *Nickleby* provides the beginnings of what in *Martin Chuzzlewit* becomes a sustained satire on the pastoral idea, a satire showing nature as a darker reality than pastoral poetry pretends. Hence the echoes of *Paradise Lost* that Dickens summons in telling the story of Smike, whose pathetic life underscores how unparadisial man's fate is, and whose dying vision of Eden, our archetypal image of benevolent nature, firmly puts *Nickleby*'s Eden beyond the grave.

While Dickens writes often enough of nature's beauty and sublimity—as when, for example, he paints a majestic sunset, or the solemn fog in the Kentish marshes, or the pleasures of a country walk or coach-ride—such scenes as delight him are of humanized and cultivated nature, in which plowed fields and antique church spires testify that man's harmony with the natural world is arduously earned. Unmodified nature, by contrast, like the Alpine landscape in *Little Dorrit*, almost always makes Dickens the city-dweller uneasy, and in *Nickleby* nature is consistently imagined as squalid and cruel. In this novel it is far from true that nature never did betray the heart that loved her. What other lesson to draw from the pupils of Dotheboys Hall?

Pale and haggard faces, lank and bony figures, children with the countenances of old men, deformities with irons upon their limbs, boys of stunted growth, and others whose long meagre legs would hardly bear their stooping bodies, all crowded on the view together; there were the bleared eye, the hare-lip, the crooked foot, and every ugliness or distortion that told of unnatural aversion conceived by parents for their offspring, or of young lives which, from the earliest dawn of infancy, had been one horrible endurance of cruelty and neglect. (8)

Nature produces deformity and injustice. Nature can make mistakes.

2

Polite Forms and Ceremonies

For aggression of this magnitude, traditional political philosophy offers the social order as an antidote, and by *Barnaby Rudge* Dickens himself had come to prescribe the same potent cure. But in *Nickleby* his understanding of society had not yet reached that point. Writing in 1911, A. S. G. Canning takes note of this failure of therapeutics in an observation about Dotheboys Hall that is equally applicable to the novel as a whole. It is a wonder, he splutters, that no one interfered with Mr. Squeers's trade in children's misery. "[W]here were the clergymen of the parish, or the nearest magistrates?" he demands. Surely they had to know what was going on, and emphatically "[t]heir utter neglect of duty, and wilful ignorance of such long continued barbarity to helpless children deserved nearly as much blame as the cruelty of the schoolmaster." But "the school is and has evidently been for many years as completely neglected as if in some deserted island, instead of in one of the chief English counties." Even John Browdie, and even Nicholas after he leaves Dotheboys Hall, do nothing "to relieve the miserable crowd of sufferers left behind them," not so much as troubling to rouse those clergy or magistrates in whom Mr. Canning reposes such confidence. In fact, "[h]ad Squeers been some child-eating ogre in an enchanted castle, or a savage chief in a remote country, he could hardly have been more independent of all civilised control or supervision." He and his wife are "in almost despotic power over their wretched little kingdom of suffering children, virtually monarchs of all they survey, and apparently responsible to nobody."[1]

In fact, of course, "civilised control or supervision" is hard to find anywhere in the world of *Nicholas Nickleby*, for the most telling sign of this novel's immaturity is its inability to see society, the source of that control, as a coherent structure. In *Nickleby*, a book viewing each man as "a mere unit among a busy throng, all utterly regardless of him" (16), the separate individuals do not add up to a unified whole. Each man is a negatively charged atom, jostling and repelling all the rest.

When callow Lord Frederick drawlingly praises his friend Hawk as "the most knowing card in the pa-ack" (19), he is hardly original in comparing society to a card game. But however conventional the idea, the particular color it takes when Dickens more than once invokes it in *Nickleby* shows how ingrained in this novel's texture is the image of society as a mere agglomeration of unconnected units. The game played in *Nickleby*—at the Kenwigses' (14) and at Fanny Squeers's tea party (9)—is Speculation: which, Dickens explains at the novel's very beginning, "is a round game; the players see little or nothing of their cards at first starting; gains *may* be great—and so may losses" (1). In other words, the game that is *Nickleby*'s metaphor of society is a game played blindly, at the mercy of chance; but more important, a "round" game is one pitting each player against every other player, and this image suggests how persistently Dickens, looking out into the social world at this moment in his career, sees little more than a ritualized version of the war of all against all. A century earlier, Jonathan Swift had elaborated virtually the same conceit: "QUADRILLE in particular bears some Resemblance to the State of Nature," he observed, "wherein every Woman is against every Woman: The Unions short, inconstant, and soon broke; the League made this Minute without knowing the Ally; and dissolved in the next." Similarly, Charles Lamb opined in "Mrs. Battle's Opinions on Whist" that a round game is "a mere naked war of every man against every man, as in cribbage, without league or alliance." Square games are better, being authentically social. In them you "glory in some surprising stroke of skill or fortune . . . because your partner sympathises in the contingency. You win for two, you triumph for two. Two are exalted. . . . Two losing to two are better reconciled, than one to one in that close butchery. The hostile feeling is weakened by multiplying the channels. War becomes a civil game." [2]

The largest social unit Dickens can see in *Nickleby*—when he can see any unit larger than the individual—is a "little world," like the "little world of the theatre" (29) or the "little kingdom" of Madame Mantalini's workshop (18). And these worlds he imagines to be self-enclosed and autonomous. "[L]et it be remembered," he remarks, "that most men live in a world of their own, and that in that limited circle alone are they ambitious for distinction and applause."

Thus, cases of injustice, and oppression, and tyranny, and the most extravagant bigotry, are in constant occurrence among us every day. It is the custom to trumpet forth much wonder and astonishment at the chief actors therein setting at defiance so completely the opinion of the world; but there is no greater fallacy; it is precisely because they do consult the opinion of their own little world that such things take place at all, and strike the great world dumb with amazement. (28)

These little worlds, virtually by definition, fail to add up to any larger reality.

Even Parliament proves this rule, as a visit to Mr. Gregsbury, MP, amply establishes (16). His fatuous self-interest and sniggering contempt for his constituents suggest how completely government in *Nickleby* is just one more little world, connected to nothing beyond itself. As a result, society's chief institution of "civilised control or supervision" is powerless to mediate aggression.

In *Nickleby*, London too appears in disjointed fragments. Dickens succeeds wonderfully in clarifying the social structure of a single lodging house or a distinct neighborhood like Golden Square or Cadogan Place, anatomized, as in the *Sketches by Boz*, with surgical deftness. But less sure is his grasp of the metropolis as a whole. "Streams of people apparently without end poured on and on, . . . while vehicles of all shapes and makes, mingled up together in one moving mass like running water, lent their ceaseless roar to swell the noise and tumult" begins his set-piece description, which ends by observing, "Life and death went hand in hand; wealth and poverty stood side by side; repletion and starvation laid them down together" (32). The energy and movement of Victorian London are here, but the only structure Dickens sees is the unmistakable opposition of glaring contrasts. A short time later he had learned to perceive the structure of an urban order so complex as to look to the innocent observer like chaos; but in *Nickleby* that illuminating eye, still maturing, could not resolve the city's overall organization into focus.

. . .

Though Dickens is not yet able to see the social order as aggression's most effective curb, he nevertheless marshals throughout the novel an energetic if somewhat diffuse opposition to man's propensity for violence. For example, without clearly seeing how society operates to defuse aggression, he sees and condemns features of his own society and culture that perversely contribute to aggressive atomism rather than restraining it. So in representing Parliament as anything but a force for coherence and order, he is implying a criticism of government—run by the windbag Gregsburies of the world—for refusing to do the fundamental task it ought to do. Parliament *intends* to do nothing, Dickens senses; and indeed by the time of *Nickleby*'s 1848 preface he makes explicit what is only dimly adumbrated in Gregsbury's *laissez-faire*-tinged rhetoric of independence, material improvement, and prosperity:

Of the monstrous neglect of education in England, and the disregard of it by the State as a means of forming good or bad citizens, and miserable or happy men, private schools long afforded a notable example. Although any man who had proved his unfitness for any other occupation in life, was free, without examination or qualification, to open a school anywhere; . . . and although schoolmasters, as a race, were the blockheads and impostors who might naturally be expected to spring from such a state of things, and to flourish in it; these Yorkshire schoolmasters were the lowest and most rotten round in the whole ladder. Traders in the avarice, indifference, or imbecility of parents, and the helplessness of children; ignorant, sordid, brutal men, to whom few considerate persons would have entrusted the board and lodging of a horse or a dog; they formed the worthy cornerstone of a structure, which, for absurdity and a magnificent highminded *laissez-aller* neglect, has rarely been exceeded in the world.

It would be hard for Dickens to imagine a more nonsensical politics than one whose charge to government is *Laissez-faire, laissez-aller*. How can anyone suppose that leaving each man alone to follow his rational self-interest will advance the common good willy-nilly, thanks to the intervention of a benign mechanism imbedded in the order of nature? Such propositions are diametrically opposed to *Nicholas Nickleby*'s basic assumptions, for not just nature but also human nature in *Nickleby* is radically different from the beneficent picture painted by the *laissez-faire* theorists. Far from being Adam Smith's reasonable creatures governed by rational self-interest, men as Dickens sees them are beset by dark, extravagantly irrational, inborn impulses, which often lead them to imprudent, antisocial, or self-destructive actions. When human affairs are left alone to take care of themselves, in the absence of any real government,

they are not guided by an invisible hand. Instead, they tend naturally toward oppression, exploitation, and inhumanity, for the world is full of
"ignorant, sordid, brutal men," whose most salient constitutional trait is
cruelty. Hence governments must govern and societies must educate.

Explicit enough in the 1848 preface, this criticism of the ascendant English theory of government as a force intensifying aggressive atomism is
still incubating in the novel itself. But fully developed is Dickens's critique
of another such disruptive influence, the Regency ideal of masculinity.
George Ford nominates *Oliver Twist* as the first Victorian novel because it
perfectly embodies that emerging moral earnestness Elizabeth Barrett so
favorably contrasted with the waning *ethos* of "gentlemen topers, with
their low gentility and 'hip hip hurrahs,' and wine out of wine-coolers."
But I am backing *Nicholas Nickleby* for this distinction, for, in his hostility to the callous gentlemanly code of manners and morals Sir Mulberry Hawk, Baronet, inherits from the Baron of Grogzwig, it is an active agent of the change in sensibility that George Ford outlines.[3]

In no uncertain terms does Dickens dissociate his hero from the Regency male ethic:

And here it may be observed, that Nicholas was not, in the ordinary sense of the
word, a young man of high spirit. He would resent an affront to himself, or inter-
pose to redress a wrong offered to another, as boldly and freely as any knight that
ever set lance in rest; but he lacked that peculiar excess of coolness and great-
minded selfishness, which invariably distinguish gentlemen of high spirit. In
truth, for our own part, we are rather disposed to look upon such gentlemen as
being rather incumbrances than otherwise in rising families, happening to be ac-
quainted with several whose spirit prevents their settling down to any grovelling
occupation, and only displays itself in a tendency to cultivate mustachios, and
look fierce; and although mustachios and ferocity are both very pretty things in
their way, . . . we confess a desire to see them bred at the owner's proper cost,
rather than at the expense of low-spirited people. (16)

An ideal of manhood defined by ferocity, swaggering, and patrician selfishness is a mindless glorification of mere masculine aggressiveness,
Dickens thinks. Doubtless appropriate when the Baron of Grogzwig
hunted bears and warred with his neighbors, it has no place in the modern world. If it is unseemly in aristocrats like Verisopht or Hawk, it is
ludicrous in the bourgeois dandies this passage censures. Not that chivalry is to be a thing of the past, as the emphatically middle-class example
of Nicholas goes to show. But it is to be a defensive chivalry; unlike the

knights of medieval romance, Nicholas does not go looking for trouble for the fun of parading his prowess.

Certainly by the late 1830s this was by no means an idiosyncratic judgment. Indeed, a growing resistance to rakish Regency aggressiveness was only one manifestation of the "refinement of manners" and "progress of civilization" that the Victorians believed their age was affecting and of which Lord Macaulay, for instance, was so fluent a spokesman. William Hazlitt drew attention to this change early, remarking, "Modern manners may be compared to a modern stagecoach: our limbs may be a little cramped with the confinement and we may grow drowsy; but we arrive safe, without any very amusing or very sad incident, at our journey's end."[4] More trenchant is Thomas Carlyle, speaking of the vast material and moral progress stalwartly made in Britain since its Saxon beginnings: "This mild Good-morrow which the stranger bids thee, equitable, nay, forbearant if need were, judicially calm and law-observing towards thee a stranger, what work has it not cost?"[5] When, in 1869, Matthew Arnold characterized the whole aristocratic class that produced the likes of Mulberry Hawk as "barbarians," this cultural devaluation of masculine aggression as an energy opposed to the workings of culture and the progress of civilization was a long-established fact.

. . .

But these criticisms are secondary to the main thrust of *Nickleby*'s opposition to aggressive atomism, for the book offers a wide range of antidotes to the primary aggressiveness of human beings, though no one of them is as convincing as Dickens's description of the problem itself.

First, one can fight fire with fire and oppose the wicked with force—like Nicholas, who often seems an impetuous embodiment of the corollary to John Locke's Law of Nature, giving every man a right to punish an offender.[6] With a vengeance does he punish Squeers and maim Hawk, providing two of the story's most satisfying moments. Young Frank Cheeryble is a similar scourge of offenders, while poor Newman Noggs, righteous but weak, is reduced to punishing the egregious Ralph in pantomime, hidden behind a door.

Or else one can counter human nature's dark promptings by taking to a fanatical extreme the advice Mr. Squeers, with brutal humor, gives his famished pupils to "subdue your appetites, my dears, and you've conquered human natur" (5). Such is the purpose of Nicholas and Kate in refusing (temporarily) to marry the people they love for fear of appearing predatory.

Or there are the Cheeryble brothers, Dickens's simplest answer to the problem of aggression. These profoundly civil, inexhaustibly benevolent twins have quite simply escaped its taint altogether, being made, one supposes, almost genetically incapable of any radically individualist impulse by virtue of being parts of an inseparable pair, like andirons. Dickens emphasizes this by affording them the luxury of endlessly counterfeiting angry violence. Shouting "Damn your obstinancy!" at their loyal old clerk while regarding him with faces "radiant with attachment" and "without the faintest spark of anger," for instance, they generously announce plans to make him a partner—threatening that "if he won't submit to it peaceably, we must have recourse to violence" (35). So pacific a statement couched in such vehement language provides an appropriate if heavy-handed emblem of violence redeemed by civility; and indeed the Cheerybles' office contains *Nickleby*'s explicit, poignant symbol of aggression disarmed:

Everything gave back, besides, some reflection of the kindly spirit of the brothers. . . . Among the shipping-announcements . . . which decorated the counting-house wall, were designs for alms-houses, statements of charities, and plans for new hospitals. A blunderbuss and two swords hung above the chimney-piece for the terror of evil-doers, but the blunderbuss was rusty and shattered, and the swords were broken and edgeless. Elsewhere, their open display in such a condition would have raised a smile, but there it seemed as though even violent and offensive weapons partook of the reigning influence, and became emblems of mercy and forbearance. (37)

This rusty blunderbuss, which had already made an appearance in the same deliberate capacity in Mr. Wardle's kitchen in *Pickwick*,[7] demonstrates how inexorably instruments of violence crumble in the Cheerybles' militantly benign atmosphere. If the brothers cannot quite beat their swords into plowshares, they can at least transform them into the quaint wall-decorations that are the stock-in-trade of the old curiosity shop.

Humphry House may be a bit hard on the Cheerybles when he sniffs that "even children have a horror of their smiles and hand-rubbing seen through glass, of their placid unremitting unctuousness,"[8] but surely no reader has failed to express at least a sigh of impatience with these characters, who so frequently ring false. In the novel's own terms their lack of aggression makes them too good to be true. But so pressing does the problem of aggression appear to Dickens here, and so imperfectly is he able to focus on institutions that mediate and contain it, that he is inclined at moments to see rooting it out altogether as the only satisfactory way to neutralize it, impossible as he knows that to be.

Similarly false is Dickens's idealized picture of the House of Cheeryble Brothers, an all-in-one combination of home, brotherhood, and business, in which all relationships are personal ties of affection, and doing business is chiefly a matter of vigorous corporate philanthropizing punctuated by ceremonial staff dinners of the kind Fezziwig & Co. reserved for Christmas alone. To the extent that economic life is a theater of conflict, Dickens's wish to show how it might easily be an arena of sociability and harmony is central to his impulse to disarm hostility in this aggression-haunted novel. But to do this he falsifies the nature of business, as a glance at the Cheerybles' books discloses. These sacred documents, over which Tim Linkinwater presides, transcend any individual life, assuring, as Tim proudly says, that "the business will go on when I'm dead as well as it did when I was alive—just the same . . ." (37). This is a moving thought; but to achieve the vision of order and continuity incorporated in these ledgers, Dickens has had to ignore the fundamentals of bookkeeping, which depends, in Max Weber's words, on "the most complete possible separation of the enterprise and its conditions of success and failure, from the household or private budgetary unit and its property interests." The familial organization of the Cheeryble firm is an attempt to deny the need "to separate the sphere of private affairs from the business."[9] For the Cheerybles, economic life and communal life are wholly reconciled with each other.

Moreover, in double-entry bookkeeping

there is introduced the fiction of exchange transactions between the different parts of a single enterprise; or, between different accounts in order to develop a technique of estimating the bearing of each particular measure on the profitability of the enterprise. Thus the highest degree of rational capital accounting presupposes the existence of competition on a large scale.[10]

In other words, the competition that is the *sine qua non* of capitalism is imbedded in the internal structure of any single enterprise. By trying, in Tim's books, to make whole what is in fact divided and competitive, Dickens has had to make the Cheerybles businessmen who do not practice capitalism: the ledgers can only contain large debits for munificent charitable donations and small ones for turkey and champagne and works of "art" made by Madeline Bray and Co. In this way, the Cheeryble sections of *Nickleby*, like the dead stevedore whose widow the brothers so generously aid, are fatally crushed under a heavy load of sugar (35).

The same cannot be said of the Kenwigses, a lower-middle class family (like Dickens's own) who provide, under the affectionate comedy with which *Nickleby* treats their thirst for gentility, the novel's most convincing answer to aggression. For they are determined to make over human nature, to refine and civilize it, to retailor it by means of dancing lessons, French lessons, genteel manners, pretty dresses, hairdos, and so on, all according to the latest middle-class pattern. Committed to the very opposite of Ralph Nickleby's notion of authenticity, they are ceaselessly making themselves up, tirelessly dramatizing themselves according to their image of what solidly middle-class people, one rung above them on the social ladder, should be. Pretending to a reality that can only be authenticated by society, they are as a result anxiously attuned to the opinions and needs of others, before whom their whole ambition is to sparkle. For the Kenwigses "the honour of the family was involved in . . . making the most splendid *appearance* possible" (emphasis added), and they ache to have their children "achieve that signal triumph over the daughters of all other people, anything less than which would be tantamount to defeat" (52). By enlisting their competitiveness wholly in the service of civilization and its values they redeem aggression, making its energy creative. This is a far cry from the Cheerybles, who have no aggression to be redeemed, and who, having no problem, can offer no solution.

But the Kenwigses do resemble the Cheerybles in their attention to ceremony and celebration, intended to invest the common milestones of ordinary life with virtually a religious significance. Thus the brothers, in what seems a dress rehearsal for Christmas, annually commemorate both "The Memory of our Mother" and the birthday of their clerk in a ritual dinner whose order is as fixed as liturgy. Similarly, the Kenwigses enter the novel in the midst of just such a ritual celebration of their anniversary, and later, when Mrs. Kenwigs has a baby boy, every ceremony surrounding childbirth is scrupulously honored. Mr. Kenwigs of course thinks of "having it in the papers," and just before the baby is born, he muffles the street-door knocker, with "some pomp and much excitement," in a white kid glove. There was, Dickens explains, no

obvious cause or reason why Mr. Kenwigs should take the trouble of muffling this particular knocker, . . . because . . . the street-door always stood wide open, and the knocker was never used at all. . . . As a question of mere necessity and usefulness, therefore, this muffling of the knocker was thoroughly incomprehensible.

But knockers may be muffled for other purposes than those of mere utilitarianism. . . . There are certain polite forms and ceremonies which must be observed in civilised life, or mankind relapse into their original barbarism. No genteel lady was ever yet confined—indeed, no genteel confinement can possibly take place—without the accompanying symbol of a muffled knocker. Mrs. Kenwigs was a lady of some pretensions to gentility; Mrs. Kenwigs was confined. And, therefore, Mr. Kenwigs tied up the silent knocker on the premises in a white kid glove. (36)

Warmly affectionate in spite of its defensive armor of mannered irony, this description, one of *Nickleby*'s central passages, demonstrates beneath its comedy how consciously Dickens is examining the difference between "civilised life" and mankind's "original barbarism," and it registers his belief that society evolved out of a barbarous, Hobbesian state of nature. Moreover, the dark instincts inherent in man's precivilized constitution remain latent in his civilized personality: it is always possible for us to "*relapse*" into "original barbarism," as *Barnaby Rudge* stresses. And finally Dickens notes that the civilization he sees as the counterprinciple to the "original barbarism" in which human aggression has its roots is not simply a "utilarian" reality—it is not, in other words, merely a mechanical, material, rational fact. How could it be, if its essential ingredients include ritual, ceremony, and a concern for prestige?

Though the nonutilitarian aspect of civilization (along with the larger question of the nature of society and its relation to aggression) certainly comes more sharply into focus in *Barnaby Rudge* and *American Notes*, it is nevertheless so plain a theme in *Nickleby* that a reader is brought up short by Hillis Miller's complaint that the "consolations" offered in the novel "reveal themselves as just what they are: mere human conventions, resting on nothing, and validated by nothing."[11] Human conventions, Miller appears to think, are not "natural"—and so, far removed from fixed eternal truth, they are epiphenominal and ultimately meaningless. But that conventions, manners, rituals, social roles, and the like are not merely natural is just the point. Essential elements of social life in Dickens's view, they are a constant affirmation of civilization as something opposed to and better than the state of nature. Thus in our manners we maintain that we are not mere animals absorbed in brutish nature. Table etiquette, marriages, funerals—by clothing the brute facts of our lives in man-made conventions, we domesticate and (to use one of *Nickleby*'s own words) humanize them (31).

The web of convention in which civilization is suspended offers one essential barrier to the aggression that is the novel's subject. Certainly Dickens has this in mind when he says that Kenwigs's conventional, ceremonial muffling the knocker is a "symbol": aside from symbolizing Kenwigs's pretentions to gentility, it also symbolizes, in cushioning that which strikes, the softening of violence. One can't help hoping that Kenwigs has one of those door knockers formed like a clenched hand—then he would be literally as well as symbolically gloving the fist.

.   .   .

The story of the Five Sisters of York, told to unite "strangers . . . thrown unexpectedly together" into a temporary "little community" by means of this eminently social activity, offers in a nutshell the novel's central opposition between aggression and its antidotes. Set in 1402, the tale unfolds against the backdrop of Hotspur's rebellion, in which the sisters' husbands play leading roles. And this historical moment is crucial to the story's point, for the Wars of the Roses and these incessant rebellions leading up to them are, along with the civil wars of the seventeenth century, the only notable instances in English history when the social fabric was dramatically unravelling. Thus the social situation at the story's center, as in *Mother Courage*, is a state of anarchy that really existed, "a time of Warre, where every man is Enemy to every man," to use Hobbes's words characterizing the state of nature.[12] And in these lawless times, as Dickens understands them, man's primitive barbarism has free rein, trampling all before it, so that at last, as a monk harshly crows to one of the now widowed and humbled sisters:

The gallant youth who looked into thine eyes, and hung upon thy very breath . . . , lies buried on a plain whereof the turf is red with blood. Rusty fragments of armour[,] once brightly burnished, lie rotting on the ground, and are as little distinguishable for his, as are the bones that crumble in the mould! (6)

Given a world of all-corroding violence, according to the monk, one's only reasonable response is contemptuous rejection of the whole meaningless spectacle. Any other view of life is vanity and self-deception. As angry and as life-denyingly "authentic" as Ralph Nickleby, who sees a world peopled only by Squeerses and a skull beneath every pretty face, the monk looks out and discerns nothing but loathsome animals living and dying in aimless isolation, tearing each other into putrefying pieces. For these two characters, this world is a dunghill; and indeed the monk embodies in his profession that extreme tradition in the Western imagination that sees man's earthly life as given over to blind violence and aggression, as utterly fallen into evil on account of original sin, beyond hope of earthly redemption. If there be any meaning, it does not have its abode in the pathetic lives of men.

This vision the beautiful sisters firmly reject. The world is indeed filled with aggression; but instead of responding with scorn, the sisters untiringly create counterprinciples to violence, loss, and death, chief among which is the community they have steadfastly forged. By successfully preserving those "holy ties" that bind them together, they have surrounded their lives with a redeeming meaning. "To die is our heavy portion," says one sister; but as if in refutation of Ralph Nickleby's belief that the meaning of life is death, she goes on to wish that "when our cold hearts cease to beat, let warm hearts be beating near."

Essential to their sustaining communal life are art and memory, virtually modes of each other in this story. Their embroidery (art has humble avatars in *Nickleby*) is an agency of association, binding them together with links of affection and connecting their present with their past lives. It even links them to the future, for the York Minster windows still glow with their patterns, and the story of their lives, now part of the tradition associated with a great monument of art and community, is remembered centuries later, giving the lie to Mrs. Squeers's assertion that "it will be all the same a hundred years hence." When the gray-headed gentleman says of them that "time passed away as a tale that is told," he is not just saying that time passed quickly, but that, like stories, it had structure and meaning. For the sisters, time has been socialized and transformed into history.

A principal lesson of "The Five Sisters of York" is that, "If our affections be tried, our affections are our consolation and comfort; and memory, however sad, is the best and purest link between this world and a better" (6). Amply illustrated by the tale, the statement about our affections needs no comment. But the point about memory, refuting the approach to life adopted by Ralph Nickleby and Ebenezer Scrooge, comes more clearly into focus when contrasted with Dickens's most explicit examination of that impoverished outlook in the Christmas book for 1849, *The Haunted Man*, which reworks and enlarges upon the central themes of *A Christmas Carol*. Here the protagonist, Mr. Redlaw, is haunted by the memory of the sorrow and wrong he has suffered in his past. A Ghost offers to cancel those painful remembrances and will cancel along with them "the intertwisted chain of feelings and associations, each in its turn dependent on, and nourished by, the banished recollections" (1). Moreover, Redlaw's presence will henceforward have the power of obliterating the memories of sorrow and wrong in everyone he meets. Redlaw assents, only to discover that "the intertwisted chain of feelings and associations" he has given up are precisely his feelings of sympathy and compassion for his fellow men; he has lost what *Nickleby* calls "the best and purest link between this world and a better." And those whom the power of his presence affects also lose, in losing their memories of sorrow, those inextricably associated feelings of gratitude, love, and unselfish compassion which bind them to their friends and families. Deprived of the memories of their shared suffering, of help and comfort given them in their sorrow, they instantly become selfish and isolate, beginning to hate where once they loved. And at last in the Tetterby family, poor but loving like Bob Cratchit's family, the result is that "the hand of every little Tetterby was against the other little Tetterbys" (3), in a juvenile version of the war of all against all.

The only creature not poisoned by Redlaw's infection is a parentless, homeless, ragged child of the worst slums: "a baby savage, a young monster, a child who had never been a child, a creature who might live to take the outward form of a man, but who, within, would live and perish a mere beast" (1). Redlaw's "influence is powerless here, because from this child's bosom [he] can banish nothing." For this child, as the Ghost tells Redlaw,

is the last, completest illustration of a human creature, utterly bereft of such remembrances as you have yielded up. No softening memory of sorrow, wrong, or trouble enters here, because this wretched mortal from his birth has been abandoned to a worse condition than the beasts, and has, within his knowledge, no one contrast, no humanising touch, to make a grain of such a memory spring up in his hardened breast. All within this desolate creature is barren wilderness. (3)

Here, in short, is an authentic wild boy; *this* is the "Noble" Savage. And his defining characteristic is his total lack of that faculty of memory that nourishes the affections linking us to our kind and permitting our participation in a community, the feelings Charles Cheeryble says in his speech on culture "must be reared and fostered." These are the feelings that the Five Sisters of York have in such abundance and that *Nicholas Nickleby* offers as one essential antidote to isolate, aggressive savagery.

. . .

Having said that Dickens offers art as a major counterprinciple to aggressive atomism in the "Five Sisters," I hasten to add a couple of necessary explanations. "Embroidery?" one might object—"that's art?" A borderline case, granted; but Dickens readers are used to seeing art in modest, sometimes even sleazy, embodiments, such as Mr. Sleary's horse-riding in *Hard Times*. And that is because Dickens makes no rarified, Pater-like claims for art. For him, art is a preeminently social, even popular, matter, a realm of shared emotion and shared significance, and consequently it has to keep both feet on the ground. In becoming too refined or arcane, it becomes pointless; and Dickens emphasizes the necessary communal rootedness of art by habitually embodying it not in lieder recitals but in circuses or Punch and Judy shows.

The Five Sisters, of course, are by no means the humblest of *Nickleby*'s artists. Certainly Miss La Creevy, the miniaturist, is no artistic Prometheus, galvanized by art's agony and ecstasy. But however unassuming, she unmistakably shows how art helps remedy aggressive atomism by her efforts to combine fragments into unified wholes and her success in correcting nature and holding up to her clients' ideal (and therefore partly false) images of themselves. Still, for authentic shabbiness, who can compare with Vincent Crummles and his travelling theatrical troupe, *Nickleby*'s most glorious and irrepressible practitioners of art? What artist can compare with them for having both feet on the ground—do they not require Nicholas to write them a play to include a real pump and two washtubs bought cheap to serve as props? Seldom, surely, does art begin more straightforwardly with the "given" of reality.

Most important, who can compare with them for retailoring human nature? Taming aggression is their stock-in-trade, in creaky melodramas like *The Mortal Struggle* or *The Blood Drinker's Burial* or their hilarious pantomime of *The Indian Savage and the Maiden*, in which the civilizing power of love subdues wild ferocity in broad gestures (23, 25). Nothing, though, can top the play Nicholas translates for them, involving a man who stabs his son, throws his wife and child out of the house, and relents in the end, when a clock striking ten interrupts his suicide by reminding him of a similar clock in his infancy, making him burst into tears, drop his gun, and become an exemplary citizen for ever after (24). The Crummleses, in other words, can retailor even the villainy of a character like Ralph Nickleby, who in "real life" remains undeterred and untransformed by the tolling bell he hears in his final moments.

Mr. Crummles explains the principle of his troupe's theater when

Nicholas, watching a swordfight in rehearsal, suggests the performance might be better if one actor were not so much taller than the other. Nonsense, says Crummles:

Why, it's the very essence of the combat that there should be a foot or two between them. How are you to get up the sympathies of the audience in a legitimate manner, if there isn't a little man contending against a great one—unless there's at least five to one, and we haven't hands enough for that business in our company. (22)

All the conventions of this theater, and melodrama is made up of nothing but conventions, go to insure the triumph of justice over aggression, of right over brute force—like the conventions of society, but more dependable. And like the whole effort of human culture, the Crummles theater strives to hold up an ideal, however simple or fustian, of what life should be to be fully human. Surely these conventions and ideals retain their power undiminished. After all, *Nicholas Nickleby*, whose most melodramatic situations the Crummles plays often mirror, is itself a melodrama of the higher kind—an unusually comic one, that uses humor as yet another antidote for aggression. What reader can fail to take pleasure in its forthright sureness in meting out just deserts?

It is fitting that this novel's most satisfying answer to the problem of aggression should be offered by a troupe of actors, further emphasizing how remote a truly human existence is from Ralph Nickleby's grim authenticity. A fully human identity is necessarily stagey and contrived: how can it not be, if we live in a society and are continually playing to others? Though most of us do not go around in the full regalia of "false hair, false colour, false calves, false muscles" like the Crummles company (24), we are theatrical enough—even histrionic—in our own way; and, like the Crummleses (though in different proportions), the roles we enact are at one and the same time factitious and real. No wonder, from Nicholas disguised as "Mr. Johnson" or as Madeline Bray's customer, to Mrs. Wititterly languid on her sofa, to Mr. Mantalini with his kisses and poison bottle, almost everyone in *Nickleby* keeps staging his own little drama. Even Dickens, to gather material for the novel, went to Yorkshire in disguise.

Indeed, like the Infant Phenomenon—her growth purposely stunted by late nights and gin—we all become most fully ourselves by being pushed out of nature. In *Nickleby*, this is all matter for cheerful comedy. In *Barnaby Rudge*, the deformation involved in self-realization becomes ground for more somber reflection.

.   .   .

Everyone knows the story of Dickens's "hard experiences in boy-hood"[13]—how he was put to work in a blacking (i.e., shoe-polish) factory when he was twelve years old and how two weeks later his improvident father, as bankrupt as the Mantalinis, was clapped in the Marshalsea Prison for debt. Allusions to this trauma of being temporarily declassed and abandoned pepper all Dickens's novels, but so insistent are they in *Nickleby* as to demand notice. A brief biographical excursus, though not essential to an understanding of the novel, will provide still another level of insight into it and afford an intriguing glimpse of Dickens interpreting his own experience and turning it to artistic account.

Nicholas, virtually compelled by his uncle to go to work at Dotheboys Hall just as Dickens was forced by his father into the blacking factory, denounces Ralph after returning to London in terms that reverberate with the language Dickens later used to describe his own youthful misery. "You . . . heaped every insult, wrong, and indignity, upon my head," he accuses Ralph. "You . . . sent me to a den where sordid cruelty . . . runs wanton, and youthful misery stalks precocious; where the lightness of childhood shrinks into the heaviness of age, and its every promise blights, and withers as it grows" (20). So Dickens, recalling how he became a working boy among working-class boys, says:

No words can express the secret agony of my soul as I sunk into this companionship; compared these every day associates with those of my happier childhood; and felt my early hopes of growing up to be a learned and distinguished man, crushed in my breast. The deep remembrance of the sense I had of being utterly neglected and hopeless; of the shame I felt in my position; . . . cannot be written.[14]

Dickens's own childhood unhappiness, one feels, provided him with a point of reference for imagining not only Nicholas's depression but also the plight of the Dotheboys pupils. And indeed Nicholas's sad fantasy of those boys as "the young noblemen" (8) recalls how Dickens's factory co-workers spoke of him as "the young gentleman."

It is curious that, as a condition for providing for Mrs. Nickleby and Kate, Ralph forces Nicholas into exile in Yorkshire, so that lonely separation from his family compounds the misery of this odious job. "To have committed no fault," Nicholas reflects,

and yet to be so entirely alone in the world; to be separated from the only persons he loved, and to be proscribed like a criminal, when six months ago he had been surrounded by every comfort, and looked up to as the chief hope of his family—this was hard to bear. (20)

No less hard did Dickens find his analogous exile. For, like Little Dorrit's father, Dickens's father also took his family to live with him in debtor's prison—leaving Dickens himself behind, however, lodged in the house of a woman who, like Mr. Squeers, also "had under her care . . . somebody's natural children, who were very irregularly paid for; and a widow's little son." Sundays only did Dickens visit in the prison, and he "felt keenly . . . being so cut off from my parents, my brothers, and sisters"— "small Cain that I was, except that I had never done harm to any one." [15] How well he must have known the loneliness he gives to Nicholas—"the agony of separation in grief and poverty when we most needed comfort and support from each other" (43). How often, like Nicholas, must he have come home to his "poor room," thrown himself on the bed, turned his fact to the wall, and wept (20).

Kate Nickleby undergoes no actual exile; her uncle permits her to live with her mother in a dismal warehouse in Thames Street that resembles that rat-infested blacking factory at Hungerford Stairs. But her employment at a dressmaker's—as menial, exacting, and degraded below her station as Dickens's pasting labels on shoepolish bottles—is made yet more bitter by her foreman's spiteful order prohibiting co-workers from speaking to her. Her next job, as Mrs. Wititterly's companion, chiefly involves suffering the persecutions of Mulberry Hawk. Her endurance exhausted, she appeals to Ralph: "I have gone on day after day . . . in the hope that this persecution would cease; I have gone on day after day, compelled to assume the appearance of cheerfulness, when I was most unhappy. I have had no counsellor, no advisor, no one to protect me." One hears reverberating in this sentence Dickens's description of his childhood exile: "I certainly had no other assistance whatever. . . . No advice, no counsel, no encouragement, no support from anyone that I can call to mind, so help me God." [16]

Kate continues: "Mamma supposes that these are honourable men [Hawk and his toadies], rich and distinguished, and how *can* I—how can I undeceive her—when she is so happy in these little delusions . . . ?" (28) And again Dickens's account of his employment at the blacking factory rings in one's ears: "My father and mother were quite satisfied. They could hardly have been more so, if I had been twenty years of age, distinguished at a grammar-school, and going to Cambridge." [17] Moreover, Mrs. Nickleby, who encourages Hawk's attentions to Kate, utterly oblivious of her misery, calls to mind Dickens's mother's behavior when he was fired in the wake of a quarrel between his father and the blacking factory manager. Mrs. Dickens patched up the quarrel, and, Dickens grimly reports, "I shall never forget, I never can forget, that my mother was warm for my being sent back." [18] He did not go back, though; but he in part settled this score with his mother by creating Mrs. Nickleby in her image. [19]

The large conclusion it is tempting to draw from all this is that Dickens in *Nickleby* is inclined to see the world as teeming with aggressive, even ferocious, individuals in part because he sees his own parents, especially his father, as capable of sweeping, malevolent hostility. At this moment in his life, he seems fitfully to imagine that his father put him in the blacking factory not because of the force of circumstances—not because he himself was weak, imprudent, and victimized—but because of anger and malice worthy of a Squeers, a Snawley, or a Ralph Nickleby. And in response to imagined parental malevolence combined with emphatically real suffering, it is hard to think that Dickens did not harbor anger enough of his own.

But the hyacinths "blooming in old blacking-bottles" in Tim Linkinwater's courtyard (40) bear witness to Dickens's effort in *Nickleby* to come to happier terms with these memories and feelings. Thus Nicholas, in taking Smike under his care and making himself protector of the novel's archetypal victimized son, becomes (oddly enough) Dickens's object lesson in how a good parent ought to behave. When Nicholas's prospects look their bleakest and fill him with despair, Smike tearfully stammers: "You—you—are not rich: you have not enough for yourself, and I should not be here. You grow . . . thinner every day. . . . I cannot bear to see you so, and think how I am burdening you." To this, Nicholas stalwartly gives the reply Dickens doubtless wishes his father had made in similar poverty and misfortune:

The word which separates us . . . shall never be said by me, for you are my only comfort and stay. I would not lose you now, for all the world could give. The thought of you has upheld me through all I have endured today, and shall, through fifty times such trouble. . . . My heart is linked to yours. . . . What, if I am steeped in poverty? You lighten it, and we will be poor together. (20)

But Nicholas's care of Smike is more than a reproach to Dickens's father. For to the extent that both these characters are imaginative versions of their creator, their relationship shows how much Dickens's response to all this was to become his own father and take responsibility for himself. Moreover, when Nicholas takes Smike home to the ancestral Nickleby village to die, what he is laying to rest is Dickens's image of himself as a creature broken by these sorrows.

Dickens's coming to terms with the blacking factory has one final expression in the novel. When Mrs. Nickleby fusses that Nicholas is leaving for his job in Yorkshire without breakfast, Ralph snarls, "When I first went to business, ma'am, I took a penny loaf and a ha'porth of milk for my breakfast as I walked to the city every morning; what do you say to that, ma'am? Breakfast! Pshaw!" (5). Such a loaf and a pennyworth of milk, bought out of his own wages, made Dickens's breakfast throughout his blacking factory exile.[20] Not just this resemblance but also the ambivalence with which Ralph is presented in the novel suggest that he is an example of what Dickens—himself a man not without a certain hardness—*might* have become as a result of this experience. But Ralph, having pushed aside the painful remembrances of his youth, has, like the Haunted Man, lost their humanizing influences as well, whereas Dickens is able to look back on the blacking factory and recognize "how all these things have worked together to make me what I am."[21] Unlike Ralph, he was always ready to say amen to the prayer that ends *The Haunted Man*, "Lord, keep my memory green."

Part Two

Barnaby Rudge

Events are written lessons, glaring in huge hieroglyphic picture-writing, that all may read and know them: the terror and horror they inspire in us is but the note of preparation for the truth they are to teach; a mere waste of terror if that be not learned.

(Thomas Carlyle, *Chartism*)

3
The Civilized Condition

Nickleby groped toward a recognition of society as our chief defense against aggression; *Barnaby Rudge* triumphantly achieves that understanding and dramatizes it with brilliance. The novel is an elaborate demonstration—two demonstrations, actually, corresponding to the book's division into two parts—of a deeply meditated political philosophy which takes this insight as its central truth.

The first demonstration sheds light on the nature of the civilized, social realm, as embodied in two idealized households, the Maypole Inn and the Golden Key. Despite the idealization, though, Dickens's representation does not omit all the shadows. These two examples—along with a third embodiment of civilized life in the household of Mr. Chester—show how inseparable social life is from a repression of impulse that entails on each individual an inescapable measure of unhappiness.

If a Dickens Christmas is an annual reconsecration of all the values of the human community, a Dickens inn might be called a secular temple dedicated to the daily celebration of those values; and the Dickens inn *par excellence*—the very epitome of Dickensian snugness and coziness and the pure distillate of the Dickensian social spirit—is the Maypole Inn in *Barnaby Rudge*. This lovingly described building, which Dickens is at pains to establish not just as a vital center of man's civilized life but as a symbolic representation of civilization itself, would warm the cockles even of John Ruskin's fastidious heart, so completely does it conform to his notion of good architecture as the pure creation of man himself, "born of his necessities, . . . expressive of his nature, . . . [and], in some sort, the work of the whole race."[1] Indeed, so far is this building an embodiment of the human community that it seems on the verge of becoming human itself. It looks "as if it were nodding in its sleep," and an observer needs "no very great stretch of fancy to detect in it other resemblances to humanity" (1).

Its great age gives it an especially resonant human meaning: steeped in history, the building is an emblem of the English national past. Queen Elizabeth slept there, and the house dates from "the days of King Henry the Eighth." Dickens's description of the maypole that is the inn's sign as being "straight as any arrow that ever English yeoman drew" links the inn with Merrie England, Robin Hood, and Agincourt—and therefore with powerful beliefs about the high worth of the English communal achievement. Dickens's imagination takes the inn back to the dawn of history to another utterly humanized realm—that of legend: on the Maypole's ancient porch stand "two grim-looking high backed settles, which, like the twin dragons of some fairy-tale, guarded the entrance to the mansion" (1).

Guarded it against what? Against the fury of nature, first and foremost, for Dickens begins each of *Barnaby Rudge*'s two halves with a ferocious storm howling round the inn, threatening the company within with "a hoarse roar as if the sea had risen," and with "such a swirl and tumult that the air seemed mad." The Maypole thumbs its nose at such an assault:

Blessings on the red . . . old curtain of the window; blending into one rich stream of brightness, fire and candle, meat, drink, and company, and gleaming like a jovial eye upon the bleak waste out of doors! . . . Blessings on the old house, how sturdily it stood! How did the vexed wind chafe and roar about its stalwart roof; . . . how . . . did it drive and rattle at the casement, emulous to extinguish that cheerful glow, which would not be put down and seemed the brighter for the conflict. (33)

This emblem of civilized society, protecting men from the wild "bleak waste," constitutes a fabricated, artificial realm, distinct from the natural

world, with whose hostile and destructive energies it exists in a state of
perpetual conflict. Accordingly, the Maypole even generates its own man-
made weather, far kinder than the inhospitable climate out of doors.
What greater comfort than to watch the punch "simmer and stew" before
the fire, so that "its fragrant steam, rising up among [the company] and
mixing with the wreaths of vapour from their pipes, might shroud them
in a delicious atmosphere of their own, and shut out all the world" (11)?

Let's go in with Mr. and Mrs. Varden and explore this "genial" realm
up close:

All bars are snug places, but the Maypole's was the very snuggest, cosiest, and
completest bar, that ever the wit of man devised. Such . . . gleaming tankards
dangling from pegs at about the same inclination as thirsty men would hold them
to their lips; . . . so many lemons hanging in separate nets, and forming [a] fragrant grove . . . , suggestive, with goodly loaves of snowy sugar stowed away
hard by, of punch, idealised beyond all mortal knowledge; . . . such drawers full
of pipes, such places for putting things away . . . , all crammed to the throat with
eatables, drinkables, or savoury condiments; lastly, and to crown all, as typical of
the immense resources of the establishment, and its defiances to all visitors to cut
and come again, such a stupendous cheese!

. . . [I]t must have been the poorest, weakest, and most watery heart that ever
beat, which would not have warmed towards the Maypole Bar. Mrs. Varden's did
directly. She could no more have reproached John Willet among those household
gods . . . than she could have stabbed him with his own bright carving-knife.
The order for dinner too—it might have soothed a savage. "A bit of fish," said
John to the cook, "and some lamb chops (breaded, with plenty of ketchup), and a
good salad, and a roast spring chicken, with a dish of sausages and mashed po-
tatoes, or something of that sort." Something of that sort! The resources of these
inns! To talk carelessly about dishes, which in themselves were a first-rate holiday
kind of dinner, suitable to one's wedding day, as something of that sort: meaning,
if you can't get a spring chicken, any other trifle in the way of poultry will do—
such as a Peacock, perhaps! (19)

No reader could fail to recognize this as a quintessentially Dickensian
vision, conjured up in novel after novel—a vision, that Dickens never
ceased to cherish, of a man-made world where man is utterly at home: a
social world which answers every human need, and in which, not surprisingly, the heart rejoices. In this artificial "fragrant grove," as much a
production of human art as the fragrant groves of pastoral poetry, all is
order, comfort, and plenty. Even the eatables owe as much to human con-

trivance as to mere nature: consider the beer, the cheese, the gin (itself further "idealised" into punch), the loaf sugar, and—this is England remember—the lemons.

Nor could any reader fail to catch the characteristic tone Dickens so often takes in describing scenes like the Maypole: a tone whose affectionate warmth is qualified with irony and, at moments, ever so slightly tinged with condescension; a good-humored, comic tone, full of the freedom, exaggeration, and broad gestures of comedy, which becomes at moments parodic or satirical, and in which the note of pleasure *in* the thing occasionally merges into a smile at its expense. It is, moreover, a distancing tone, complex and ambivalent, which partly asserts a realistic, worldly awareness that these values are ideals, or fantasies, not ever permanently attainable and always qualified with much dross; but which nevertheless confesses—in spite of all this hard-headed skepticism—a genuine belief in them, a genuine susceptibility to being moved profoundly by them, which Dickens finds slightly embarrassing. But, after all, it is indeed a poor heart that "would not have warmed towards the Maypole," a heart (like Scrooge's or Ralph Nickleby's) on which what Louis Cazamian called "the philosophy of Christmas"[2] can make no impression whatever.

A sign of *Barnaby Rudge*'s greatly matured understanding of society as compared with *Nicholas Nickleby* is the part of this description that reminds us how in civilization even *human* nature has been retailored. In the world of the Maypole, as the joke about Mrs. Varden and the bright carving knife tells us, human aggression is disarmed; and Dickens's immediate reference to savages, their need to be soothed, and the Maypole's ability to soothe them expands the context far beyond this single character. It telegraphs to us that the primary function of civilization is the circumscription of our inborn aggression. Thus the hostile and destructive nature against which civilization protects us is to be found not only outside in the nonhuman world but also inside, bound up in every human heart. And the tumult of aroused human nature is perhaps more to be feared than the fury of the elements, for if the Maypole easily withstands the storms which open each half of *Barnaby Rudge*, it is not so fortunate in the face of the human storm which in the second part of the novel engulfs both it and the civilized realm it represents.

The bar that might have soothed a savage is an infinitely more assured and unsentimental emblem of aggression disarmed than the Cheerybles' rusty blunderbuss, for here the tamed aggression is real. And in this civilized realm that grows out of the circumscription of aggression, Dickens observes, one eats "a first-rate holiday kind of dinner, suitable to one's wedding-day." His point is that a Maypole dinner succeeds famously in humanizing a merely animal function by transforming it into a social ritual. Indeed, a Maypole dinner is, as Dickens says dinners in general ought to be, a "social sacrament,"[3] like those more momentous social sacraments—holidays and rites of passage like "one's wedding day." These are the observances by which men celebrate and reconsecrate their social existence: by which they reaffirm the reality of a human realm of value, rooted in their own communal existence, in which alone their lives acquire purpose and significance. This of course is exactly what all those social sacraments which together comprise religion do, and it is in this sense that Dickens's reference to the Maypole's "household gods" in our present passage and his earlier description of the bar as "that solemn sanctuary" (10) must be understood as not simply comic figures of speech.

Thus there is more to the Maypole than a mere physical fabric of bricks and mortar, for a no less essential component of this building's reality, as of society itself, is that spiritual dimension which includes the shared beliefs and common values fostered here and includes also the intangible web of social relationships which bind the Maypole regulars into a tightly woven community. The Maypole is inspired with a social soul (to use Marx's phrase), of which the Maypole regulars have daily experience, as the following description of them smoking together while uttering not a single word makes clear.

Whether people, by dint of sitting together in the same place and the same relative positions, and doing exactly the same things for a great many years, acquire a sixth sense, or some unknown power of influencing each other which serves them in its stead, is a question for philosophy to settle. But certain it is that old John Willet, Mr. Parkes, and Mr. Cobb, were one and all firmly of opinion that they were very jolly companions—rather choice spirits than otherwise; that they looked at each other every now and then as if there were a perpetual interchange of ideas going on among them; that no man considered himself or his neighbour by any means silent; and that each of them nodded occasionally when he caught the eye of another, as if he would say "You have expressed yourself extremely well, sir, in relation to that sentiment, and I quite agree with you." (33)

In this silence, in other words, plenty is being communicated: the chief message exchanged among these rather dull men is that they are important to each other, they are deeply interested in each other's fate, they respect and value each other, and all will stand by each. The sense of well-being they derive from this communication suggests that from their social relations men do indeed acquire "some unknown power of influencing each other," and the sixth sense—the social sense—that is attuned to this influence is, as our passage indicates, one of the sources of their feelings of worth and dignity.

Thus the Maypole is a community as well as a building, and like all communities, it has among its social sacraments its traditional legends. Chief among these

was a legend . . . that Queen Elizabeth had slept there . . . [and] that next morning, while standing on a mounting block before the door . . . , the virgin monarch had . . . boxed and cuffed an unlucky page for some neglect of duty. The matter-of-fact and doubtful folks, of whom there were a few among the Maypole customers, as unluckily there always are in every little community, were inclined to look upon this tradition as rather apocryphal; but whenever the landlord of that ancient hostelry appealed to the mounting block itself as evidence, and triumphantly pointed out that there it stood in the same place to that very day, the doubters never failed to be put down by a large majority, and all true believers exulted as in a victory. (1)

Legends, of course, do not have to be true in order to serve their complex social function of knitting together a "little community." What makes this attractive story so effective is that it introduces the mildest possible offense by a servent against the authority of a master, the meekest undutifulness of a subject to his sovereign (and *what* a sovereign), in order to tell us not to worry, no harm is done. Thus we enjoy a little shiver in seeing the social and political order momentarily out of whack, which shiver immediately gives way to satisfaction in seeing order at once restored with a reproof so harmless that it roars as gentle as any sucking dove.

It is hardly surprising that the legend of a "little community" should have a content so explicitly *about* the social order and the forces that upset it as this, but this story does double duty in *Barnaby Rudge*, for it introduces on the novel's very first page its governing complex of themes. And if it does so in a playful way, the other traditional "Maypole story" told in the first chapter—the story of the murder of Reuben Haredale by his servant—casts those same themes in a far more lurid and sinister light, more appropriate to the quite dreadful assault which later in the novel will be directed against that civilized order Dickens so affectionately delineates here.

.   .   .

The Maypole is unquestionably Dickens's primary symbolic representation in *Barnaby Rudge* of the civilized realm, but Gabriel Varden's
combined house and workshop, at the sign of the Golden Key, falls unmistakably into this same category. Whereas the Maypole is Dickens's
holiday representation, the Golden Key is its weekday counterpart. Here
at the locksmith's Dickens takes account of the fact that men have to work
for a living and Maypoles and the rest of the man-made world do not rise
out of the ground spontaneously. This is not to say that the Golden Key is
any less idealized than the Maypole: far from it. But in describing this
old, picturesque house, Dickens takes note of the unremitting effort required to maintain the values these two buildings embody. For instance:

There was not a neater, more scrupulously tidy, or more punctiliously ordered
house, in Clerkenwell, in London, in all England. There . . . was not more rub-
bing, scrubbing, burnishing and polishing, in the whole street put together. Nor
was this excellence attained without some cost and trouble and great expenditure
of voice. . . . (4)

"Beauty, cleanliness and order," as so unsentimental a theorist as Sigmund Freud remarked, "obviously occupy a special position among the
requirements of civilization. No one will maintain that they are as important for life as control over the forces of nature. . . . And yet no one
would care to put them into the background as trivialities."[4]

But more important than this labor is the work required to earn a live-
lihood; and here, in his depiction of the economic life which is an inseparable component of the civilized condition, Dickens casts on the Golden
Key an especially idealized glow. In the first place, Gabriel Varden's work
is entirely a mode of self-realization, not self-alienation. "For some centuries after the late Gothic period," observes Siegfried Giedion, "the
locksmith was known as the artisan of a most elaborate handicraft. He
united mastery of hand with the gift of untiring inventiveness," not only
in the locks and keys of his manufacture, but also in his other "artistically
wrought ironwork," such as "gates, grilles [for public squares, country-
house parks, and so on], knobs, handles, and the fantastic iron ornamen-
tation of chests."[5] This craft reached its apogee of refinement exactly at
the time in which *Barnaby Rudge* is set. Gabriel is a craftsman, not a laborer, making useful and beautiful objects with his own hands, to his
own constantly varying designs, according to his own methods, and at
his own pace. He is self-employed and has control over every step of production: he is his own salesman, bookkeeper, and purchasing agent.

What he makes is truly his own work, bearing his imprint, the product of his hand and his brain alike. No wonder, then, that Dickens imagines Gabriel's labor to be strenuous but not toilsome, and pictures him—by contrast with those whose work is "a dull monotonous duty"—"working at his anvil, his face all radiant with exercise and gladness, his sleeves turned up, his wig pushed off his shining forehead—the easiest, freest, happiest man in all the world" (41).

If we are doomed to live by the sweat of our brow, this kind of work is not such a terrible fate. It is an example of the work men *ought* to do, as many people at the time *Barnaby Rudge* was written believed. For around this time the debasement and mechanization of skilled handicrafts like this was completing itself, making men conscious of what was being lost. Indeed, "[b]etween 1825 and 1845, as observed in the report of the jury of the Paris International Exhibition of 1867, the highly skilled [lock]smiths disappeared from the big cities. Grilles, railings, and balconies had come to be made of cast iron."[6]

Moreover, the economic organization characteristic of such an enterprise as Varden's was likewise becoming extinct in England in 1841, so that many who believed it to be best—especially in comparison to the factory organization that had substantially replaced it—already looked to it with the kind of nostalgia that surrounds, for instance, Fezziwig's ball in *A Christmas Carol* or the House of Cheeryble Brothers in *Nicholas Nickleby*. This preindustrial, even precapitalist unit of production, composed of a master, his wife, children, apprentices, and servants, was described at the time as a "family," whose head was "father to some of its members and in place of father to the rest," with "no sharp distinction between his domestic and economic functions," in Peter Laslett's slightly rose-tinted description. Workshop and house were one and the same place, and "economic organization was domestic organization." Thus, "[w]e may feel that in a whole society organized like this, in spite of all the subordination, the exploitation and the obliteration of those who were young, or feminine, or in service, everyone belonged in a group, a family group. Everyone had his circle of affection: every relationship could be seen as a love relationship."[7] The qualifications in the middle of this statement concede that even in this garden lurks the inevitable serpent, as we will see when we consider Sim Tappertit's complaint; but even so, the kind of social and economic organization that Dickens depicts in the Golden Key is presented in *Barnaby Rudge* as one in which a man could be fulfilled and contented if he would, and find such happiness as human life affords.

Barnaby Rudge, Steven Marcus has observed, is obsessed with the father-son relationship, each one of which in this novel, he remarks, "suffers from a profound disorder."[8] Indeed, this sense of general disturbance in the father-son relationship finds expression even in the most local details of the narrative. For example, there are two symmetrical vignettes which at first appear to have as their point the deep love between father and son. One describes a prisoner in Newgate, condemned to be hanged in forty-eight hours, who is rescued by his two sons. In their frenzy to save their father, the young men perform almost superhuman feats, finally standing "in—yes, in—the fire" set by the rioters, "striving to prize [the prison gate] down, with crowbars" (64). Needless to say, their father was the first condemned prisoner to be freed; he was carried out "a mere heap of chains . . . with no sign of life" (65). Related to this story is the glimpse we catch of a father's love for his guilty son: when a rioter "was hanged in Bishopsgate Street," his

aged grey-headed father waited for him at the gallows, kissed him at its foot when he arrived, and sat there, on the ground, until they took him down. They would have given him the body of his child; but he had no hearse, no coffin, nothing to remove it in, being too poor; and walked meekly away beside the cart that took it back to prison, trying, as he went, to touch its lifeless hand. (77)

These are the only places in the novel where Dickens suggests such love between fathers and sons, and that he can conceive of such a thing only in association with guilt and gallows suggests how deeply troubled this relationship is in *Barnaby Rudge*'s world.

Of the three unhappy father-son relationships that are central to Dickens's story, two have as their setting the two embodiments of civilization just considered, and the third is associated with another (rather questionable) version of civilization—the character of Mr. Chester—to be discussed in the next chapter. Dickens presents these relationships as three variations of the same theme, the issue in all of them being the oppression of a son by his father, and all taking essentially parallel courses. And the connection of each with an embodiment of civilization, rather than an accidental feature, is crucial, for as the novel elaborately dramatizes, civilization requires of everyone a repression of natural instinct which is brought about by paternal oppression. Thus if *Barnaby* is obsessed with the father-son relationship, it is because Dickens imagines that relationship as essential to the process of civilization, which is one of this novel's major themes. And if the relationship is disturbed, it is not fortuitously but inherently so: fathers civilize their resisting sons by compulsion.

It is clear enough what is troubling Joe Willet, the "heir apparent to the Maypole," for certainly "a broad-shouldered, strapping young fellow of twenty, whom it pleased his father still to consider a little boy, and to treat accordingly," has a justifiable complaint (1). John Willet's delusion is so entrenched that, after Joe has run away from home, he has a missing-person advertisement printed,

describing his son as a "young boy" . . . eighteen inches to a couple of feet shorter than he really was: two circumstances which perhaps accounted . . . for its never having been productive of any other effect than the transmission to [the Maypole] . . . of some five-and-forty runaways varying from six years old to twelve. (33)

And what kind of behavior does Dickens have in mind when he says that old John treated his son in accordance with this willfully distorted conception? There is, to begin with, John's literal enforcement of the precept that children should be seen and not heard. "Silence, sir!" he roars, when Joe protests that his father surely cannot expect that he is never to open his lips: "No, you never are. When your opinion's wanted, you give it. When you're spoke to, you speak. When your opinion's not wanted and you're not spoke to, don't you give an opinion and don't you speak" (1). And, though Joe is evidently a full-time employee of the Maypole, John gives him neither allowance nor wages. Joe at last protests:

Look at other young men of my age. Have they no liberty, no will, no right to speak? Are they obliged to sit mumchance, and to be ordered about till they are the laughing-stock of young and old? . . . I say . . . that before long I shall be driven to break such bounds, and that when I do, it won't be me that you'll have to blame, but your own self, and no other. (3)

One might think all this would be humiliation enough, but old John, impelled by "his strong desires to run counter to the unfortunate Joe," goes on to "goad and chafe his son and heir" still more flagrantly. He puts Joe "upon his patrole of honour . . . not to leave the premises," which, translated, means that Joe is under house-arrest. "And what's more . . . he won't be off his patrole for a pretty long time to come, I can tell you that" (29). From here on, things go from bad to worse, until "there never was an unfortunate young fellow so bullied, badgered, worried, fretted, and browbeaten; so constantly beset, or made so tired of his life, as poor Joe Willet" (30).

The central issue in this situation, according to the elder Willet, is "who's the master of this house, and who isn't. We'll see whether boys are to govern men, or men are to govern boys" (30). But, in addition to the primary question of authority and government (of major concern throughout the novel), the conflict between the Willets has a sexual dimension, too, as one of Willet's cronies makes clear enough in accusing Joe—"metaphorically," Dickens assures us—of "[p]utting himself forward and wringing the very nose off his own father's face!" (1). Willet evidently feels he has weathered these attacks unscathed: as he rather ungraciously tells the same crony the next time he offers Willet his help in tyrannizing over Joe, "I can stand pretty firm of myself, sir, I believe, without being shored up by you" (30). But in this sexual conflict Joe is not so lucky. For if old John is opposed "as a general principle to all matters of love and matrimony," he is, in particular, quite decided in his mind that "We want no love-making here, sir, unbeknown to parents" (29). Consistent with this policy, and with an instinct so sure it is better than cunning, he insults Joe's manhood in front of his sweetheart, Dolly Varden, by sending Hugh the ostler to protect him on the road. "'My father!' said poor Joe; adding under his breath, with a very unfilial apostrophe, 'Will he never think me man enough to take care of myself!'" (22).

.   .   .

The case of Gabriel Varden and Sim Tappertit vividly illustrates, with appropriate emotional detail, what is meant by saying that in the preindustrial world an apprentice's master stood him in place of a father. These two are in this sense the second of *Barnaby Rudge*'s troubled father-son pairs, and their trouble derives first of all from the measure of paternal oppression that is built into the structure of the apprentice system. Not only does an apprentice engage himself to total obedience to his master, but also his freedom is limited by little leisure, scanty pocket money, and the provisions of his indentures which ban drinking and gambling and forbid him all sexual relationships, including marriage. The authority of the master thus extending to virtually every department of his apprentice's life, it is no metaphor to say that an apprentice is "bound" by his indentures.[9] Any apprentice could hardly avoid moments of feeling oppressed, even under so good a master as the easy-going Gabriel Varden.

But over and above all this, still another potential source of conflict and discontent inheres in the master-apprentice relationship. For the preindustrial "family" is liable, as nostalgic conservatives and radicals alike sometimes forget, to all the emotional ills afflicting the modern nuclear family. As Laslett points out, "if a [preindustrial] family is a circle of affection, it can also be the scene of hatred. . . . In the traditional, patriarchal society of Europe, where practically everyone lived out his whole life within the family, . . . tension . . . must have been incessant and unrelieved, incapable of release except in crisis." [10] In a culture which saw a master's authority as virtually identical to a father's, any boy who brought with him into his apprenticeship unresolved problems with paternal authority could find in his master a made-to-order father-figure on whom to project them.

This is precisely the case with Sim Tappertit, and it largely explains why he feels so inordinately resentful toward the genial Varden. Sim seethes with cravings for power—his "soul was forever feasting and regaling itself" on gargantuan fantasies of command and domination, to which his "swelling sense of wrong and outrage" is directly proportional. Dickens unmistakably indicates the focus of these fantasies when Sim draws "from the right hand, or rather right leg pocket of his smalls, a clumsy large-sized key, which he insert[s] cautiously in the lock his master had secured" (7). This unwieldy "master key" is a copy Sim has secretly made of his master's "master key" (8): the sexual power he covets is the power he ascribes to Varden as his surrogate father, and it is chiefly the fact of not having that power that makes him deem himself the oppressed "victim of [Varden's] tyrannical behaviour" (59). His swollen fantasies of power are part and parcel of his fantasies of oppression; and that his fantasies of sexual power center on "his master's daughter" (4)—whom he believes Varden, in a yet more fiendish act of tyranny, has forbidden to him—suggests that behind this whole system of delusion lies a recognizable version of the family romance.

Varden himself has an astute insight into the character of Sim's aspirations. When the rioters drag Gabriel to Newgate to make him open the main-gate lock, Sim tells him that he must perform this act—which would liberate what is imprisoned and grant entry into what is sealed shut—"with your own hands." "'When I do,' said the locksmith quietly, 'my hands shall drop off at the wrists, and you shall wear them, Simon Tappertit, on your shoulders for epaulettes'" (63).

·   ·   ·

If the oppression about which Sim so vigorously complains exists largely in his own mind, the oppression of Edward Chester by his father, like that of Joe Willet by old John, is real enough. Mr. Chester professes to believe that, "[i]f there is anything real in the world, it is those amaz-

ingly fine feelings and natural obligations which must subsist between father and son"—so much so that "[t]he relationship between father and
son, you know, is positively quite a holy kind of bond" (12). But in these
lofty sentiments he is, though more refined, no more sincere than Mr.
Squeers and Mr. Snawley on the subject of parental instinct. He comes
much closer to his true feelings when explaining to Edward that a son,
"unless he is old enough to be a companion—that is to say, unless he is
some two or three and twenty—is not the kind of thing to have about
one. He is a restraint upon his father, his father is a restraint upon him,
and they make each other mutually uncomfortable." Accordingly, he
kept Ned away at school until his twenty-third year, seeing him only for a
week or two at a time, when they "disconcerted each other as only such
near relations can" (15).

But Chester is not enthusiastic about the idea of a grown-up son, either. When Ned addresses him not as "sir" but as "father," he responds
with horrified astonishment, exclaiming, "For heaven's sake don't call me
by that obsolete and ancient name. Have some regard for delicacy. Am I
grey, or wrinkled, do I go on crutches, have I lost my teeth, that you
adopt such a mode of address? Good God, how very coarse!" (32). He too
seems to feel that it is in the nature of a son to put himself forward and
wring the very nose off his own father's face: no less intensely (though
more self-consciously) than John Willet, John Chester worries that having
a grown-up son must make him a diminished man.

Chester, though, who makes the best of every situation, is resolved
upon turning Ned to the best possible account for himself. However
much it may appear that he relinquished control by cavalierly sending
Ned off to school, it turns out that this paternal nonchalance is compatible
with paternal domination. He has intentionally given Ned an education
bound to make him his father's creature by not preparing him for a career.
"I have been, as the phrase is, liberally educated, and am fit for nothing,"
Ned concedes to his father. "I find myself at last wholly dependent upon
you, with no resource but in your favour" (15).

This is bad enough, Ned feels, but he learns that his father plans to
abridge his autonomy further. Ned, Mr. Chester explains, has been "bred
upon a careful principle" to "succeed in the pursuit for which I destined
you." He has been brought up to be what he indignantly terms "a mere
fortune-hunter," expected to catch an heiress equal to his father's enormous debts and expensive style of life (15). Himself a successful fortune-
hunter in his day, Mr. Chester has brought Ned up to go into the family
business.

Had Ned turned out to be the cynical man of the world we might ex-

pect as the product of such an education, none of this would be so terrible. An aristocratically bred young man of the *ancien régime*, desirous
of ease and confident that his moneyed wife's claims would be limited,
would recognize the wisdom of doing as well for himself as possible. But
in Edward, by spontaneous generation perhaps, a middle-class, Victorian
morality straight out of *Nicholas Nickleby* has sprung up, in terms of
which Mr. Chester is trying to exploit and oppress Ned shamelessly.
Moreover, this oppression (as in the case of the Willets) is partly sexual in
character. In the matter of sexual choice, Chester tells Mrs. Varden, to
countenance any "encouragement for young persons to rebel against their
parents . . . is particularly injudicious" (27). Accordingly, refusing for fi-
nancial reasons to sanction Ned's marrying his beloved Emma Haredale,
he sets out to destroy their relationship. As Dickens presents all this,
Chester is trying to keep control of his son's sexuality forever by choosing
its object to further his own self-interested motives. Thus Dickens applies
to the Chesters a sexual symbolism as blatant as Sim Tappertit's cumber-
some key. At the beginning of their last interview, which ends with the
father throwing the son out of the house, Mr. Chester (seated in Browne's
illustration under a painting of Abraham poising the knife over Isaac) asks
Edward to pass the nut-crackers, and the whole conversation is punctuated by the grating sound of Mr. Chester cracking and "eating his nuts
meanwhile" (32).

.   .   .

Rigorous indeed is the training in filial obedience these sons receive,
being made again and again to renounce their own freedom in submission
to civilizing paternal authority. The fathers, as Dickens imagines them,
are active agents of repression, vigilantly maintaining their power by unremitting exercise: extravagantly so in the case of the Willets, insidiously
so with the Chesters, and conventionally, institutionally so with Varden
and Sim, where however the intensity is amplified by Sim's paranoia.

Reflected, to be sure, in Mr. Willet's and Mr. Chester's obdurate concern with their own authority is no small measure of narcissism, but all
these men also sense a deeper threat from their sons, a threat whose
nature is specified clearly enough in that warning of Mr. Willet's crony
about keeping a son from "wringing the very nose off his own father's
face." Certainly, as Sim Tappertit's career shows, sons do have it in them
to try to wring their fathers' noses: when Sim breaks into open rebellion,
seeking to get what he thinks Varden has been denying him, he comes

within an ace of becoming responsible for Varden's murder. And Dickens's large point in making Sim's revolt a part of the anarchic Gordon Riots is that the threat presented by the impulses these fathers repress is not just to the father but, more important, to the whole social order for which he stands.

Unquestionably, therefore, the efforts of fathers to defuse the aggressive and sexual impulses standing in diametrical opposition to the civilized order are in Dickens's view imperative. But he also sees that such necessary efforts are no less liable to exceed all bounds than the forbidden impulses themselves, with the result that every manifestation of independent will on the part of the sons is seen as an affront to paternal authority. What freedom is left is the liberty to do what John Willet recommends to Joe—"to go to the top of the Monument, and sit there. There's no temptation there" (13).

It is because Dickens imagines the repressive father as the essential agent of the son's socialization that *Barnaby Rudge* so insistently presents civilized life and its values in connection with oppressive father-son relationships in this novel. The point, simply put, is that if you want to have civilization, then you must resign yourself to enduring the repression, often enough excessive, out of which civilization is born and by which it is perpetuated.

Apart from these three oppressive father-son relationships, there is a further grouping of characters in *Barnaby* exemplifying the necessary civilizing function of paternal restraint. Lord George Gordon, whose anti-Catholic agitation precipitates the riots bearing his name, has a scheming, manipulative secretary, Gashford, and a bluff, faithful servant, John Grueby, who, Dickens suggests, stand in relation to him as a bad father and a good. And what determines this valuation is precisely the degree to which each is concerned to restrain his darker impulses—the "something wild and ungovernable" in him "which broke through all restraint" and of which the Gordon Riots are the ultimate expression (35). Gashford, interested in Gordon only because he can exploit him, vociferously encourages his will to power; whereas Grueby, seeing only danger in the young lord's megalomania, firmly opposes his grandiose ambitions.

Unfortunately, Gashford, not Grueby, holds sway, and the Gordon Riots follow in due course. But in his caring though finally ineffectual devotion, John Grueby shows that fathers make their civilizing demands for restraint not just out of John Willet's brontosaurian grandiosity or John Chester's reptilian selfishness but also out of love.

It does not take three fathers named John to tell us that Dickens is still coming to terms with the element of aggression in his feelings about his own father, John Dickens. And central to this sorting out are feelings akin to those impelling Lord George Gordon (or even Sim, who aspires to be something very like another Lord George). Who should know more about Gordon's megalomaniacal ambition to "move" men, to leave them "stricken" by the "magic of his eloquence," to "raise this human sea and make it swell and roar at pleasure" (35) than the world's most popular novelist, who had just completed a book so wildly successful that multitudes in England and America hung breathlessly on every turn of Little Nell's fate, and mature men wept like children over her death?[11] Who should understand this more than the man who wore himself out by a compulsively heavy schedule of impassioned public readings from his works, including the reading of "Sikes and Nancy" from *Oliver Twist* that actually caused ladies to faint.[12] "There's nothing equal to seeing the house rise at you," he said of the readings, "one sea of delightful faces, one hurrah of applause!"[13] Surely the man who *wrote* Sikes's murder of Nancy and read it in public like a man driven—surely a man who boasted while writing *Barnaby Rudge* that "I think I can make a better riot than Lord George Gordon did," and who kept Forster posted with dispatches about how "I have just burnt into Newgate, and am going . . . to tear the prisoners out by the hair of their heads" and how "I have let all the prisoners out . . . , burnt down Lord Mansfield's and played the very devil"— such a man surely knew something about the even darker impulses that lay behind Lord George's and Sim's ambitions.[14]

He always loved the power, but clearly in *Barnaby* he was accepting the concomitant responsibility of a preeminent public figure. Yes, he can raise the human sea: the point is not to let it—or himself—surge out of control. The point is not to use the power merely to satisfy one's craving for adulation or to feed one's need to feel immeasurably elevated over the rest of mankind—to feel, like Lord George, "called and chosen and faithful" (35). Nothing gratifies such feelings quite so well as a rapturously cheering audience. But Dickens, when the cheering had only just begun, was already rejecting feelings like these in *Nickleby*, where he scoffed at Miss Knag's brother, "who took to scorning everything, and became a genius."[15] He intensifies the rejection in *Martin Chuzzlewit*, where he jeers at the vermicular Cheevy Slyme's claim, on the basis of his "infinite taste" and "true greatness of soul," to be one of "Nature's Nobs," licensed to scorn everyone.[16]

The focus ought not to be on your inner feelings, which in Lord George and especially Sim are something akin to blurry modern adolescent fantasies of being a rock star and which produce, if anything at all, confusion and disorder in the world. The conviction of special gifts, in other words, may be only an expression of the craving for power, even among the gifted. The point is to produce something worthwhile in the real world, by means of hard work—as Dickens explained to an aspiring young poet just before *Barnaby* began to appear. You say, writes Dickens, that you can write better verse than what you sent me:

How can I judge of that, upon you[r] mere assurance that you have the power of writing regular verse, but have not taken the trouble to exert it? For aught I know, a great many men may *think* poetry—I dare say they do—but the matter between us, is, whether you can write it or no.

Do not suppose that the entertaining a distaste for such extremely light labour as reading and revising your own writings, is a part of true poetical temperament. Whatever Genius does, it does well; and the man who is constantly beginning things and never finishing them is no true Genius, take my word for it.[17]

.   .   .

Given this novel's generational discord, it is a wonder any son in it grows up to be both civilized and a man. But sons do; and the rough paths Joe Willet and Ned Chester take to autonomous manhood show how much trouble and unhappiness go into forging the necessary compromise between (on the one hand) the instinctual drives their fathers are trying to crush in them so absolutely as to unman them and (on the other) their powerful wish to please and emulate their fathers by meeting their demands. The resolution they reach is well worth achieving, *Barnaby Rudge* unhesitatingly affirms, but it necessarily falls short of perfection and rings with an undertone of disappointment and regret.

Joe and Ned earnestly seek accommodation with their fathers, patiently tolerating indignities which, as Joe tells Willet, "are hard enough to bear from you; from anybody else I never will endure them any more" (30). But finally, when their efforts leave them fixed in self-annihilating unfreedom, they have no choice but to rebel. As Edward Chester says, "it is sad when a son, preferring his love and duty in their best and truest sense, finds himself repelled at every turn, and forced to disobey" (32). But neither son revolts in Sim Tappertit's fashion, squaring off in a mortal struggle with parental authority. They simply go away, unable to become men in their fathers' houses.

Their quest for manhood takes a significant course, for their self-exile makes each of them defenders of an authority analogous to their fathers'.

Both engage themselves in the maintenance of imperial power over the colonies, to which England stands in a parental relation. The father-son relationship thus exists even on a geopolitical level in *Barnaby*—as did the main theme of aggression in *Nicholas Nickleby*, in Mr. Gregsbury's complacent vision of the imperial adventure as a "boundless prospect of conquest and possession." Ned takes part in the British exploitation of the West Indies—an exploitation as onerous as the rule of sons by fathers in this novel and similarly rationalized as oppression in the service of civilization. Joe identifies himself even more directly with paternal authority by fighting in an army combatting a revolt against the parent country— the American War of Independence. This war was a key cause of the general unrest out of which the Gordon Riots grew, and although Dickens thought the American Revolution a forward step in human progress, he gives no hint of that sympathy here, so suspicious is he of revolts against parental authority in this novel.[18] Thus Joe and Ned become grown-up men by a familiar paradoxical process: their revolt against paternal authority is simultaneously an identification with it. And when they return from exile, we first see them as defenders of social authority, taking a resolute stand against the rioters (64).

But in *Barnaby Rudge*, no rebellion goes unpunished. Sim Tappertit's almost parricidal rebellion against paternal authority meets a correspondingly violent retribution when the legs onto which he has displaced his measureless phallic narcissism—"his perfect legs, the pride and glory of his life, the comfort of his whole existence—[are] crushed into shapeless ugliness" in the riots (71), leaving him to "stump" about on a pair of wooden legs, which his wife sometimes takes away as a chastisement (Ch. the Last). But even such mild, equivocal, and necessary revolts as Joe's and Ned's exact considerable penalties in the process: exile, danger, and for Joe, who loses an arm in the American War, a mutilation like Sim's. This is the dilemma of civilized sons, as Dickens sees it. To comply with your father's demands unmans you, so revolt ultimately is inescapable; but rebellion, however mild and partial, entails impairment and diminution. You lose no matter what choice you make. Most sons, like these two, take both courses—and lose twice.

Readers of the English novel, with examples like Square B in *Pamela* or Mr. Rochester in *Jane Eyre* before them, are familiar with the idea that becoming a true gentleman involves a diminution of free, aggressive, masculine potency, sometimes even to the point of mutilation. What is new in *Barnaby Rudge* is that this process of socialization is seen in the context of the father-son relationship, where it becomes the experience, Dickens suggests, not only of gentlemen-heroes but of men in general.

Joe returns from exile to marry his sweetheart and to be reconciled with his father, with whose blessing he takes over the Maypole—rightfully succeeding to the inheritance of civilization and also, as the maypole that is the inn's sign suggests, to the potency his father had hitherto been trying to deny him. But to win all this, he had to submit to his father's tyranny and undergo exile and mutilation: the price and the reward are inseparable.

Reconciliation between father and son, like every positive value in *Barnaby Rudge*, is qualified and imperfect. Before Joe's return his father suffers a shock from which he never recovers when the rioters not only vandalize his house but also chop down his maypole and derisively shove it through his window. His manhood symbolically violated, Mr. Willet is in every way a reduced version of his former self when reconciliation with his son becomes possible.

A son's entry into full manhood is unquestionably a threat to his father; as Mr. Chester well knows, when sons grow to full maturity, fathers begin to grow old and must relinquish authority. Still, Mr. Willet's hunger for power remains unabated to the end:

It being accidentally discovered . . . that Mr. Willet still appeared to consider himself a landlord by profession, Joe provided him with a slate, upon which the old man regularly scored up vast accounts for meat, drink, and tobacco. As he grew older this passion increased upon him; and it became a delight to chalk against the name of each of his cronies a sum of enormous magnitude, and impossible to be paid: and such was his secret joy in these entries, that he would be perpetually seen going behind the door to look at them, and coming forth again, suffused with the liveliest satisfaction. (Ch. the Last)

In this way he retains the illusion of the unlimited power he craves, and, because of the confusion of his mind, this illusion satisfies him, saving him from confronting the extent of his loss. But the loss is real, though Joe poignantly tries to paper over its actuality by providing his father with a little house disguised as a miniature Maypole Inn and "plant[ing] in the little garden outside the front-door a fictitious Maypole" (Ch. the Last). Yet this maypole is indeed fictitious, being only the symbol of a symbol.

Nor can Willet, perpetually trying and failing to understand that Joe has lost an arm, come to terms with his own responsibility for this loss.

But the blame that attaches to him, as Dickens presents it, is mitigated and indirect. He is no villain, after all—no Claudius of Denmark—and the situation between him and Joe, with all its comic exaggeration, is not something out of *Hamlet*. What he bears is only a version of the blame inseparable from the responsibility of fatherhood.

4

Natural Man

Disturbed, excessive in its intensity of conflict, the father–son relationship is nevertheless essential to civilization, as Dickens makes clear not only in the cluster of situations just discussed but also in his presentation of the effects of its absence in two of the novel's central characters, Maypole Hugh and Barnaby Rudge, both abandoned by their fathers before they were born. Hugh, who is in fact Mr. Chester's illegitimate son by a gypsy girl, grew up "in utter ignorance of his father" (75); he "never knew, nor saw, nor thought about" one (23). Barnaby's father, wrongly supposed to have been murdered on the night before Barnaby was born, has never been heard of since, and so Barnaby too has grown up fatherless. What the lesson of these two sons teaches is that to be deprived of a father is to be victimized more calamitously than the three "oppressed" sons could ever dream of being; for, as a result of their fatherless condition, Hugh the "natural [i.e., illegitimate] child" and Barnaby the "natural" [i.e., idiot] both lack certain essential characteristics of socialized men. Both these creatures, as Dickens conceives of them, have remained uncivilized, a fate this novel imagines as horrible. Indeed, in these characters Dickens explicitly presents two alternative representations of that mythical figure who lives outside civilized society, Natural Man.

Early in the novel, Dickens mentions the story of Valentine and Orson, a childhood favorite of his, which tells of a pair of twin brothers lost in the woods moments after their birth, and which was clearly very much on Dickens's mind throughout the writing of *Barnaby*. Found by King Pepin, Valentine grows up a knight in the French court. The other twin, Orson, reared as a "savage boy" in the forest by "ruthless beares" (in the words of the ballad in Percy's *Reliques*), matures into a club-wielding creature who "drinks the blood of men" and, in his "fierce and mortal rage," terrorizes the countryside. Sir Valentine overcomes his "brutal" brother in a furious battle, bringing him back to court to be tamed and civilized.

The main point of this story is the confrontation between the civilized and the wild brother, and in this sense *Barnaby Rudge* as a whole is truly (to use Mr. Chester's phrase) "quite a Valentine and Orson business" (15).[1] The contrast between civilized Ned and his savage brother Hugh is central to the novel no less than to the ballad, though Dickens's Orson never does get civilized. Moreover, because Dickens conceives of Ned always in relation to Joe and Sim, and Hugh always in relation to Barnaby, the opposition between the Valentine and the Orson figures is a theme that *Barnaby Rudge* extends beyond Mr. Chester's two sons, giving us not one Valentine and Orson but rather three civilized figures contrasted to two wild counterparts. And the juxtaposition eloquently demonstrates that however high the personal cost of becoming civilized may be, it is worth it.

Orson, as we know from Richard Bernheimer,[2] is a full-fledged representative of a stock figure in medieval (and later) literature, painting, and folklore—the "wild man"; a bestial, hairy, club-wielding creature, alone in the forest, living a life of ceaseless violence. "If he was to survive, he had to be the physical equal, if not the superior, of creatures such as dragons, boars, or primeval bulls." Nor is his violence merely defensive, for his superhuman strength "is the mainspring of his actions, driving him in a continuous effort to release the explosive force which is in him by trying it out in combat. No beast . . . is ever secure against the wild man's perpetual aggressiveness." Moreover, "when several wild men meet, the result is usually a battle of all against all, fought fiercely, without regard for those rules which medieval custom imposed on the knight."[3] The wild man's sexuality is as peremptory as his aggressiveness and is so salient a feature of wild man lore that Bernheimer devotes a separate chapter to his "erotic connotations."

This creature, "compounded of intransigence, lust, and violence," is a "commentary on the bestial side of man's nature," Bernheimer rightly points out. "Devoid of all those acquired tastes and patterns of behavior which are part of our adjustment to civilization," the wild man "embodies a negative ideal in all its harshness and one-sidedness," representing the "disturbing, untried, elementary forces in each of us." He is related to such classical representations of man's aboriginal personality as satyrs and centaurs, regularly identified in the Middle Ages and Renaissance as wild men.[4] And he merged into the figure of that later embodiment of uncivilized human nature, the "natural man" of seventeenth- and eighteenth-century political philosophy, as is clear from this 1590s description of the wild man's world:

> In time of yore, when men like brutish beasts
> Did lead their lives in loathsom celles and woodes,
> And wholy gave themselves to witlesse will,
> A rude unruly rout, then man to man
> Became a present praie; then might prevailed
> The weakest went to walles:
> Right was unknowen, for wrong was all in all.[5]

What is this if not "the life of man, solitary, poore, nasty, brutish, and short" that Hobbes imputes to his natural man?[6]

This whole cluster of figures stands behind the vision of man's pre-civilized character that Dickens dramatizes in Hugh. Living in the stable with the horses he tends, he shows the wild man's traditional mastery over animals, and he is described by Dickens as "a handsome satyr" (21) and by Mr. Chester as a "centaur" (23). The handsomeness, moreover, glances at a strand in wild man lore not yet enumerated—the notion of his having preserved intact all those physical powers that civilized man has lost as a result of too much soft living in sophisticated and therefore degenerate society. Dickens is not profoundly impressed by these qualities, thinking their dilution a small enough price to pay for not being an otherwise squalid, treacherous creature like Hugh, but he enumerates them dutifully nonetheless. "[N]imble, strong, and swift of foot" (21), keen-sighted as a hawk (34): with his "muscular and handsome proportions," his "hale athletic figure," and his "giant's strength," Hugh "might have served a painter for a model" (11), so well-developed a sample of our physical nature is he. But the handsomeness of this satyr goes no way to qualify Dickens's overwhelmingly negative valuation. Indeed, if the satyr of classical antiquity is half human, half bestial, Dickens's satyr calls himself "more brute than man" (77).

What does his life consist of? To "eat, and drink," he reports (74), and in addition, as Willet observes, to sleep "in the sun in summer, and in the straw in winter time" (10). He loves drunkenness, which does not so much change as intensify his ordinary, purely physical mode of being. After all, he has nothing to regress from. And finally, he has the wild man's powerful, peremptory sexual and aggressive impulses, which in wild-man fashion he is not accustomed to restrain from the pitch of ferocity they are capable of reaching.

For example, when he accosts Dolly Varden in the fields beyond the Maypole, what is threatened is rape, as Dolly—correctly interpreting the "something of coarse bold admiration in his look, which terrified her very much" (21)—is well aware. The threat of rape is renewed when Hugh and a band of rioters kidnap Dolly and Emma Haredale, who, says Dickens, "in their being borne they knew not whither, by a band of daring villains who eyed them as some among these fellows did," justifiably found "reasons for the worst alarm" (59). Nor in this instance is Hugh abashed by Dolly's distress or resistance. Her scorn only excites him further, for his cave-man sexuality, as Dickens emphasizes in this encounter even more than in the scene in the fields, is supercharged with aggression.

It is Hugh's aggressiveness that Dickens takes as his defining characteristic. Hugh himself says that he would "sooner kill a man than a dog any day," and his matter-of-fact threat of murderous violence to Dolly Varden's friends, added to his sexual aggression, convinces Dolly "that his ferocious nature, once roused, would stop at nothing" (21). Dickens underlines his aggression by referring to him as a "hungry wolf" (59) or a "wild beast" (74). But the term Dickens thinks most appropriate is "savage" (e.g., 21, 34), a word, as *Barnaby Rudge* uses it, that not only describes Hugh's aggressiveness but also implicitly explains it. "Savage" means "ferocious and cruel," of course, but it also means "in a state of nature" or "wild"; and a "savage" is not just "a cruel or fierce person" but, more usually, "a person living in the lowest state of development or cultivation; an uncivilized, wild person."[7] The word itself contains a theory of human nature—a pessimistic theory which tells us that precivilized man is inherently ferocious, with aggression his most salient characteristic. The extreme violence Hugh displays in the riots is the violence definitive of his character, there revealed in its full magnitude, when his "ferocious nature" really is "roused."

Dickens goes still further in outlining what the absence of civilization means in this exemplary figure. Hugh, says John Willet, because he "has never had much to do with anything but animals, and has never lived in any way but like the animals he has lived among, *is* a animal. And . . . is to be treated accordingly" (11). If we put aside Willet's cockeyed conclusion, there is a sense in which his diagnosis is not so farfetched. Bernheimer's further comments on the wild man are to the point here: frequently this creature is

without the faculty of human speech, the power to recognize or conceive of the Divinity, or the usual meaningful processes of mind. What remains, after losses of this kind and magnitude, is a creature human only in overall physical appearance, but so degenerate that to call him a beast were more than an empty metaphor.[8]

It is in this sense that we are to understand Hugh's inability to read or write. And perhaps this is also the point of Hugh's claim of seeing no difference between the room where Reuben Haredale was murdered and any other room that keeps out rain and snow (34): to his undeveloped consciousness, the world is mere material, unhaunted by a social soul.[9]

That the wild man lacks man's highest faculties provides an explanation for both Hugh's scoffing at the notion of prayer and John Willet's response to that derision. "He's quite a animal, sir," Willet pronounces. "You'll excuse him, I'm sure. If he has any soul at all, sir, it must be such a very small one, that it don't signify what he does or doesn't in that way" (12). Everything that comes out of Willet's oracular mouth is suspect and needs to be scrutinized; but since Dickens himself makes precisely the same declaration about Barnaby's defect of soul, we have to consider seriously Willet's statement about Hugh. For here Willet hits on what Dickens takes to be a truth—that natural man possesses only in the most rudimentary form that spiritual faculty which distinguishes man from the beasts and confers upon him his human dignity. What we take to be the primary source of our human value is inherent in our nature only as a potentiality: it depends on our life in civilization for its realization.

Such, we saw, is the lesson of *The Haunted Man*: The "baby savage" is lacking in an inner faculty which can germinate only in the medium of the social life he has been denied. "All within this desolate creature is barren wilderness," Dickens says of him; he is "a creature who might live to take the outward form of a man, but who, within, would"—like Hugh— "live and perish a mere beast."

.   .   .

According to the Lord Monboddo whose "doctrine" Dickens invokes in the first chapter of *Martin Chuzzlewit*,

however ingenious Mr. Hobbes may have been, (and he certainly was a very acute man . . .), it is plain to me, that he did not know what man was by nature, divested of all the habits and opinions that he acquires in civil life; but supposed, that, previous to the institution of society, he has all the desires and passions that he now has.[10]

If we really want to reconstruct man's primitive, original nature, according to Monboddo as well as the whole Rousseauean tradition to which his thought belongs, we must look at the barbarian peoples of America, Africa, and the South Sea Islands, at deaf people, at infants, at idiots, and at Orang Outangs. And what we find is a creature like the "natural" Barnaby Rudge—"a completely unintelligent, unsocial, and non-moral though good natured beast" in "a state of virtual idiocy."[11]

One of the sixty-six meanings of the word "nature" distinguished by Arthur O. Lovejoy is "that *in* man which is not due to taking thought or to deliberate choice; hence, those modes of human desire, emotion, or behavior which are instinctive or spontaneous, in contrast with those which are due to the laboring intellect, to premeditation, to self-consciousness, or to instruction."[12] This is one of the primary senses, beside the sense of "natural fool," in which Barnaby may be said to be a "natural." The "light-hearted idiot," remarks Forster of him, is "as unconscious of guilt as of suffering, and happy with no sense but of the influences of nature."[13] He is an artless and "undesigning creature" (49), with a "wayward and capricious nature" (25), who, like the natural man of Rousseau's *Second Discourse*, "is given over to the sole sentiment of [his] present existence, without any idea of the future, however near it may be."[14] So Barnaby is "soon forgetful of the past" (47) and has "no recollection" of the stories his mother tells him; "the tale of yesterday was new upon the morrow" (45). And his lack of memory brings him pleasure, for all his experience wears the charm of novelty. Wholly at home in the natural world as he is, his unselfconscious integration into it provides him with another inexhaustible reservoir of pleasure. "The world to him was full of happiness; in every tree, and plant, and flower, in every bird, and beast, and tiny insect whom a breath of summer wind laid low upon the ground, he had delight" (47).

Though these are sufficiently benign traits, Dickens has by no means set out to represent in Barnaby a natural man in the mold of the eighteenth-century noble savage, that creature "of uncorrupted rationality, knowing intuitively all essential moral and religious truths,"[15] who makes a dignified appearance in Epistle III of Pope's *Essay on Man*, for example, or in the pages of Diderot's *Supplement to Bougainville's "Voyage."* Rationality is exactly what Barnaby lacks.

In our own time we distinguish carefully between idiots or mentally retarded people like Barnaby, on the one hand, and lunatics on the other; but such a sharp distinction was not made at the time Dickens's novel was written. Both groups were lumped into the category of "persons insane (in which class . . . are to be included idiots who have had no understanding from their birth, as well as lunatics who . . . have lost the use of their reason)."[16] The absence of reason, in the words of Michel Foucault, was conceived as "dispossess[ing] man of what is specifically human in him," of reducing him to the status of mere animal, and "establish[ing] him at the zero degree of his own nature."[17] "Why is man alone subject to becoming imbecile?" asked Rousseau. "Is it not that he thereby returns to his primitive state . . . ?"[18] In this vein, too, Hobbes also placed idiots and lunatics outside the civilized condition, for

[o]ver naturall fooles, children, or mad-men there is no Law, no more than over brute beasts; nor are they capable of the title of just or unjust; because they never had power to make any covenant, or to understand the consequences thereof; . . . as they must do that make themselves a Commonwealth.[19]

Just as Dickens briefly flirts with the notion of unconscious, artless innocence when considering Barnaby's lack of reason, so too does he momentarily wonder if a lack that we assume to be an affliction may not instead be a mark of special grace. Consider this apostrophe on Barnaby's pleasure in the natural world:

It is something to look upon enjoyment, so that it be free and wild and in the face of nature, though it is but the enjoyment of an idiot. It is something to know that Heaven has left the capacity of gladness in such a creature's breast; it is something to be assured that, however lightly men may crush that faculty in their fellows, the Great Creator of mankind imparts it even to his despised and slighted work. Who would not rather see a poor idiot happy in the sunlight, than a wise man pining in a darkened jail! (25)

Some alternatives! But the general point—that his lack of reason protects Barnaby from having the shades of the prison house that is social life and self-conscious identity close around him—is familiar enough.

Though Dickens never explicitly repudiates this notion of the grace of affliction in relation to Barnaby, he goes out of his way to show that as a general principle there is no such thing. Mr. Stagg, the blind gin-cellar keeper, makes an analogy between his sightlessness and Barnaby's "blind-ness of the intellect" (45), but even without this explicit indication it is clear that these characters are, with respect to their defects, analogous. "[W]e are accustomed," remarks Dickens of Stagg's blindness, "to see in those who have lost a human sense, something in its place almost divine" (45); and so, he continues, Mrs. Rudge was the more shocked by Stagg's disclosure of his villainous intentions toward herself. Stagg reads these thoughts in her voice and answers them:

I know what you would say: you have hinted at it once already. Have I no feeling for you, because I am blind? No, I have not. Why do you expect me, being in darkness, to be better than men who have their sight—why should you? Is the hand of God more manifest in my having no eyes, than in your having two? It's the cant of you folks to be horrified if a blind man robs, or lies, or steals; oh yes, it's far worse in him, who can barely live on the few half-pence that are thrown to him in your crowded streets, than in you, who can see, and work, and are not dependent on the mercies of the world. A curse on you! (46)

An affliction is an affliction, not a mark of grace; a loss is a loss, not a sign of innocence. If it is true for Stagg, it is true for Barnaby.

Dickens has about the natural man he represents in Barnaby the same kind of ambivalence that Rousseau has about the natural man of the *Second Discourse*. Both writers see qualities to value positively in their natural men—health, strength, freedom from guilt and vainglory, exemption from modern social life's perversions and insincerity—but both ulti-mately take a stand on the same essentially negative judgment. For both writers, natural man is "a narrow, stupid animal," whom only civilized society transforms into "a creature of intelligence and a man." [20] Dickens shares Rousseau's conviction that except for the capacity for develop-ment, which at this stage is an entirely unrealized potentiality, "nothing that is distinctive of man was primitive, and nothing that is most excel-lent in him comes by nature alone." [21]

The loss of reason restores man to his aboriginal state—where, how-ever, he ceases to be man in all but outward appearance. Dickens, though full of ambivalence and misgiving, means all this when, coming to the very core of his understanding of what civilization confers, he tells us that for all intents and purposes Barnaby has no soul. "[T]he absence of a soul is far more terrible in a living man than in a dead one," he says in his very first description of Barnaby; "and in this unfortunate being its noblest powers were wanting" (3). Terrible indeed: for Barnaby is deficient in that spiritual endowment which is the specific differentiation between "a narrow, stupid animal" and "a creature of intelligence and a man."

Hence the elaborate interplay between Barnaby and his pet raven, Grip. For Grip is "a creature of mere brute instinct" (47)—who talks! and who moreover listens to conversations "with a polite attention and a most extraordinary appearance of comprehending every word" (6). He seems such a "knowing blade," such a "deep customer," that Gabriel Varden says there is "no doubt he can read and write and cast accounts if he chooses" (5). Grip and Barnaby are "strange companions" Gabriel says, for "the bird has all the wit," to which Barnaby adds that "he's the master, and I'm the man" (6). The disquieting point—the reason for Dickens's original notion of having Barnaby "always in company with a pet raven immeasurably more knowing than himself"[22]—is that it is hard to differentiate between these two. Each of them is capable of a caricature of rational discourse; each inhabits an ambiguous realm between the animal and the human. Grip, an animal who is, as we say, "almost human"—disturbingly so, when we consider that some thinkers have made speech the specific quality distinguishing man from beasts—is a satirical commentary on Barnaby, who with his defect of soul is a man who is not quite human.[23]

        ·   ·   ·

I have said that Dickens, in his ambivalence over Barnaby, is occasionally tempted to see in him a childlike innocence. But after one of the novel's central suggestions to that effect—the statement, already quoted, affirming how much better it is to see "a poor idiot happy in the sunlight, than a wise man pining in a darkened jail" (25)—he immediately denies those suggestions with a vehemence no less startling than the juxtaposition of two such starkly contradictory points of view in as many pages. Mrs. Rudge is suddenly flooded with recollections of Barnaby's early childhood:

How often . . . had she sat beside him night and day, watching for the dawn of mind that never came; how had she feared, and doubted, and yet hoped, long after conviction forced itself upon her! The little stratagems she had devised to try him, the little tokens he had given in his childish way—not of dullness but of something infinitely worse, so ghastly and unchildlike in its cunning—came back to her as vividly as if but yesterday had intervened.

What she sees in his "wild and vacant eye" and "old and elfin-like" face that is infinitely worse than dullness is the stupid, untrustworthy cunning of the beast (25). It is ghastly in its inhumanity.

Here a darker tone falls over the question of Barnaby's animality, making him a more sinister figure than Rousseau's nonmoral though good-natured beast. Here too we come face-to-face with a perplexing problem in Dickens's conception of this character, a problem whose solution shows that even within this representative of fundamental human nature Dickens imagines, in spite of all his Romantic flourishes, a nucleus of impulses corrosive of the human order. Throughout the novel, Dickens generally portrays Barnaby as a version of natural man differing signally from the version embodied by Hugh not only in a lack of sexual impulse but, more important, in an apparent lack of aggressiveness. And yet Barnaby ends up fighting alongside Hugh and Dennis at the head of the furiously destructive mob in the riots. We have to ask why this is.

In rather a fanciful way, Dickens begins to answer this question by dressing this "natural fool" in ribbons, lace, ruffles, "motley scraps" (3)—in short, the motley of the Fool, that folk-figure who is associated, in jest, with lawlessness and the abolition of morality and order. The Feast of Fools, "in which mighty persons were humbled, sacred things profaned, laws relaxed and ethical ideals reversed," was, according to Enid Welsford, "an annual interruption of the ordinary routine, marked by a temporary suspension of law and order and a temporary reversal of moral judgements."[24] Thus Barnaby is linked to the standard-bearer of a mock collapse of civilized life and a playful breaking out of the normally repressed primitive instincts of which the Gordon Riots offer an instructive example, not in play, but in earnest.

Of course by placing the idiot along with the "obscene animals," Hugh and Dennis (52), in the vanguard of the rioters, Dickens insists on the mob's moral idiocy. Indeed, his original plan was to present as the mob's leaders three lunatics escaped from Bedlam, to emphasize that such destructiveness is a form of madness.[25] But this is not enough to explain Barnaby's active involvement, *fighting* in the thick of things: indeed, why is it Barnaby who strikes the first blow for the rioters (49)? Behind such actions is there really no aggression?

We know that Barnaby is closely connected to the act of aggression whose recital begins this novel and whose memory broods over the whole first part, for in some complex, unexplained way, his idiocy has been caused by his father's murder of Reuben Haredale, in whose house the elder Rudge was steward. Indeed, to his father, Barnaby seems "a creature who had sprung into existence from his victim's blood" (69). This crime appears to be modelled on a notorious contemporary case, the murder of Lord William Russell by his valet, François Courvoisier, in May of 1840. Having slit his master's throat with a carving knife, Courvoisier was convicted after a celebrated trial, which Dickens discussed in a letter to the editor of the *Morning Chronicle*; he also went to see the execution in July.[26] This crime so gripped Dickens, it is fair to guess, not just because it was the murder of a master by a trusted servant but also because the victim was a representative of legitimate public authority as well, being both a peer and the uncle of Lord John Russell, the Prime Minister. All crimes are committed against society, in that each is a breach of the social contract; but the special circumstances of this crime, in which "venerable blood" was "most savagely, barbarously, and inhumanly shed,"[27] make it seem an unusually overt assault upon the whole structure of social authority.

Rudge's master occupied no such exalted station; but that the Courvoisier case stands behind Rudge's crime strengthens a reading of this fictional murder as a domestic analogue of the public overthrow of social order that Dickens depicts in the Gordon Riots. Moreover, how terrible, how fundamental an act of aggression Dickens conceives Rudge's crime to have been is apparent from the fate to which he consigns him. Though Rudge is at last executed by the civil authorities, he spends the quarter-century before he is caught living the life of a "hunted beast," being so absolutely outcast that he is excluded even from the society of conventional criminals, who fear and shun him (16). Indeed, right at the outset Dickens tells us (with a meaning more literal than at first sight appears) that he "looked unsociable enough" (1), for Rudge's violent crime has in effect condemned him to a life outside civilization, which truly is solitary, poor, nasty, brutish, and (as it happens) short.

In this dreadful act of aggression, Dickens makes plain, Barnaby is somehow implicated. He bears the imprint of his father's crime in his birthmark that "seemed a smear of blood but half washed out" (5), as well as in his darkened intellect. Dickens at moments even seems to identify him with his father: trying to impersonate the elder Rudge, Barnaby makes himself look "so like the original he counterfeited, that [his father] might have passed for his own shadow" (17). And Rudge himself knows that he and his son are "inseparable" (69). More than just its victim, Barnaby, in a confused and unexplained way, bears the guilt for his father's crime. Thus, since his life comes into being stained with violence and the novel keeps recurring to his association with so brutal a murder—since, moreover, his career in the book culminates in his deep implication in the riots' fearsome rage—a reader is surely justified in thinking that violence and aggression are inseparable from Dickens's conception of Barnaby, however much he himself is inclined at times to resist that conclusion.

A convinced Freudian would have a ready explanation for this puzzling association of Barnaby with his father's violence and his father's victim. True, such a critic would say, Dickens makes Barnaby the victim of his father's violence in that his defect is caused by his father's crime—and indeed on one occasion in this novel his father tries to kill him (17). But Dickens also makes an identification between Barnaby and his father, saddling Barnaby with a measure of the elder Rudge's guilt for a crime that is, at least symbolically, parricidal and the negation of the civilized condition. Moreover, Barnaby engrosses the total attention of his mother, who lives for him and complies with her husband's criminal demands on her simply to protect her beloved son from his violence. What is this, an orthodox Freudian would say, but a massive expression of the Oedipus complex? Here are the various Oedipal wishes and fears all mixed up together: Barnaby bears the guilt for parricide, has been maimed by his father (presumably in retaliation for parricidal wishes), and possesses his mother. So Barnaby is indeed imbued with murderous, anticivilized, Oedipal violence. And *of course* Dickens is ambivalent, such an analysis would conclude: he is projecting his own Oedipal fantasies onto Barnaby, where they are at once revealed and denied.

A non-Freudian is hard-pressed to find an alternative order for making sense of this confused complex of elements. The present critic cannot but note that the virtue of Freud's theory here is that it takes exactly the same elements that are so puzzling in Dickens's novel and finds a meaning in them that is utterly consistent with *Barnaby Rudge*'s whole drift. Surely *something*, one feels, connects civilization, aggression, and the specific father-son disturbances described both here and in Freud. And if the Oedipus complex is faulty and extreme in Freud's formulation, if it is hardly applicable to all eras and places, it nevertheless undoubtedly sheds some light on the deepest feelings of sons who grew up in a particular family structure in Western Europe in the nineteenth century—especially sons who in later life were so obsessed with understanding the relations between fathers and sons as these two men.

Hedged round with ambivalence and equivocation as Barnaby is, he is a figure on whom Dickens nevertheless places an unquestionably negative judgment, even though he finds this version of natural man only disturbing, whereas he finds Hugh frightening and hateful. But what I hope is now clear is that although Dickens seems to imagine a sharp contrast between Barnaby and Hugh, the differences between them are by no means as great as at first sight they appear. The fundamental conception underlying both characters, fully conscious in the case of Hugh, dimly and distortedly perceived in the case of Barnaby, is essentially the same. Both figures, with their undeveloped or defective souls and their imperfect humanity, shock and repel Dickens, in spite of his flicker of interest in certain aspects of their purely instinctive character. What disturbs him most of all in these figures is his sense that an innate, fundamental feature of natural man, blatantly obvious in Hugh and covert in Barnaby, is his built-in, peremptory aggressiveness.

5

Lord Chesterfield's Conscience

One of the two essential ways civilized men differ from natural men in *Barnaby Rudge* is that they have different histories, having experienced a specific relation to their fathers not afforded natural men. This experience—vexatious and painful—is what socializes them. The other definitive difference is that social men have souls and natural men do not, making for a fundamental *internal* difference—a difference in the basic structure of personality—between the two, as well.

Dickens establishes that civilization is an inner quality largely by a negative strategy—by an elaborate demonstration that the defining essence of a civilized individual is not a mere matter of externals. Mr. Chester, Dickens's satire on the famous fourth Earl of Chesterfield, provides the case in point, and to this exceptionally interesting character we must now attend, to grasp what civilization is not, before we examine the "soul" that Dickens takes to be a civilized man's essential characteristic.

Mr. Chester, *au courant* in all things, has read with admiration the latest best-seller, Lord Chesterfield's *Letters to His Son* (published in 1774, the year before *Barnaby Rudge* opens). He pronounces that nobleman "the writer who should be his country's pride," for his *Letters* contain "the most masterly composition, the most delicate thoughts, the finest code of morality, and the most gentlemanly sentiments in the universe!" (23). Because Dickens has modelled Mr. Chester so closely on Lord Chesterfield as to have given him an abbreviated version of his name, it is worth pausing to consider that "Pharasee's Pharasee," who teaches, Dr. Johnson judges, "the morals of a whore, and the manners of a dancing-master."[1] Doing so, too, will make clear the large, cultural significance of Dickens's satire, for it registers an important development in the history of the idea of conscience, of which Chesterfield's *Letters* and *Barnaby Rudge* represent two quite different stages. The movement inward of the defining faculty of civilization taking place in *Barnaby* exemplifies a decisive shift away from the Chesterfieldian conception, and this reinterpretation of conscience is itself part of a changing conception of the relationship between the self and society. Here the inquiry into the nature of civilization takes on a psychological dimension: Dickens's satire of Chesterfield signals his discovery that it is in the nature of society to transform the nature of the self.

Dr. Johnson aside, it is Mr. Chester who expresses the opinion of the great majority of Chesterfield's first readers, who saw in him the perfection of the man of the world, civilized man *par excellence*. He was, according to the *Monthly Review* of April 1774, "a complete gentleman," and even Johnson, on another occasion, was willing to grant that with the immorality excised the *Letters* might well be given to any young gentleman.[2]

Chesterfield's ethical viewpoint—already lucidly formulated in antiquity by Adeimantus in Plato's *Republic*—can best be understood in relation to the "love of fame" theory of conscience, central to eighteenth-century thought.[3] This theory has been eloquently analyzed by Lovejoy in his *Reflections on Human Nature*, whose argument runs as follows. Why do men act in ways judged to be moral? Not out of any self-subsisting love of virtue, and not because such actions are reasonable, for reason operates only in the realm of facts, not motives, and is regularly led astray by the passions. Nor can we impute to human nature any primitive, disinterested love of others, for everyone loves nothing so much as himself. But men have an irrational and morally ambiguous inborn craving for fame and distinction, for the good opinion, applause, and admiration of others, and this craving is "the sole objective prompting of good conduct." Through this impulse "the interests of other men and the moral

standards of a society get their hold upon the conduct of the individual."
Thus "pride" (in this sense of a desire to win approval) "leads the individual to act as other individuals, or the community in general, desire him to act—in other words to subordinate his private desires and interests to the public interest. It is, in fact, . . . the only dependable . . . motive for the behavior which is generally described as moral. If it is not a virtue"—if, indeed, it had been condemned by moralists of every period as a fundamentally vicious impulse—"its overt effects are, in the main, the same as those of virtue."[4]

But there is a danger inherent in this situation, for if the source of moral validation lies outside ourselves, lies in the judgment of other people, it is almost inevitable that we shall compromise our authenticity even as we try to behave in ways our society regards as moral. In the first place, the craving for approval and distinction which generates moral behavior takes us outside of ourselves and makes us live too much through the eyes and in the opinions of others. As a result, our inner lives tend to be corroded in the medium of public opinion. Second, morality comes to be a matter more of appearance than reality; behavior, not motive, is at issue. We create a public persona, which need not correspond to our inner self (so far as we manage to maintain an inner self), and so moral behavior is peculiarly liable to decline into hypocrisy.[5]

Chesterfield begins the *Letters* a wholehearted subscriber to the "love of fame" theory, but as the *Letters* progress, he unconsciously modifies and finally transforms it. Whereas this whole structure had during most of the eighteenth century virtually the status of a law of nature—whereas it was thought to operate in an essentially automatic and unconscious fashion—with Chesterfield it becomes conscious to the extent that it is subject to systematic manipulation. Why not take advantage of necessity and turn it to our own account, by consciously directing our inescapable desire for approval into the service of our personal advancement? For while pleasing others is of great benefit to society, it is also of great benefit to the successfully plausive: society best rewards those who best please. "[T]he art of pleasing is, in truth, the art of rising, of distinguishing one's self, of making a figure and a fortune in the world."[6]

To gain men's approval, you must address yourself to their self-love rather than to their judgment, often going so far as to "dupe the understanding."

Mankind . . . is more governed by appearances, than by realities. . . . Few people have penetration enough to discover, attention enough to observe, or even concern enough to examine, beyond the exterior; they take their notions from the surface, and go no deeper.[7]

Neither your inner worth nor your true motives are given their proper weight in the opinion formed of you by your fellows; it is the external man, the mask, that is judged.

Therefore, "in everything, the Manner is full as important as the Matter."[8] "The solid and ornamental united are undoubtedly best; but were I reduced to make an option, I should, without hesitation, choose the latter."[9] So to learn to please is to learn the ornamental, rather than the substantive, virtues—to learn to flatter and pamper, to be all "gentleness, affability, complaisance, and good-humour." The purpose always is to manipulate others to gain one's own goals. One's fellow men constitute a vast magazine of raw materials, lying ready to hand, for the "man of parts" to exploit in the furtherance of his own interests: "there is scarcely anybody who is absolutely good for nothing."[10]

Chesterfield, in other words, ends by turning the "love of fame" theory of conscience inside out. What is so interesting about that theory is that it reconciles the competitive, aggressive aspects of human nature with the everyday sociability of men by deriving both impulses from that complex element of human nature described by the equivalent terms, "pride" and "self-love." While it is self-love that impels the individual to be egotistical, self-serving, and antisocial, to devalue other men and ignore their interests in favor of his own, the very same self-love defuses and transforms these tendencies, because it depends for its satisfaction on the authentication accorded it by others and thus requires the individual to conform his behavior to the real interests and standards of his society. Here, this theory of conscience discloses its consanguinity with the economic theory of *laissez-faire*, in that it seeks to establish that individuals, while variously pursuing their self-interest, advance willy-nilly, through some mechanism established by the Architect of the universe, the interest of the community.

By the time the theory reaches Chesterfield's hands, it seems to have become so well assimilated that Chesterfield has forgotten its origin as an explanation for the transformation of potentially, even fundamentally, antisocial tendencies into social impulses. Thus, while the theoreticians of conscience were relieved to find that the desire to serve yourself regularly mutates into the desire to serve society—that you cannot rationally serve yourself without at the same time serving society—Chesterfield, as

I have pointed out, reverses the terms and observes with satisfaction that, since you must serve society, you can also learn to use the means of doing so to serve yourself in the process. Here we have come full circle and are back at Square One and, as *Oliver Twist*'s Noah Claypole would say, Number One.

To manipulate people successfully you have to be an acute observer of men, for you need to "know them thoroughly in order to manage them ably." [11] You should learn their weaknesses in order to know "what to bait your hook with to catch them," remembering always that "[e]very man is to be had one way or another, and every woman almost any way." [12] You must, therefore, "like the chameleon, be able to take every different hue," because you "must, like St. Paul, become all things to all men, to gain some." [13]

To all this, Chesterfield points out, "[i]t may be objected that I am now recommending dissimulation to you; I both own and justify it. . . . [W]ithout some dissimulation no business can be carried on at all." [14] One is always consciously playing one role or another, and to do this requires *sang-froid*, clear-sightedness, and self-control. You have always "to be upon your own guard, and yet, by a seeming natural openness, to put people off theirs." [15] One has to develop

the mastery of one's temper, and that coolness of mind, and serenity of counte-nance, which hinders us from discovering . . . those passions or sentiments by which we are inwardly moved or agitated. . . . You will say, possibly, that this coolness must be constitutional, and consequently does not depend upon the will; . . . [b]ut a man may as surely get a habit of letting his reason prevail over his constitution, as of letting, as most people do, the latter prevail over the former. [16]

That desirable coolness Chesterfield displays often enough toward his illegitimate son, Philip Stanhope, to whom he addresses these letters. Claiming to be the author not only of his son's being but of his identity as well, Chesterfield tells young Stanhope:

The best authors are always the severest critics of their own works. . . . Consider-ing you as my work, I do not look upon myself as a bad author, and am therefore a severe critic. I examine narrowly into the least inaccuracy or inelegancy, in order to correct, not to expose them, and that the work may be perfect at last. [17]

His sense of his son as an extension of himself is as literal and absolute as any of the fathers in *Barnaby Rudge*. While he assures his son, as Mr.

Chester likewise observes to Ned (15), that he does not "mean to dictate as a parent; I only mean to advise as a friend, and an indulgent one too," he nevertheless reminds him, in the very next breath, "how absolutely dependent you are upon me"—just as Ned, as he complains, is absolutely dependent upon his father—and therefore, Chesterfield suggests, "I believe it would do you no harm if you would always imagine that I was present, and saw and heard every thing you did and said."[18] Indeed, Chesterfield outdoes even Polonius by having, not one Reynaldo, but many "Arguses, with a hundred eyes each, who will watch you narrowly, and relate to me faithfully [whatever you do on your travels]."[19] Freud's superego is hardly more vigilant and omniscient than this: young Stanhope is truly "on his patrole."

That spontaneous love plays any part in the relations between father and son is not to be thought. Thus, Chesterfield reminds his son, "as I have no womanish weakness for your person, your merit must, and will, be the only measure of my kindness."[20] Indeed, should his son be lacking in merit, says Chesterfield, with the paralyzing fatuity that Dickens has appropriated from him for Mr. Chester, "we should not converse very much together; . . . it would endanger my health."[21] And, by the same token, his son's "affection for me can only proceed from your experience and conviction of my fondness for you (for to talk of natural affection is talking nonsense)."[22] Even between father and son, affection is not spontaneous but payment for services rendered. No sentiment could be less Dickensian: for example, Mr. Cheeryble's speech in *Nickleby*, pointing out that natural affections need to be fostered in order to survive, takes it for granted that natural affections do indeed exist. The whole spirit of Dickens's work bears witness to this truth, as do specific situations, such as Barnaby Rudge's spontaneous impulse of love toward his father when the elder Rudge first reveals his identity (an impulse immediately crushed, however).[23] On this question, Dickens most strenuously takes Mr. Chester and the whole Chesterfieldian ethic to task. And one cannot but wonder to what extent Dickens, preoccupied in *Barnaby* with the relations between fathers and sons, was moved to satirize Chesterfield not just for his failure as a moralist but also for his failure as a father.

. . .

Chesterfield may have been a hypocrite and an opportunist, frigid both ethically and emotionally, but Mr. Chester is after all a real villain, and Dickens demonstrates through him not merely the distastefulness and bankruptcy of the Chesterfieldian sensibility but the positive menace of its extreme implications as an active source of evil. Chester embodies the

Chesterfieldian ideal of the gentlemanly persona as if he were a statue of
it. His identity is the product of his own dexterous workmanship, a caricature of both artist and work of art at once. When he rides into the novel
on horseback,

[n]either man nor beast had turned a single hair; and, saving for his soiled skirts
and spatterdashes, this gentleman, with his blooming face, white teeth, exactly-
ordered dress, and perfect calmness, might have come from making an elaborate
and leisurely toilet, to sit for an equestrian portrait at old John Willet's gate. (10)

His is an art like Mrs. Jarley's—"calm and classical"; he is "always the
same, with a constantly unchanging air of coldness and gentility."[24]
    But his characteristic calmness is, like Chesterfield's, instrumental; his
self-command "[i]s not to be disturbed, when it will serve my purpose"
(12). He controls himself in order to control others; with the accomplished gracefulness of his manner, he plays others as skilled musicians
play instruments. He practices his manners constantly, even on beggars
and servants, and his dexterity is always perfect when he puts it to use.
His conquest of Mrs. Varden (27) is a *tour de force*; his subjugation of
Hugh is a success still more spectacular. Even the King cannot resist the
insinuating efficacy of "[s]uch elegance of manner, so many graces of deportment, such powers of conversation." Recognizing that "Mr. was too
common for such merit," His Majesty authenticates both the perfection
and the potency of Mr. Chester's manners by rewarding them with a
knighthood (40).
    Mr. Chester is hardly unique in his single-minded devotion to satisfy-
ing his wishes, as he points out.

All men are fortune-hunters, are they not? The law, the church, the court, the
camp—see how they are all crowded with fortune-hunters, jostling each other in
the pursuit. . . . [Y]ou would be nothing else . . . if you were the greatest cour-
tier, lawyer, legislator, prelate, or merchant, in existence.[25] (15)

Nor should this sordid reality surprise us: "each of us has himself for the
first article in his creed" (40). As Chester believes along with Lord
Chesterfield, there is no such thing in human nature as natural affections
or good-heartedness to supply selfless motives for behavior:

"Now . . . *do* not," said Mr. Chester, . . . "talk in that monstrous manner.
About to speak from your heart! Don't you know that the heart is an ingenious

part of our formation—the centre of the blood-vessels and all that sort of thing—
which has no more to do with what you say or think, than your knees have?
How can you be so very vulgar and absurd? These anatomical allusions should be
left to gentlemen of the medical profession. They are really not agreeable in society." (32)

Dickens wrote this shortly after completing his novel of the "good heart,"
and what he thinks of it goes without saying; but for Chester, as for
Ralph Nickleby, "the spirit does but mean the breath." No less consistent
than Ralph, Chester reduces all complex motives to their basest and most
mechanical elements, until at last he makes Ralph Nickleby's monstrous
assertion that "there's no such thing, I assure you," as love (15). He would
agree with one of Laclos's dangerous acquaintances, a sensualist like himself, that love is merely a name we use to dignify the sordid pleasures of
our appetites. Noble emotions are only empty words; as Chester remarks, "I wonder no philosopher has ever established that our globe itself
is hollow. It should be, if Nature is consistent in her works" (12).

The denial of the existence of "natural affections" has two important
aspects. In the first place, while Chester, like Lord Chesterfield, claims to
be merely representative in his heartlessness, he nevertheless deems himself unique in his honest consciousness of that heartlessness, and his unflinching self-recognition gives him, in his view, a claim to a highly superior authenticity. "Men who are thoroughly false and hollow," Dickens
says of him,

seldom try to hide those vices from themselves; and yet in the very act of avowing
them, they lay claim to the virtues they feign most to despise. "For," say they,
"this is honesty, this is truth. All mankind are like us, but they have not the can-
dour to avow it." The more they affect to deny the existence of any sincerity in the
world, the more they would be thought to possess it in its boldest shape. (23)

We have met with this argument before in Ralph Nickleby, and what
these two complex and gifted villains, who fascinate Dickens so keenly
even while he condemns them, have most in common is the interconnec-
tion in each of them of a denial of natural affection with an insistence on
personal authenticity—an equation completed by the license this superior authenticity gives them to despise utterly the vast mass of weak and
stupid other men. Dickens presents the workings of the equation in
Chester thus:

The despisers of mankind—apart from the mere fools and mimics, of that creed—are of two sorts. They who believe their merit neglected and unappreciated, make up one class; they who receive adulation and flattery, knowing their own worthlessness, compose the other. Be sure that the coldest-hearted misanthropes are ever of this last order. (24)

In Chester, who is a cynic of this second category, one has not only the modern paradox of a fraud whose consciousness of his fraudulence constitutes his authenticity, but also the further paradox that it is the consciousness of his worthlessness that makes him authentic, and his authenticity redeems and therefore cancels the worthlessness on which it is founded and replaces it with a superiority so lofty that all other men become despicable by contrast.

In the second place, the denial of natural affection forms part of a larger assertion of radical freedom for Chester no less than for Lord Chesterfield or Ralph Nickleby. It is another instance of the claim that nothing in one's character is determined or fixed, and one is free to do and be whatever one wants. This idea comes together with Chester's right to despise his fellow men and his belief that all men are as unscrupulously self-interested as himself to form a world view in which he is licensed to make use of everybody in any way he likes.

Thus the Chesterfieldian ethic, insofar as Dickens's satire of it exposes its ultimate consequences, is by no means sociable. Chesterfield and Chester take the forms of sociability and reverse their sign; they transform the ceremonies of community into instruments of radical individualism. Consider for example this reflection of Chester's:

". . . And here is one of the inestimable advantages of having a perfect command over one's inclinations. I have been tempted in these two short interviews, to draw upon that fellow, fifty times. Five men in six would have yielded to that impulse. By suppressing mine, I wound him deeper and more keenly than if I were the best swordsman in all Europe, and he the worst. You are the wise man's very last resource," he said, tapping the hilt of his weapon; "we can but appeal to you when all else is said and done. To come to you before, and thereby spare our adversaries so much, is a barbarian mode of warfare, quite unworthy any man with the remotest pretensions to delicacy of feeling, or refinement." (27)

Chester's "refinement" is only a parody of the essential self-restraint required in civilized life, for both the general deferral of immediate gratification which is characteristic of civilization, and the specific renunciation of aggression which makes civilization possible, are here turned upside-down. If Chester restrains himself, he by no means gives up his aggression; the future good for which he postpones present gratification is, perversely, the certainty of a more complete satisfaction of his malice, like the legendary sadist who refuses to comply with the masochist's plea to be beaten.

Or consider one further example—the confrontation between Chester and his hostile illegitimate son. Hugh, from the moment he steps into Mr. Chester's finely decorated room, is "humbled and abashed" by his father's manner and by "all the unaccustomed luxuries and comforts of the room." "Hard words he could have returned, violence he would have repaid with interest; but this cool, complacent, contemptuous, self-possessed reception caused him to feel his inferiority more completely than the most elaborate arguments." In the course of the interview, Mr. Chester's "consummate art" vanquishes Hugh entirely. "The ascendency which it was the purpose of the man of the world to establish over this savage instrument, was gained from that time. Hugh's submission was complete. He dreaded him beyond description" (23). For here Mr. Chester has wielded the graces of civilization like a bludgeon and used his refinement to quell and subdue more effectively even than Sim Tappertit could dream of doing by the urgent power of his gaze.

In Mr. Chester's hands, manners are essentially a weapon, and society ultimately is, for him and Lord Chesterfield alike, a scene of universal conflict, different from the original war of all against all only because in society, as Chesterfield tells us, "[v]igilance, dexterity, and flexibility supply the place of natural force; and it is the ablest mind, not the strongest body, that prevails there." [26] And as Geoffrey Haredale rightly decides: "The very last man on this earth with whom I would enter the lists to combat with gentle compliments and masked faces, is Mr. Chester, I do assure you. I am not his match at such weapons, and have reason to believe that few men are" (12). However delicate and refined the weapons, the battle, Haredale recognizes, is deadly; and "men of the world" like Chester and Chesterfield, however graceful and ceremonious, are not just unscrupulous but radically antisocial. Their Chesterfieldian code, providing both a disguise and a rationalization for predatory selfishness in its claim that the depredations of radical will become praiseworthy by becoming smooth and elegant, is at bottom the negation of morality.

To just such a claim Hazlitt objected that in his view "[i]t does not appear . . . (whatever it may do in the genteel letter-writing of Lord Chesterfield, or the chivalrous rhapsodies of Burke) that vice by losing all its grossness loses half its evil." Hazlitt himself "prefer[red] a bear-garden to the adder's den." [27] Dickens concurs in this judgment, demonstrating through the example of Mr. Chester that etiquette is no substitute for ethics. Chester is implicated among those responsible for perpetrating the riots; Haredale says, with much truth, that Chester, Lord George Gordon, and Gashford "are the essence of your great Protestant Association, in yourselves" (43). Dickens thereby emphasizes that Chester's "morality" does not stop at mere private villainy but is subversive of the possibility of collective life. This *soi-disant* highly civilized man constitutes a danger to civilization: social bonds come unstuck wherever he touches them: and Dickens repudiates through him the notion that the external refinement Chesterfield professes can make men civilized, that manners are all we need to make social life possible.

.   .   .

Of the soul, that *internal* faculty whose presence Dickens believes to be the real distinguishing feature of civilized man, somewhat more can be said beyond what we have learned from examining the effects of its absence in Hugh and Barnaby. Though in this novel Dickens never explicitly represents what the soul *is*—he is much franker on that subject in *American Notes*—the fact that he always connects the soul with the oppressive father-son relationship provides us with enough information to permit reconstruction of the whole organism from these few actual bones.

The idea that the soul is not part of the original endowment of natural man certainly is not new with Dickens. Taking a step further Rousseau's belief that only civilization makes of a "narrow, stupid animal . . . a creature of intelligence and a man," Lord Monboddo, for instance, was perfectly willing to plead guilty to the charge that he himself believed man's "chief prerogative, the rational soul, . . . to be of our own acquisition, and the fruit of industry, like any art or science, not the gift of nature." Natural man has a soul only as a *potential*; he needs to participate in society to awaken what is otherwise merely latent and dormant. We know this is true, Monboddo argues, from observing children; "for, in our infancy, where is the rational soul, but in the possibility or capacity of acquiring it?" [28]

But putting aside Dickens's predecessors, we can find perhaps the best gloss on the notion of the soul in *Barnaby* in a later work, Freud's *Civilization and Its Discontents*, which collects together so many of those currents of eighteenth- and nineteenth-century thought about society and the individual's psychological relation to it that flowed through *Barnaby*

Rudge at an earlier point in their history. Like Dickens, Freud believed that the process of socialization transforms the individual by endowing him with an inner faculty of civilization, which, wishing to speak in the authoritative voice of Science, he called by the grandiloquent, Latinate name of "superego." But Friedrich Nietzsche, who anticipated large portions of Freud's concept in his discussion of "bad conscience" in *The Genealogy of Morals*, called it by its old-fashioned name: he speculates that the turning inward against himself of man's instinct of aggression is what "provides the soil for the growth of what is later called man's *soul*." [29]

Freud's theory is helpful here, because, as the latest development of that strain in the history of the idea of conscience to which *Barnaby Rudge* also belongs, it makes systematically explicit much that is latent and implicit in Dickens's notion of the soul. The superego, the institutionalization of civilization in the mind itself, is the faculty which makes social life possible, Freud argues. "Like a garrison in a conquered city," it is the agency within the mind that keeps watch over and largely neutralizes that aggressive instinct "which constitutes the greatest impediment to civilization." The cost is high, for the superego does this by turning one's aggressive impulse back against oneself. [30] Moreover, the superego is, according to Freud, the internalization of precisely the kind of father-son relationship that we have seen functioning in *Barnaby Rudge*. The relationship both brings the superego into being and is at the same time eternally preserved within it.

One's father, Freud postulates, is the indispensable element required for the superego's formation. In the early stage of life before the superego is developed, the relation of the child to the father is exactly the oppressive relation of Willet to Joe, in which the external authority of the father proscribes the forbidden impulses and compels the son to repress them. The next stage of development brings the superego into being, when the son, through love of his father, comes, like Joe, to identify with him and thus internalizes the father's demand for the renunciation of instinct. By this process of identification, he incorporates the authority enforcing moral behavior into himself. The self, now compounded of two competing energies—the demands of instinct of the unsocialized son, and the civilizing demands for the renunciation of instinct formerly made by the father— becomes as a result an arena of perpetual conflict. Whatever may be the further vicissitudes of the actual father-son relationship, this early, oppressive shape of it remains forever after preserved within the self. Against this reality of the divided self, the self that has institutionalized within it something originally foreign and "other," Ralph Nickleby was so vehemently in revolt in *Nicholas Nickleby*. Dickens knew in *Nickleby* that

Ralph's psychology of radical individualism was wrong and dangerous; by *Barnaby* he sees it is simply false.

The superego differs from older theories of conscience not only in that it is unambiguously internal, a constituent part of the self, but also in that is it not placated by renunciation of the forbidden wishes. Unable to distinguish between deeds and thoughts, it accordingly punishes one for forbidden thoughts as well as for forbidden acts. Thus the superego puts one in the same double-bind that Joe is in *vis-à-vis* his father: it punishes one whether one does or does not act out the forbidden impulses.

Moreover, every renunciation of instinct produces vengeful rage directed at the repressing authority, which the superego turns back against the ego.[31] For the rage one feels when the superego compels a renunciation is itself a forbidden impulse, which the superego must punish by a feeling of guilt. Thus the superego is megalomaniacal after Mr. Willet's fashion; its calls for renunciation are absolute, and every compliance with them provides it with increased energy to make further and ever-increasing demands. Suffering under it, one feels as "bullied, badgered, worried, fretted, . . . browbeaten" and "tired of . . . life" as "poor Joe Willet" (30), and one is tempted to protest, in *Barnaby*'s words, that "[t]here are bounds to human endurance" (4).

Surveying such a state of affairs, Freud observes that although men established communities in order to promote happiness and secure the advantages of mutual cooperation by circumscribing "the constitutional inclination of human beings to be aggressive towards one another," nevertheless the inner repression on which society rests is a threat to that happiness. Once civilized, men must forego the satisfaction of their aggressive impulses, submit to a severe inhibition of their sexual instinct, and endure an excessive, debilitating sense of guilt, regardless of the scrupulosity of their behavior. "We are led," Freud remarks, "to make reproaches against the super-ego. . . . In the severity of its commands and prohibitions it troubles itself too little about the happiness of the ego, in that it takes insufficient account of the resistances against obeying" its demands. Indeed, he says, "[i]t almost seems as if the creation of a great human community would be most successful if no attention had to be paid to the happiness of the individual." "What a potent obstacle to civilization aggressiveness must be," he concludes, "if the defense against it can cause as much unhappiness as aggressiveness itself!"[32]

Though Dickens perceives in *Barnaby Rudge* that socialization takes place in the context of a particular relationship with the father, and that

this process transforms the self by endowing it with a social faculty
within the mind, he does not take Freud's final step of seeing the father-
son relationship as preserved within that new mental faculty. But his description of the civilizing relations between the harried young men and
their insatiably demanding fathers describes essentially what Freud described as the workings of the superego. One of the novel's central passages, Dickens's most succinct characterization of the relationship between Willet and Joe, is a case in point:

A homely proverb recognises the existence of a troublesome class of persons who,
having an inch conceded them, will take an ell. Not to quote the illustrious examples of those heroic scourges of mankind, whose amiable path in life has been
from birth to death though blood, and fire, and ruin, and who would seem to
have existed for no better purpose than to teach mankind that as the absence of
pain is pleasure, so the earth, purged of their presence, may be deemed a blessed
place—not to quote such mighty instances, it will be sufficient to refer to old John
Willet.

Old John having long encroached a good standard inch, full measure, on the
liberty of Joe, and having snipped off a Flemish ell in the matter of the parole,
grew so despotic and so great, that his thirst for conquest knew no bounds. The
more young Joe submitted, the more absolute old John became. (20)

Like the superego, John Willet tries to make his son renounce all "liberty"
and "exuberance," and—also like the superego—with every submission
Willet gains energy and becomes more absolute. The language of impairment and injury in the passage recalls Freud's view that the repressing authority requires a radical abridgement of sexuality, enforced by the son's
fear of mutilation: old John "snips off" and "trims off" and "shears
away" to the extent of "yards, furlongs, [and] miles."

Nor, Dickens senses, is this the full extent of the diminution that socialization produces. One of Willet's cronies testifies that

when he was [Joe's] age, his father thought no more of giving him a parental
kick, . . . or some little admonition of that sort, than he did of any other ordinary
duty of life; and he would further remark, with looks of great significance, that
but for this judicious bringing up, he might have never been the man he was at
that present speaking: which was probable enough, as he was, beyond all question, the dullest dog of the party. (30)

The repression required for socialization abridges your energy, your spontaneity, your venturesomeness. In proscribing even certain fantasies it fetters your imagination and inventiveness. In its tendency to excess, it un-
necessarily binds vital energies and blights creativity. "What would any
of us have been, if our fathers hadn't drawed our faculties out of us?" John
Willet asks the Maypole cronies (11). He means how lucky we were our
fathers encouraged our capabilities, but his sentence also says that our fathers forcibly extracted out of us our incipient talents and powers and left
us empty.

In associating Willet's paternal authority with the authority of society
at large, the long passage quoted a moment ago uses terms for political
authority that are hardly neutral. Willet "conduct[s] himself . . . with as
much high mightiness . . . as the most glorious tyrant," and his assertion
of power is insistently compared to the "despotic" power of "heroic
scourges of mankind." This invocation of tyranny in public life looks forward to the second half of *Barnaby*, which recognizes in public authority
the same tendency toward oppression as the private authority of the father
displays. All forms of civilizing authority in *Barnaby* have this tendency
toward tyranny. The civilizing demands of religion, for instance, became
megalomaniacal and life-denying in the acrid Protestantism of Mrs. Varden and her servant, Miggs. Mrs. Varden thinks her husband's morning
mug of ale, like most of his innocent indulgences, "should be shunned by
the righteous as a work of sin and evil" (19). Classing mankind as "sinful
fellow-beings—mere . . . worms and grovellers," she incites Miggs to
declare, "I hope I know my own unworthiness, and that I hate and despise
myself and all my fellow creatures as every practicable Christian should"
(13). This joke points to a grim reality: there *are* people who, as a result
of the repression they have undergone, feel only self-loathing. And there
are plenty of people, who, out of self-indulgent religious vanity, manage
to deprive others of innocent pleasures—people against whom Dickens
inveighed in *Sunday Under Three Heads* (1836), an attack on a bill to enforce strict Sabbath observance on the whole nation. Dickens is very well
aware of "our fallen nature"; but his God "detects amidst our own evil
doings, a redeeming quality," for we still have in us "something . . . of
the divine spirit" (47).

Or take the case of Mr. Haredale. Recognizing the positive value of
immersion in social life, he is yet unable to tolerate the potential for suffering such involvement opens to the individual (79). Saint Augustine had
the same perception, in his obsessive apprehension that the more friends
we have, the more racked with continual worry we must be that death or

illness or some other of "the mass of evils of this present world" will be-
fall them, or (worse) that their friendship will be turned to enmity.

Anyone who forbids such sadness must forbid, if he can, all friendly conversation, must lay a ban on all friendly feeling or put a stop to it, must with a ruthless
insensibility break the ties of all human relationships, or else decree that they
must only be engaged upon so long as they inspire no delight in a man's soul.[33]

Such was the view *Nickleby's* monk outlined to the Five Sisters of York,
who nevertheless do not withdraw from social life and *do* derive much
suffering from it—along with all their happiness. Mr. Haredale, by contrast, enters a monastery "known throughout Europe for the rigour and
severity of its discipline," which "thenceforth shut him out from nature
and his kind" (Ch. the Last). Here is a grim parody of the renunciation
and self-discipline required for civilized life. And here is a parody of society, too—for this is a community which is no community. It is as totali-
tarian in its way as Mr. Dennis, as we shall see later, is in his. Thus these
positive values—renunciation, self-denial, social authority—turn by excess into negative values. Most positive values in *Barnaby Rudge* have the
potentiality of doing just that. The past is both venerable and oppressive.
Liquor is both sociable and anarchic. The sense of a social soul turns into
mystification. And even the Maypole Inn has a gloomy bedroom in it.

6

The Riots 1: Down with Everything!

Turning to the novel's second half brings us face-to-face with the chief critical difficulty *Barnaby Rudge* poses: how are the two parts of the novel connected? What makes matters so complicated is that the connection is implicit rather than stated, a structural peculiarity familiar enough in contemporary novels or in dreams, but heretofore not adequately explained in this early Dickens novel.

The first thing to notice about the complex logic of connection between these two parts is that Dickens makes a double reversal as he moves from one to the other. First, he reverses the *scale*: whereas the earlier part is conceived in terms of the personal and domestic, the latter half expands to the public and political and reexamines on the level of society as a whole the same themes Part I considered in terms of individuals. This juxtaposition of public and private has been fully anticipated by Part I, which insisted throughout on the interdependence of those two realms in its examination of the process by which the social becomes an inseparable constituent of the personal. The existence of an internal faculty of civilization once granted, there ceases to be any such thing as a purely private life. This unremitting insistence in Part I prepares us to see that the shift in scale is not arbitrary or willful on Dickens's part; the connection between the public panorama that now opens before us and the private realm we have just left is, in the terms the novel has already established, inescapable.

To see how the two parts of *Barnaby* come together "so as to have life" (as Ruskin would say), we must look at the second reversal Dickens makes, a reversal of emphasis. Part I, as it presents examples of "natural" men in order to contrast them with civilized men, reveals the unsettling possibility of a kind of human life unmodified by that dimension of socialization which the first half of the novel, all things considered, so positively values. Also, the tenacious resistance this process of civilization encounters in Part I makes us aware of the operation of a powerful counterprinciple which has, so to speak, a negative existence there, for it is glimpsed only as it is overcome. Yet this very counterprinciple, so insistently and in so many senses repressed in Part I, is set free at the beginning of Part II and allowed thereafter to rule the novel almost to the very end.

What occurs at the novel's center, in other words, is a reversal in the balance of power between two dialectical opposites: whereas the organizing principle of Part I is, broadly speaking, civilization, the emphasis shifts in Part II to the absolute negation of that principle, to the unrestrained anarchy that erupts in the Gordon Riots. These two terms truly form a dialectical symbiosis: neither of them can be defined without invoking the other. And this dialectical relationship generates the energy of opposition that turns the logical machinery of *Barnaby Rudge*.

Not only are the two parts of the novel firmly rather than fortuitously connected, but, more important, their relationship implies a single, complex logical argument. The very structure of the novel advances an idea— the controlling idea of *Barnaby Rudge* as a whole. Each half of the novel offers one term of a pair of alternatives, and the fundamental proposition of *Barnaby Rudge* is that if you do not have the first of these alternatives, then you must inescapably have the other; if you do not want the second of these alternatives, then you are required by the nature of reality to have the first.

On the one hand, you can have the state of affairs depicted in the first half: the life of man in society, which requires a sweeping transformation of individual human nature, brought about by wholesale oppression and repression and having as one of its direct results ineradicable personal discontent, diminution, and guilt. The benefits of civilization are immeasurably great, for (among other advantages) by becoming civilized you become fully human; but, just as surely, you also become unhappy, for that is the incalculably high price you are obliged to pay.

Is the price perhaps too high? In answer, *Barnaby Rudge* asks us to confront, in the Gordon Riots of the novel's second half, the alternative. These riots, in Dickens's view, provide a concrete, historical example of what actually happens when civilization breaks down; they demonstrate what you are left with if you take civilization away. As Dickens understands them, the riots constitute a momentary restoration of the state of nature; in them the true character of precivilized human life is unambiguously revealed. This character has of course been intimated in the essentially Hobbesian conception of natural man Dickens develops in the novel's first half, where we glimpse the danger threatened by those inborn impulses of violence and aggression that the civilizing effort is so strenuously trying, not to abolish (for that is impossible), but to repress and defuse. But what is initially presented as a mere latent possibility becomes in Part II an actuality, when the riots conclusively demonstrate that there indeed does inhere in human nature a tendency of every man to be enemy to every man, a tendency which results, if unmodified and unrestrained, in primeval universal warfare.

As Dickens sees it, it is to prevent *this* that civilization has been called into being. The entirely consistent vision on which the whole of *Barnaby Rudge* is constructed, the thesis of which it is an elaborate and coherent dramatization, is that if you do not have civilization with its concomitant personal oppression and unhappiness, then you must have universal anarchy and brutality, the war of all against all. Between these two alternatives, Dickens does not find it hard to choose. If Freud, in his Olympian mood at the end of *Civilization and Its Discontents*, icily wonders if the whole effort of civilization has been worth the trouble, Dickens, with an equally profound intuition of the enormity of the cost, has no such misgivings, for he sees (as Freud does not) that it is only through this effort that man has realized the specifically *human* essence that gives him his unique value.

Now of course not all commentators have read the riots in *Barnaby Rudge* in this way. Jack Lindsay's essay on the novel is an obvious case in point. Lindsay speaks of how Dickens's first conception at last evolved into the book as we have it:

The hearty romance became an epical novel with a philosophy of history permeating it. From Carlyle Dickens gained the concept of revolt and revolution as an elemental upsurge of the oppressed: a necessary stage, though in itself an explosion of blind retaliatory violence. He could not but respond with every fibre of his being to Carlyle's attacks on the class that monopolised suffrage, land, press, religion, and imposed the Poor Law. . . .

Dickens is chary about showing what is driving the people into revolt—though at a few points he is so overcome by his emotion that he breaks through his petty-bourgeois cautions and reticences, and makes the underdog speak in accents that are in accord with the fundamental Carlylean theme: when Stagg utters his bitter comments to Mrs. Rudge and when Hugh bursts out before his hanging. . . .

Barnaby and Gordon thus represent the future striving to be born, the wild confusion of hopes and desires which can as yet be articulated only in the tones of "wild animals, in pain."[1]

This argument is an extreme and therefore unambiguously instructive example of the resistance often opposed to a clear perception of what Dickens is doing in this novel by the ideological pieties of a large spectrum of the political left, including the mechanical radicalism typified by Lindsay's essay. Our usual notion of Dickens the man and the novelist tends to emphasize his reforming spirit, his profound sympathy with the poor and unfortunate, his "generous anger" at institutional abuses and stupidity, as well as his own declarations—coupled with the pronouncements of his contemporaries—about his "radical" inclinations. Thus one can understandably feel that one recognizes in him liberal or radical sympathies, and—forgetting the extreme indeterminacy of these political labels; forgetting that in our own time there have been myriad liberalisms and radicalisms, which are different from the various liberalisms and radicalisms of the 1830s and 1840s; forgetting in particular G. A. Sala's remark that Dickens characteristically spoke of political subjects "always from that which was then a strong Radical point of view, but which at present [1894] I imagine would be thought more Conservative than Democratic"[2]—one can be tempted to impute to Dickens one's own particular brand of liberal ideology with its concomitant reading of history.

But here one runs the risk of taking literally the metaphor that it is *we* who are Dickens: at which point criticism becomes mere introspection and issues forth in claims of what Dickens "could not but" feel—for *we* feel it. Thus, if Dickens does not show us what is driving "the people" into "revolt," we know—or at least Lindsay knows—what it "could not but" have been; we hear the allegedly Carlylean "accents," and Dickens "could not but" have agreed with Carlyle on all points. As for Barnaby and Gordon, if they do not articulate what we know must be on their minds, still, they "could not but" mean it. I need not further dissect the tissue of unsupported assertions based on unexamined assumptions that here takes the place of thought. What is important is that Lindsay's distortion of *Barnaby*, however idiosyncratic in its extremism, nevertheless

typifies the intense reluctance of not a few readers to confront the painful
conclusions about human nature and the nature of social and political reality that Dickens puts forth in this novel—conclusions inconsistent with
the liberal optimism of many academics and Dickensians alike.[3] One cannot but wonder if *Barnaby Rudge* has attracted relatively little (and chiefly
unfavorable) critical comment because of this essentially ideological
resistance.

In any event, we can reject Lindsay's view that the Gordon Riots are at
least the beginnings of a progressive, political movement—that in them is
discernible the future striving to be born. Insofar as they are a quasi-
political event at all, the riots in *Barnaby* are, as Avrom Fleishman has observed, "not a revolution but a pogrom."[4] Such, certainly, is Dickens's
own unequivocal judgment of their politics, explicitly stated in the preface to the novel. The riots are described there as a series of "outrages,"
and, the preface declares, there can be no question that "these shameful
tumults . . . reflect indelible disgrace upon the time in which they occurred, and all who had act or part in them." As for the rioters themselves, that miscellaneous collection of furious featherless bipeds which
Lindsay sees as "the people" is in Dickens's eyes only "the mob." But it
has to be added in the same breath that, although Dickens discusses the
riots in the preface as a political event of the most benighted and reactionary character, he did not conceive of them (as we shall see in a moment) as
primarily or essentially a political event at all.

Nevertheless, the value of Lindsay's reading is in serving to remind us
how the interpretation of such outbreaks tends to be a matter of unresolved controversy. The assumption of Lindsay's kind of thinking is that,
since the exploited and oppressed have real political grievances, any "elemental upsurge of the oppressed" is therefore *necessarily* an expression of
precisely these grievances and nothing else, an "inarticulate" expression
insofar as the oppressed have not yet attained consciousness of the true
nature of their oppression. Thus, whatever form these popular outbursts
may take and however mindlessly destructive or reactionary they may appear, their latent message is in all times and places the same. According to
this view, they are moments in that progressive realization of human freedom which is the meaning of history, and they invariably express, if
rightly understood, *political* protest against political injustice. Not to understand this is to misunderstand history or—still worse—to wish to oppose it out of rapacious or slavish or exploitative motives.

And yet, this reductive argument notwithstanding, there of course are
differences among popular uprisings: not all "inarticulate" outbursts are

trying to say the same thing. Rather, each needs to be interpreted in its individual particularity if its meaning is to be understood. Here, in order to clarify Dickens's position in *Barnaby*, it will be helpful to invoke an important distinction made by Freud in *Civilization and Its Discontents*, which differentiates the defining tendencies of such events into two widely divergent classes. In considering any "revolt against oppression," Freud cautions, we must ask ourselves what kind of oppression is being repudiated. For it has to be remembered that, prior to the existence of any specific political injustice in any given polity, oppression has already come into being as an inescapable condition of civilized life itself (as diverse thinkers, to name only Diderot and Wordsworth, had already seen); and, while we may find in this or that particular historical state a flagrantly tyrannical usurpation of human freedom, against which every feeling of justice and humanity makes us cry out, nevertheless we are forced to recognize that even in the most praiseworthy of states man's freedom is conclusively abridged, for the restriction of liberty inheres in the essence of civilization. Thus,

What makes itself felt in a human community as a desire for freedom may be [people's] revolt against some existing injustice, and so may prove favourable to a further development of civilization; it may remain compatible with civilization. But it may also spring from the remains of their original personality, which is still untamed by civilization and may thus become the basis in them of hostility to civilization. The urge for freedom, therefore, is directed against particular forms and demands of civilization or against civilization altogether.[5]

Any "elemental upsurge of the oppressed," that is, if it is a protest, however inarticulate, against political injustice and exploitation, constitutes a political event; but if it is a revolt against the general unfreedom inseparable from civilized life, if it is merely a liberation of that original aggressiveness which the program of civilization has labored to place under severe restraint, then to that extent it is antipolitical by definition.

It is as an example of this second class that Dickens understands the Gordon Riots, which he depicts in *Barnaby* as an attack on civilization itself and as a momentary, epidemic reversion of men to their precivilized character.[6] He contemptuously denies from the outset that the avowed aims of the Protestant Association, in support of whose anti-Catholic policy the rioters claimed to be demonstrating, deserve a moment's consideration as a serious political program. The wish to deny Catholics the right to hold property in their own names and to educate their children in their own schools in the Year of Grace 1780 seems to Dickens the plainest absurdity, worthy only of indignant derision if the real danger it posed to the Catholic citizens of England did not require one to dignify it with the strongest condemnation.[7] To the extent the rioters had any kind of program, before their demonstrations declined into mere anarchy, it was a program "begotten of intolerance and persecution." Devoid of a single politically progressive principle, it was, in Dickens's view, reactionary to the point of lunacy. The Gordon Riots, in other words, contrary to Lindsay's implications, are not a dress rehearsal for the French Revolution, and *Barnaby Rudge* decidedly is not an early version of *A Tale of Two Cities*.[8]

But that the disgraceful program of the Gordon Riots is without merit is of small importance, in that virtually no one connected with the riots believes in it anyway. The "No Popery" agitation, though claiming a religious justification, has in fact been fomented by "men who have no religion," says Dickens in the preface, "and who in their daily practice set at nought the commonest principles of right and wrong." This is true of Gashford, in this novel the actual director of the Protestant Association; it is true of leaders of the riots like Hugh and Dennis; and Gordon himself, while sincere (if misguided) in his religious scruples, is also unbalanced and is motivated as much by a hungry, narcissistic preoccupation with his own power as by religious conviction. The overwhelming majority of the rioters bray the "No Popery" cry without interest in its meaning, like those people described by Defoe—those "stout fellows that would spend the last drop of their blood against Popery that do not know whether it be a man or a horse."[9] "Many of those who were banded together to support the religion of their country, even unto death, had never heard a hymn or a psalm in their lives," Dickens tells us; and, asked to sing one, they "chanted any ribaldry or nonsense that occurred to them, feeling pretty certain that it would not be detected in the general chorus, and not caring much if it were" (48). When at the novel's end a number of rioters are to be hanged, it "was an exquisite satire upon the false religious cry which led to so much misery, that some of these people owned themselves to be catholics, and begged to be attended by their own priests" (77). So much for the professed political aims of the Gordon Riots; they are as specious, in Dickens's judgment, as they are shameful.

If the official pronouncements of the Protestant Association do not disclose the intention of the rioters, a wild, highly unofficial interchange that Dickens puts into the mouths of the riots' leaders provides an explicit statement of their true aim. Gordon's secretary, Gashford, and Dennis the hangman are enrolling Hugh in the Association:

> "No Popery, brother!" cried the hangman.
> "No Property, brother!" responded Hugh.
> "Popery, Popery," said the secretary with his usual mildness.
> "It's all the same!" cried Dennis. "It's all right. Down with him, Muster Gashford. Down with everybody, down with everything!" (38)

That last cry, in Dickens's opinion the real motto of the riots, confesses the rioters' appetite for universal annihilation. The whole course of the riots makes manifest what this slogan enunciates: these disturbances are an eruption of that inborn aggressiveness which it is the program of civilization to restrain but which, as *Barnaby* demonstrates so dramatically, is ineradicable from the human breast and therefore threatens, in the mere fact of its sullen and circumscribed existence, the possibility of just such a furious outbreak as we witness here.

Dennis's formulation describes this cosmic aggression in its most intense form—as pure, undifferentiated negativity—but his universality does not identify the specific avenues through which such nihilistic aggression will try to discharge itself. But Hugh's "No Property," whose appropriate context is not Marx but Locke, points to the crucial cornerstone whose dislocation will bring the whole structure of "everything" tumbling down. For chief among Locke's contributions to political theory is his argument for the virtual identity of the institution of private property with society itself. The invention of private property brings civilization into being; thereafter the preservation of property and the functioning of civilization are one and the same process.

An invasion of private property is therefore tantamount to an assault on civilization—a conclusion, enormously influential ever since its first formulation, which Hugh's "No Property" is calculated to bring to mind. That England's greatest practitioner of the bourgeois novel invokes this classic rationalization of bourgeois society should surprise no one. More important, this passage announces the target against which the rioters' primal aggressiveness will hurl itself in its campaign for universal sway: this is precisely the whole framework of civilization within which it has heretofore been imprisoned.

Although the rioters' profession of a fervent attachment to Protestantism is specious, the claim they make of being motivated by a hatred of Catholicism is much less farfetched. The fantasy they have of Catholics is a highly specific one, according to Dickens. They believe in "a dangerous confederacy of Popish powers" (36)—"a confederacy among the Popish powers to degrade and enslave England, establish an inquisition in London, and turn the pens of Smithfield Market into stakes and cauldrons" (37). Here, in other words, is a close-knit, bloodthirsty band of conspirators, professing an ancient, repudiated creed and bent on the ruination and domination of society. Their chief goal is to establish a massive apparatus of torture on the very scene of the Protestant martyrdoms of the sixteenth century. The tutelary demon of their doings is Bloody Mary—according to the Protestant Association a powerful monster utterly given over to sanguinary aggression. The Association members, says John Grueby, are obsessed with "that unfort'nate Bloody Mary" (35), and the list of that organization's contributors includes "The Associated Rememberers of Bloody Mary" (36).

This fantasy of world conspiracy is more usually projected not onto Catholics but onto Jews, and we may interpret it in the same way that Norman Cohn has interpreted the myth of the Jewish world conspiracy.[10] The Catholics, like the Jews, can be seen as a "kind of collective father figure," for, if "the Jewish religion is the parent religion out of which, and in rivalry with which, Christianity developed,"[11] Catholicism stands in the same parental relationship to Protestantism. It was easy for English Protestants to project onto Catholics their fantasies of the revenging Oedipal father, a figure armed with the child's own aggression against his father, turned by the operation of the superego against himself and thus endowed with terrifying superhuman power. A pogrom like the Gordon Riots, therefore, may be seen as a revolt against the internalized image of the oppressing father and his harsh, megalomaniacal demands, as a revolt against the sometimes tyrannical superego itself.

To test whether Englishmen of the late eighteenth and early nineteenth century could imagine Catholicism as the embodiment of a bloodthirsty superego, we have only to remember the flourishing, not long after the Gordon Riots, of the Gothic novel, which portrayed the Catholic Church precisely as a civilizing institution run amok, torturing, murdering, and making demands for submission and renunciation that were ultimately subversive of life itself. (Or remember William Blake's outrage at finding that a chapel, with "Thou shalt not" emblazoned over the door, had been built in the middle of the Garden of Love, where now "Priests in black gowns were walking their rounds, / And binding with briars my joys & desires."[12]) To a certain extent, Gothic novels may be seen as protests against the severity of a politically repressive society, but the fact that their model civilized monk keeps getting transformed into (or revealed as) the *real* monster of unbridled lust and aggression makes it hard to deny that the main issue here is psychological at least as much as it is political.

Thus the riots do constitute an "elemental upsurge of the oppressed," but in a more literal sense than Jack Lindsay intends his phrase to carry. For what is surging up is primordial aggressiveness, while the oppression being repudiated is the first systematic form in which oppression comes into the world—the oppression with which civilization tries to abridge the tendency of every man to be enemy to every man. So it is fair to say, if we continue to speak in this absolute and literal way, that the riots are indeed a struggle for freedom; but the freedom in question is not political liberty but rather the "elemental" freedom of the state of nature, which characteristically asserts itself, at least in the view of the tradition of political thought whose concepts inform this novel, as the freedom of aggression. The extreme violence that marks the riots, therefore, is not only a means but also an end. Here the fundamental liberty of aggression asserts itself with a vengeance, and freedom becomes once again unqualified and whole.

And yet because "freedom" is essentially a political concept, and because in this temporary suspension of civilization the political life is also momentarily abolished, the meaning of the idea of freedom starts to disintegrate just at the point where, no longer qualified and relative, it strives to become absolute. What these outbreaks establish in their uncompromising absolutism, therefore, is not so much a reign of freedom as a reign of aggression, which temporarily succeeds in regaining its original universality when it turns against even the rioters themselves, involving them in the general ruin they have precipitated. But before examining this final development—inevitable but unforeseen by the rioters, who are as incapable as Fanny Squeers of realizing that they are included in the "everybody" they wish to destroy—we must first trace the progress of the systematic assault on civilization which constitutes the essential meaning of the Gordon Riots.

·   ·   ·

The assault these riots launch proceeds on two separate fronts. In the external world of concrete action, it consists of the destruction of a series of buildings, each of which is presented as symbolic of an essential aspect of civilization. But simultaneous with this physical destruction, the rioters progressively obliterate in themselves those inner qualities which hitherto identified them as civilized men, until they succeed in effacing entirely their own personal inward faculty of civilization. They dismantle, along with the outward, tangible structure of civilized life, its spiritual manifestation as well.

Mesmerized by Dickens's striking representation of the psychology of the rioters, we tend not to grasp that the physical destruction they accomplish is not random but specific and significant to the argument of the novel. Nor does Dickens go out of his way in Part II of the novel to signal that the details of this destruction, and the identity of the buildings wrecked, are important enough to require close scrutiny. Proceeding by implication and suggestion, with an economy verging on terseness, he expects his reader to remember from the novel's first half how buildings such as the Maypole, wrecked by the rioters' violence, embody those crucial qualities he recognizes as definitive of civilized life. Dickens is reinvoking an old theme here, not inventing a new one, and it is as a result of setting up carefully in Part I what he later demolishes in Part II that he is able to accomplish, in his representation of the riots, such sweeping destruction with the relentless swiftness of the rioters themselves. If we have followed the development of this theme in Part I with sufficient care, we will not miss its concise reintroduction and its central significance in Part II, nor will we be confused when Dickens generalizes it to buildings not met with in Part I.

The prologue to the riots is the outrageous demonstration at the House of Commons in Chapter 49, which sounds the keynote for the destruction to follow. In invading the Legislature and roughly handling its members, the rioters direct their first attack against government. They begin, that is, with an assault on the building that houses the most visible and concrete of those large human institutions which make up the outward structure of society; and Dickens makes the most of that circumstance to give us clear warning that the subsequent objects of the rioters' violence, although they are buildings whose meaning may not be so immediately obvious, nevertheless belong to this same class.

The riots begin in earnest with the demolition of a Catholic chapel in Chapter 50, which, because it is carried out by people Dickens believes devoid of religious faith, he represents as a blow aimed not only against the Roman Church but against the institution of religion in general, for centuries almost as basic to the structure of civilized society as government itself. The sole descriptive detail Dickens notes in reporting the destruction of this "place of worship"—the "spoils" which the rioters "bore as trophies" and which were "easily recognisable for the vestments of priests, and rich fragments of altar-furniture"—affords a glimpse of how

Dickens understands religion, even in the form of the Roman Catholicism he dislikes,[13] as an institution in the service of civilization. First, such "spoils" and "trophies," remind us of the close connection between the Church and artistic achievement. The wanton destruction of any good building is a negation of human accomplishment, but the razing of a fine chapel, whose gratuitous richness of painstaking decoration testifies most eloquently, as churches generally do, to the presence of man as *man*, is a particularly gross outrage of this kind.[14]

More important, the chapel, vestments, and altar-furnishings are also concrete expressions of the human spirit in that they are holy objects, invested by men with a metaphysical but real dimension of sacredness. While we recognize among the original functions of religion its effort to explain and domesticate the mysterious, awesome operation of the natural world and, in addition, its civilizing effort, as embodied in the ethical demands lying at the heart of its teaching and summed up by the injunction to love our neighbor, we should also acknowledge religion's function as an institutionalized expression of the spiritual essence of the human community. By this I mean, first, that the celebration of communal religious rituals and rites of passage is at bottom a celebration of the idea and the existence of the human community itself, and, second, that the sacred, mysterious, spiritual power religion worships is in fact an objectification of the "social soul," a symbolic projection outward of that internal, spiritual dimension with which civilization invests each man, and through which it both establishes its power within him and at the same time confers upon him that human existence on which is based his sense of the meaningfulness and dignity of his own individual life. Thus in the realm of the sacred men have enthroned, alongside the power of the natural world, also the power of their own humanity—a transcendent power no less mysterious to them than the operation of nature; a power whose effects they everywhere perceive, while remaining as yet unconscious of its source in that communal life in and through which man is truly Man.

This assault against sacredness forms the fully articulated meaning of the sacking of the Maypole, a building painstakingly established in Part I as, in its own prosaic way, virtually a secular temple of civilized society. Dickens mobilizes all those associations in Chapter 54 in order to demonstrate that the rioters, in "wantonly wasting, breaking, pulling down and tearing up" the Maypole, are destroying not only a catalogue of material objects but also the spiritual essence emanating from the intangible tissue of social relationships enacted there and no less intrinsic to the reality of this building than the bricks in its walls or the liquor in its cellars. The scene describing its sad fate sounds the comic note habitual to Dickens in discussing the inn: it expresses his awareness that the Maypole's sacredness is a mystique existing in the minds of the Maypole cronies—all unsophisticated men. But of course this does not make the Maypole's sacredness any less real: a mystique is not necessarily a mystification.

The imagery Dickens marshals is entirely the imagery of desecration. The rioters invade the Maypole bar "—the bar that the boldest never entered without special invitation—the sanctuary, the mystery, the hallowed ground," and instantaneously it is "crammed with men, clubs, sticks, torches, pistols; changed all at once into a bear-garden, a madhouse, an infernal temple." The invaders fall into an orgy of destruction, even to the point of "cutting down the sacred grove of lemons, hacking and hewing at the celebrated cheese, breaking open inviolable drawers," until they leave the bar no more than a "despoiled and plundered room, through whose shattered window the rioters had thrust the Maypole itself—for even that had been sawn down" (54). All this, it is clear, amounts to a profanation, as Dickens later underscored by the running-title "Sacrilege in the Sanctuary" added in the Charles Dickens Edition of *Barnaby Rudge*: the temple and its hallowed grove (of lemons) are despoiled, its sacred images (the consecrated Cheese, the totemic Maypole itself) dishonored and broken, its holy mysteries violated.

When Dickens tells us that the rioters, in dismantling the Maypole, turn it for a moment into an "infernal temple," his oxymoron, bringing into explosive collision two diametrically opposed principles, reproduces in the structure of the language the real issue at the heart of this event: it reaffirms the Maypole's essential sacredness, while demonstrating, with a virtually physical gesture, that the negation of that spiritual essence is the specific meaning of this phase of the riots. When the rioters have finished, that spirit is indeed gone: the bar and its contents have been reduced to mere material objects from which the "social soul" has fled; "even the stout Dutch kegs, overthrown and lying empty in dark corners, seemed the mere husks of good fellows whose jollity had departed, and who could kindle with a friendly glow no more" (55).

The rioters move on to raze Mr. Haredale's house, the Warren, an act described in essentially the same terms as the vandalizing of the Maypole. Once again the rioters despoil a building hallowed by the communal life it houses, though the organic social unit in this case is not the village community but a single, domestic home, to use the word Dickens so often employs with the feeling, urgent emphasis of italics.[15] ("[T]hough home is a name, a word, it is a strong one," says Dickens in *Martin*

Chuzzlewit, "stronger than magician ever spoke, or spirit answered to, in strongest conjuration"[35].) This too, in spite of the smallness of its scale, qualifies as a fundamental social institution.[16] If you try to split the social compound any further, it flies apart into its constituent elements, mere atomic individuals, and ceases to exist.

Chief among the defining attributes of this home is that sacredness also inherent in the Catholic chapel and the Maypole. The "exposure to the coarse, common gaze, of every little nook which usages of home had made a sacred place, and the destruction by rude hands of every little household favourite which old associations had made a dear and precious thing" is the center of the rioters' violation of the Warren (55). And when they begin to withdraw from the now ruined house, Dickens closes his chapter with the following elegy, illuminating still further the nature of its sacredness:

Slowly, and in small clusters, with hoarse hurrahs and repetitions of their usual cry, the assembly dropped away. The . . . distant noise of men calling to each other, and whistling for others whom they missed, grew fainter and fainter; at length even these sounds died away, and silence reigned alone.

Silence indeed! The glare of the flames had sunk into a fitful, flashing light; and the gentle stars, invisible till now, looked down upon the blackening heap. A dull smoke hung upon the ruin, as though to hide it from those eyes of Heaven; and the wind forbore to move it. Bare walls, roof open to the sky—chambers, where the beloved dead had many and many a fair day risen to new life and energy; where so many dear ones had been sad and merry; which were connected with so many thoughts and hopes, regrets and changes—all gone. Nothing left but a dull and dreary blank—a smouldering heap of dust and ashes—the silence and solitude of utter desolation.

Blighted by the losses, wrongs, and sorrows suffered there, the Warren has long before this come to be a melancholy house. But all these sorrows have been twined together by the Warren's inhabitants with memories of "life and energy," of the habitual "usages of home," to form a chain of "old associations" which make even this unlucky house "dear and precious" and "sacred" to its inmates.[17] Part of this idea we have already seen coming into focus in the moral *Nickleby* draws from its tale of the Five Sisters of York: "If our affections be tried, our affections are our consolation and comfort; and memory, however sad, is the best and purest link between this world and a better." And the chain of associations conferring sacredness upon the Warren we learned about when we considered

The Haunted Man, a story in which the lack of such "humanising" associations leaves the baby savage—the direct descendent of Smike, of Barnaby and Hugh, of the children Want and Ignorance in the *Christmas
Carol*—"a mere beast."

   This passage from *Barnaby* makes especially clear that these memories,
feelings, and "associations" constitute the mental dimension of our closest social relationships. Much more than a series of confrontations in the
external world, these relationships also have a lively existence within the
mind itself; they derive their reality as much from their psychological as
from their existential dimension. For this reason, certain social relationships, particularly those we think of as personal, exist even *in absentia*,
and by the same token they have an historical existence, a capacity for
development, whose locus is memory. These relationships come to be established as part of the substance of the mind, constituting a portion of
that personal history from which each man derives a significant measure
of his own unique identity. Thus the "old associations" which concern us
here are analogous to Dickens's idea of the soul, in that they incorporate
social and especially familial relationships into the mental fabric of the
civilized individual. And the rooms in which these relationships have
been enacted—like the embroideries of the Five Sisters of York—form a
link in the chain of associations too.

   One last feature of this passage completes our understanding of the
nature and enormity of this desecration—its evocation of Thomas Gray's
Elegy Written in a Country Church-yard, whose echoes reverberate throughout these concluding paragraphs of Chapter 55. Consider the following
similarities, beginning with Dickens's language, which here recalls that of
the *Elegy*. Dickens's "blackening heap" and "smouldering heap," to take
one notable instance, echo the "mould'ring heap" of Gray's fourth stanza.
Second, the movement of the first paragraph of the *Barnaby* passage
closely reproduces the opening movement of the *Elegy*:

> The Curfew tolls the knell of parting day,
> The lowing herd winds slowly o'er the lea,
> The plowman homeward plods his weary way,
> And leaves the world to darkness and to me.
>
> Now fades the glimmering landscape on the sight,
> And all the air a solemn stillness holds. . . .

In Dickens and Gray alike, the inhabitants of the scene slowly draw off;
the sounds of their activity fade from the ear, as light fades before the

spectator's eye. At last, in Dickens's scene, "silence reigned alone" (a silence which becomes at the very end of the passage "silence and solitude"), just as the movement of Gray's first stanza "leaves the world to darkness and to me," and, in the second stanza, "all the air a solemn stillness holds." Third, Dickens's description of the "beloved dead" and their activity imitates in brief and general terms Gray's concrete, detailed summary of the daily lives and domestic affections of the now-dead "Forefathers of the hamlet" (stanzas four through seven). Fourth and last—to come to the point of this comparison—Dickens's little elegy on the Warren and Gray's poem focus on essentially the same subject: how, through their shared activity and mutual solicitude, the members of a little community make meaningful their own lives; how in this way they keep unbroken the link between the present and the past, between the living and the dead; and how this communal and historical life of man consecrates the very ground he inhabits, making it a sacred place. The effect of Dickens's appropriation of the power of Gray's poem is to suggest that the Warren embodies the same values to which Gray's churchyard is a monument and that the destruction of the Warren is as outrageous and barbaric as the desecration of Gray's churchyard would be—which any reader of English poetry knows is outrageous indeed.

Two more buildings and we are done. The first is Newgate Prison (64, 65). This prison, we recall, is the only large-scale social institution present in *Nickleby*, where its gallows starkly display the legitimate coercive force by means of which the state ultimately guarantees its own existence, if necessary *compelling* man to observe the social contract. In *Barnaby* the prison is one of the specific social institutions through which the physical power of the state is directly applied.[18] The force and violence on which the state's authority is finally based will be examined more fully later; in the meantime, however, this provisional account provides a sufficiently clear view of how, in the burning of Newgate, the rioters are trying to abolish an essential political reality.

One important detail in Dickens's picture of the assault on Newgate needs mention. The rioters drag Gabriel Varden to the prison and try to force him to pick the lock on the main gate. When he obdurately refuses, they knock him down with a blow that makes blood pour from his forehead.

Some [rioters] cried "Kill him," and some (but they were not near enough) strove to trample him to death. . . . He was down again, and up, and down once more, and buffeting with a score of them, who bandied him from hand to hand, when one tall fellow, fresh from a slaughter-house, whose dress and great thigh-boots smoked hot with grease and blood, raised a pole-axe, and swearing a horrible oath, aimed it at the old man's uncovered head. At that instant, and in the very act, he fell himself, as if struck by lightning, and over his body a one-armed man came darting to the locksmith's side. Another man was with him, and both caught the locksmith roughly in their grasp.

His rescuers are Joe Willet and Ned Chester, who pull him to safety, distracting the mob's attention by shouting, "Leave him to us. Why do you waste your whole strength on such as he, when a couple of men can finish him in as many minutes!" (64).

Dickens's point is that the rioters really did try not merely to hurt Varden but to kill him, and Joe and Ned divert them by promising to "finish"—that is, kill—him themselves. Dickens, in other words, thinks of the mob as murderers, bent on destroying not only buildings but people. Thus Hugh, according to Joe Willet, would have killed Mr. Haredale during the destruction of Landale's Distillery, had not Ned Chester knocked him off his horse (67). However, as *Barnaby* is an historical novel, and as the actual Gordon Rioters in fact did not kill anyone, Dickens is obliged to limit his portrayal of their murderousness: they unquestionably would have committed murder, he suggests; it was only fortuitous that they did not. Certainly the assault they made, *Barnaby* insists, was directed against far more than mere property.[19]

On the same night that the rioters burn Newgate and set its prisoners loose, they also demolish the townhouse of Lord Mansfield, the Lord Chief Justice, and Dickens's brief description of that outrage—an outrage summing up the whole destructive course of the riots thus far—is his most explicit statement of what exactly the riots are in process of annihilating. Having "forced an entrance according to their usual custom" into Lord Mansfield's house, the rioters

began to demolish it with great fury, and setting fire to it in several parts, involved in a common ruin the whole of the costly furniture, the plate and jewels, a beautiful gallery of pictures, the rarest collection of manuscripts ever possessed by any one private person in the world, and worse than all, because nothing could replace this loss, the great Law Library, on almost every page of which were notes in the Judge's own hand, of inestimable value,—being the results of the study and experience of his whole life. (66)

Here the rioters are symbolically destroying the whole of what is most valuable in Western civilization, for this house is the repository of the most refined accomplishments of the human spirits—art and learning and the skillfully wrought contrivances that render life not merely decent but splendid.

Lord Mansfield's law library, moreover, embodies in its highest seriousness that indispensable legal system regulating the mutual relations of men in society. Because Dickens's lawyers tend to constitute a legal vampirarchy, any Dickens scholar—with Dodson and Fogg, or Uriah Heep, or the whole legal panoply of *Bleak House* in mind—is bound to be shocked to hear Dickens speak of *any* lawyer in the tone of honor he applies here to the Chief Justice of the King's Bench. But Mansfield was neither Dodson nor Fogg: as a young man he won the admiring friendship of Alexander Pope, and he became in later years one of those half-dozen or so celebrated jurists whose achievement makes eighteenth-century England particularly distinguished for its legal thought. Any reader who, by his vivid memory of the general grotesqueness and inhumanity of Dickensian lawyers, is rendered suspicious of Dickens's sincerity in this instance need only remind himself that Mansfield is not the only lawyer who meets with unqualified approbation in *Barnaby Rudge*: Ned Chester's maternal grandfather was an "eminent lawyer" who "stood high at the bar," and Dickens offers so serious an accomplishment as the polar opposite of the frivolity and irresponsibility of Mr. Chester *père* (15). No one can mistake Dickens's habitual criticism of the abuses and imperfections of the legal system for a contempt for the law. Though frequently "the Law is an Ass, a Humbug," it is nevertheless essential in its attempt to replace the natural rule of the stronger with the artificial rule of right.

Dedicated to art, learning, and law, this house is a monument to three of the most characteristically civilized activities of man—activities which seek to refine nature, even to transcend it by opposing to nature's productions new creations that are wholly human. The rioters could not express their enmity to civilization any more clearly than they do in thus vandalizing Lord Mansfield's house: their wish to "wrap the city in a circle of flames" and "burn the whole to ashes" (67) is a more grandiose but not a more complete expression of the same thing.[20]

7

The Riots 2: As Wild and Merciless as the Elements Themselves

T his, then, is what the rioters do: the destruction of these build-ings (along with the burning of Langdale's Distillery, to be dis-cussed later) are the central actions of the Gordon Riots, and they add up to a symbolic assault on the objective, institutional structure of society itself. But, as mentioned before, this is only half the ruin the rioters accomplish, for at the same time as the destruction of these tan-gible manifestations of civilization is going forward, a disintegration of the inner quality of civilization takes place in every individual rioter. One of *Barnaby*'s finest achievements is its vivid representation of this: of how, in the midst of their frenzy of physical destruction, the rioters suffer an abrupt inner conversion and revert in an epidemic way to the status of natural men.

All the major descriptions of the riots' central events deal with this psy-chological aspect, and always in the same terms. Dickens knew that to achieve in his riot scenes the "broad, bold, hurried effect" he wanted, he had "to select the striking points and beat them into the page with a

sledgehammer,"[1] and he does this with the greatest intensity in describing the radical changes taking place within the rioters. These descriptions, in fact, are so similar as to be, in effect, alternative versions of each
other, forming five or six variations on the same underlying theme.

This theme is first announced as early as the novel's second chapter, tes-
tifying to the consistency of the imagination at work in *Barnaby Rudge*.
Here, in his reflections on a horseman galloping furiously through a
stormy night, Dickens provides a little model, complete and accurate
though on the most miniature scale, of precisely the kind of transformation the rioters undergo. Such a passage repays detailed analysis: it offers
a blueprint of the completed edifice, showing with great clarity the speci-
fications of each component and the system of subordination by which
the parts are integrated into a whole:

There are times when, the elements being in unusual commotion, those who are
bent on daring enterprises, or agitated by great thoughts whether of good or evil,
feel a mysterious sympathy with the tumult of nature and are roused into corresponding violence. In the midst of thunder, lightning, and storm, many tremen-
dous deeds have been committed; men self-possessed before, have given a sudden
loose to passions they could no longer control. The demons of wrath and despair
have striven to emulate those who ride the whirlwind and direct the storm; and
man, lashed into madness with the roaring winds and boiling waters, has become
for the time as wild and merciless as the elements themselves. (2)

This passage starts out as a conventional Byronism, but it metamor-
phoses into something quite different before it reaches its conclusion, for
it revises its first assumptions so radically as to cancel them. It opens with
the familiar Romantic storm, revealing nature in its most awesome mood.
The usual Romantic response here is admiration for the limitless energy
animating the scene, a primal energy that compels our homage even
when it discharges itself in so potentially destructive a way. As for the
audacious human figure who has heroically invaded the solitude of nature
at its most terrible—he, through his sympathetic identification with nature's cosmic energy, is put back into immediate touch with the natural energy in his own breast. Through him, too, this primal energy utters itself
forth, and here again a Romantic poet would not hesitate to bestow his
admiration, regardless of the specific end in whose service this energy is
being enlisted. Whether directed toward prodigious, creative heroism or
defiant criminality, so full a charge of energy will in any event discharge
itself in some breathtaking manifestation of fearless vitality, which—to

Blake, for instance, and for his followers down to the present day—is a sign of life and therefore of health.

While the passage starts in this direction, Dickens concedes the moral indefiniteness of such unrestrained energy only for one sentence. For he persistently senses in *Barnaby* that inseparable from the forces of nature, including human nature, is a superabundance of impersonal, merciless violence. This consciousness tends so strongly toward a belief in the essential malignity of nature that in the present passage he imagines "demons" (not "gods" or even "spirits") at the helm of whirlwinds and storms.[2] The conclusion to which we see Dickens virtually surrendering here is that man, when restored to the full exercise of the natural energy at his disposal, is as destructive as Dickens assumes the unfettered breaking out of any natural force, whether animate or inanimate, to be.

The transvaluation of Romantic values that takes place in the very tissue of the passage also involves a radical change in the idea of the relation between nature and the self. Instead of regarding the identification of the self with nature as a realization of the self, Dickens judges it tantamount to self-disintegration. Men are "self-possessed," he writes, only when those "passions" which are the fundamental energy of human nature are under "control"—an observation that sounds like a pious truism until we grasp that "self-possessed" is used with absolute literalness to mean that men have selves as a result of having gained mastery over the darker passions constitutive of their human nature. One defines one's self by a separation-out from universal, fundamental human nature, not by a total identification with it. Dickens utterly rejects that tendency of Blakean Romanticism to locate one's "real" self in one's most fundamental, primitive, and unmodified impulses. For Dickens in *Barnaby*, the full mobilization of the fundamental passions of one's nature does not put one in contact with one's "true" self but merely surrenders the self back to the meaningless chaos of nature.

A significant detail in the language of our passage sharpens the focus of these observations, clearly identifying the psychological transformation at issue here as the precipitous regression of civilized man to natural savagery. In holding up "madness" and a "wild and merciless" character as the two salient features of the violent inner existence this transformation brings about, our passage identifies that existence with the essential nature of precivilized man, minutely anatomized in Dickens's portraits of the mad Barnaby and the savage Hugh. *Both* Barnaby's madness *and* Hugh's savagery have to be added to each other to complete Dickens's theoretical reconstruction of natural man. As Dickens conceives of him, natural man is essentially mad and essentially savage—terms which at bottom denote the same utter dormancy of the specifically *human* qualities, the same total lack of a "rational soul," the same inherent aggressiveness, described however with very different emphases, or seen now in its quiescent, now in its active manifestation. So unequivocally has Dickens established the meaning of the formula "mad and savage" in the first half of the novel that we can hardly mistake its significance when we repeatedly meet with it—or with one of its variations, such as the phrase "wild and merciless" that in our present passage is the exact equivalent of "savage"[3]—in the descriptions of the riots.

Thus when Dickens insistently shows the rioters progressively reaching a state of undiluted madness and savagery, we recognize a transformation whose identity is unmistakable—citizens grow feral, civilized men are reduced to precivilized brutality, becoming as they become more and more natural proportionally less human.

One last detail: while the phrase "demons of wrath and despair" seems at first nothing more than a ready-made epithet, Dickens's evocation of the demonic introduces into the novel yet another component of the thematic framework underlying each major riot scene. The word "demonic" denotes an idea with a long, complicated history, of which three strands are important for our purposes. First, the realm of the demonic incorporates the myth of Satan's revolt, an act so senseless, negative, and malicious as to constitute only rebellion for rebellion's sake. Dickens's description of the rioters as "demonic" thus emphasizes his belief that the Gordon Riots are a revolt of the most irrational, nihilistic kind—a revolt, since Satan and his demons are at war with *God*, against unquestionably legitimate authority.

Second, implicit in the idea of the demonic is a theory of human nature similar to the one so vigorously at work in *Barnaby* and *Nickleby*. However innocent prelapsarian human nature may have been, the devil's contrivance of original sin irrevocably transformed our inner nature, which is now tainted with disobedient, brutal, even criminal impulses. Third, from the fall onward, man has found a sufficiency of demons at his shoulder to encourage these impulses. Indeed, these demons clearly "represent desires which individual Christians have, but which they dare not acknowledge as belonging to themselves."[4] Demons are personifications of that multitude of forbidden impulses generated from within ourselves—impulses so forbidden that we deny their origin in our own hearts, projecting them outward onto a host of imaginary agents.

Dickens already begins to forge a link between the idea of the demonic and the aggressiveness that is the most fundamental of these forbidden impulses in *Barnaby*'s first half. In this way may we understand the devilishness attributed to Mr. Chester (12, 29), and, following the maxim that it takes one to know one, we may also accept as accurate Mr. Chester's judgment that "any King or Queen may make a Lord, but only the Devil himself—and the Graces—can make a Chesterfield" (23). What Dickens thinks is devilish about these characters, clearly enough, is their undeviating aggressive individualism, insidiously subversive of the communal life. Such also is the meaning of the devilishness he attributes to Gashford in the novel's second half (44); and in this sense, too, we should understand the devil imagery coiled around Mr. Rudge. The novel's emblematic primal murderer, he has symbolically committed the specific act which constitutes the utter antithesis of civilized life (16, 17, 65).

But besides stipulating this relationship between the demonic and the radically antisocial, the first half of the novel also connects, in its treatment of Barnaby himself, the idea of the demonic with the idea of aboriginal human nature. Constantly flickering about Barnaby are hints of the demonic—his red hair is a traditional badge of the devil; his birthmark, that "seemed a smear of blood but half washed out" (5), recalls the devil's mark; and Phiz illustrates the phantoms who haunt his dreams as a legion of obscene demons straight out of Hieronymus Bosch (7). What is implied about Barnaby, though, is made explicit about his raven, Grip, described as an "imp" (6), an "old necromancer," and "the embodied Spirit of Evil" (25), and whose cries of "I'm a devil! I'm a devil!" resound throughout the novel or even (as its last paragraph asserts) beyond. Insofar as Grip is Barnaby's completing counterpart, the bird's explicitly demonic character confirms the existence of a demonic principle at work within the fool. This way of going about things—decomposing Barnaby still further after having already split natural man into two representative figures—is of course another reflection of Dickens's extreme ambivalence about Barnaby, whom he sometimes would like to think of as "childlike," but to whom he reluctantly feels compelled to attribute the "demonic" aggression he invariably concludes is the defining character of natural man. And so here he simultaneously asserts and tries to exorcise the demonic quality he believes is lodged in the very heart of human nature, by separating the demonic from the man and projecting it onto the animal. But if the demonic principle is partly repressed in Dickens's representation of Barnaby, Grip's habit of "drawing corks," as Dickens describes the popping noises with which the raven punctuates his speeches, provides a continuous warning throughout Part I that the demonic impulses, "bottled up and corked down" (11), will, like "certain liquors, confined in casks too cramped in their dimensions," begin at length to "ferment, and fret, and chafe in their imprisonment," and will "with great foam and froth and splutter" sooner or later "force a vent, and carry all before" them, as Sim Tappertit's "aspiring soul" is said on occasion to do (4).

These same "demons of wrath and despair" also allude to one element still missing from our blueprint. Clearly, they are cousins of that "Genius of Despair and Suicide" who materializes in *Nickleby* (6) to advise the Baron of Grogzwig to "quit this weary world at once." As such, they embody an aggression directed not only against the whole of external reality but also against the self. We noticed Dickens's belief that an identification of the self with the primal energies of nature entailed a disintegration of the self; his imagination of some sort of "death instinct,"[5] hinted at here and developed further in the riots themselves, is the logical extension of this idea, taken with undeviating literalness to its ultimate conclusion. In Dickens's view, the identification of the self with nature involves a surrender of the self to the appetite for violence at the center of human nature—an appetite which, not satisfied but rather strengthened by what it feeds on, at last devours even itself.

This insight brings into sharp focus all the anticipations of *The Birth of Tragedy* that a reader cannot but notice in *Barnaby*'s riot scenes. The Dionysian broods over this book; in particular, Nietzsche's Dionysiac intoxication figures centrally in Dickens's riots, where the collective drunkenness of the mob grows more and more obscene and absolute until the rioters really do "abrogate the *principium individuationis*" (as Nietzsche calls it) by incinerating themselves in a fiery lake of burning liquor. Though *Barnaby Rudge* presents these matters more impressionistically than does *The Birth of Tragedy*, Dickens, seeing through to the logical conclusion of what Nietzsche later called the Dionysiac principle, reveals what Nietzsche avoids—that its essence is the "One-ness" achieved in universal annihilation.

Perhaps the most "Nietzschean" passage in *Barnaby* occurs in Chapter 53:

Each tumult took shape and form, from the circumstances of the moment; sober workmen going home from their day's labour, were seen to cast down their baskets of tools and become rioters in an instant; mere boys on errands did the like. In a word, a moral plague ran through the city. The noise, and hurry, and excitement, had for hundreds and hundreds an attraction they had no firmness to resist.

The contagion spread, like a dread fever: an infectious madness, as yet not near its height, seized on new victims every hour, and society began to tremble at their ravings.

This description calls to mind Nietzsche's procession of Dionysian revellers rushing by in noisy intoxication and sweeping up into their throng ever-increasing numbers as they carouse along. The instant transformation of a "sober workman" into a rioter is analogous to the transformation of Nietzsche's Apollonian individual into an intoxicated reveller; and when Dickens's workman flings away, along with his sobriety, also his tools, one cannot help thinking of how the Dionysian reveller, in merging himself into the ecstatic throng, thus renounces the plastic, shaping Apollonian faculties, which find their most complete expression, says Nietzsche, in sculpture.

But Dickens's passage has little in common with the aesthetician's abstraction so characteristic of *The Birth of Tragedy*. The tools thrown away here are not metaphysical tools but real ones—this particular workman's own particular tools—and they cost money; they constitute this workman's capital plant. And what they build, one assumes, is not sculpture but cities. These are the instruments with which men shape their environment, express and realize their human essence, and humanize the world. If Dickens could have seen *The Birth of Tragedy*, he would have argued that what the reveller trades in for his ecstasy are his specifically human qualities—hence the uncompromising judgment expressed by the epidemic of disease imagery Dickens repeatedly uses to describe the psychology of such a mob.

No more dramatic illustration of the relationship between our blueprint passage and the riot scenes can be found than a description, fifty chapters later, that is virtually a paraphrase of the passage's last sentence. An urban mob, says Dickens, is a "creature of very mysterious existence"—few men so much as know where it comes from.

Assembling and dispersing with equal suddenness, it is as difficult to follow to its various sources as the sea itself; nor does the parallel stop here, for the ocean is not more fickle and uncertain, more terrible when roused, more unreasonable, or more cruel. (52)

Like the man at the heart of the storm, who, "lashed into madness with the roaring winds and boiling waters, has become for the time as wild and merciless as the elements themselves," the rioters have become assimilated to an elemental, violent, natural force and reduced to the "un-reasonable" madness and "cruel" savagery which are precivilized human nature's defining features. Almost as unadorned a statement of these themes is the very first riot scene, the demonstration at the House of Commons, which notes that the rioters, in their madness and savagery, are becoming bestial: "The mob raged and roared, like a mad monster as it was, unceasingly, and each new outrage served to swell its fury." A few moments later, Dickens adds, the rioters "grew more wild and savage, like beasts at the sight of prey" (49).

The ensuing riot scenes, more elaborately embellished, nevertheless beat the same few "striking points" into the page, as in this description of the rioters' departure from the ruined Catholic chapel:

Covered with soot, and dirt, and dust, and lime; their garments torn to rags; . . . their hands and faces jagged and bleeding with the wounds of rusty nails; Bar-naby, Hugh, and Dennis hurried on before them all, like hideous madmen. After them, the dense throng came fighting on: . . . some shouting in triumph; some quarreling among themselves; some menacing the spectators as they passed; some with great wooden fragments, on which they spent their rage as if they had been alive, rending them limb from limb, and hurling the scattered morsels high into the air; some in a drunken state, unconscious of the hurts they had received from falling bricks, and stones, and beams. . . . Thus—a vision of coarse faces . . . ; a dream of demon heads and savage eyes, and sticks and iron bars uplifted in the air, and whirled about; a bewildering horror, . . . not to be forgotten all through life . . .—it flitted onward, and was gone. (50)

Here in the "hideous madmen" and the "savage eyes" are the madness and the savagery. The dirtiness of the rioters, along with their tattered gar-ments, reinforces Dickens's conceit that they are regressing to the squalid, naked savagery of man's precivilized condition, where, as the detail of the "coarse faces" suggests, the human is submerged in the brutish. So too the rioters' "unconsciousness of the hurts they had received" reminds us of the bestial hardiness and lack of self-consciousness which Dickens's theory imputes to man's original, animal state. Their spontaneous aggres-siveness, directed indiscriminately at bystanders, at each other, even at inanimate objects, and operating with such an intensity as to constitute "rage"—this of course is the inherent aggression Dickens imagines as the defining characteristic of natural man, while the mention of "demon heads" places the rioters for the first time in that demonic realm which is still another nightmarish imaginative representation of man's original per-sonality. It is no wonder that this is a scene "not to be forgotten all

through life," as Dickens insists again and again of the outrages committed by the rioters. For in these riots, he believes, a fundamental truth
about the human condition, a truth usually hidden and repressed, is disclosed in a revelation that perforce transforms the observer's understanding of the nature of man and society.

The next two outrages—the plunder of the Maypole and the burning
of the Warren—are a study in contrasts. When Dickens sums up the scene
of anarchy at the inn by saying that the rioters "changed [the Maypole] all
at once into a bear-garden, a madhouse, an infernal temple" (54), his formula, placing in apposition images of the savage, the mad, and the demonic as if they were alternative versions of each other, is, we know, no
random groping for the appropriate metaphor but a specific identification: this vision of the world turned upside down, of chaos come again, is
a vision of the Hobbesian state of nature restored. As for the rioters
themselves—in describing them as "swarming on like insects" Dickens
suggests that they are casting off their specifically human qualities and, in
Tennyson's phrase, reeling back into the beast.

If the Maypole incident treats the thematic material in a concentrated
way, the razing of the Warren (55) presents a fully worked-out version.
Arriving there, the rioters, says Dickens, "poured in like water" and took
over the house "like an army of devils." Falling at once to their work of
destruction, they "plied their demon labours fiercely"—an expression
fusing together the demonic with an aspect of the savage, in that *fierce*
means "of formidably violent and intractable temper, like a wild beast."[6]
Here too the rioters are said to have "spent their fury" on inanimate objects. Nor is the element of madness lacking. One group of rioters is described as "mad for destruction," while men from another contingent of
the mob "rushed to an fro stark mad, setting fire to all they saw—often to
the dresses of their own friends." Indeed, Dickens continues, calling
forth a vision of inner transformation which has destroyed all that we
recognize as human and replaced it with the demonic, "The more the fire
crackled and raged, the wilder and more cruel the men grew; as though
moving in that element they became fiends, and changed their earthly
nature for the qualities that give delight in hell."

As the description continues, the element of self-destruction that appeared in our blueprint passage begins to assert itself too.

If Bedlam gates had been flung open wide, there would not have issued forth such
maniacs as the frenzy of that night had made. There were men there, who danced
and trampled on the beds of flowers as though they trod down human enemies;

and wrenched them from the stalks, like savages who twisted human necks. There were men who cast their lighted torches in the air, and suffered them to fall upon their heads and faces, blistering the skin with deep unseemly burns. There were men who rushed up to the fire, and paddled in it with their hands as if in water; and others who were restrained by force from plunging in, to gratify their deadly longing. On the skull of one drunken lad . . . who lay upon the ground with a bottle to his mouth, the lead from the roof came streaming down in a shower of liquid fire, white hot; melting his head like wax. When the scattered parties were collected, men—living yet, but singed as with hot irons—were plucked out of the cellars, and carried off upon the shoulders of others, who . . . left them, dead, in the passages of hospitals. But of all the howling throng not one learnt mercy from, or sickened at, these sights; nor was the fierce, besotted, senseless rage of one man glutted. (55)

"Maniacs" worse than Bedlamites; men like "savages who twisted human necks": madness and savagery—clearly identified as alternate expressions of an aggression so vehement and comprehensive as grotesquely to attack even the flowerbeds—open our passage; and madness and savagery— again subsumed under the larger category of "rage"—bring it to its conclusion. And whereas the Maypole's "bear-garden, madhouse, infernal temple" formula adds to these the element of the demonic, the "fierce, besotted, senseless rage" formula, which sums up the rioters' motivation at the Warren, supplements the mob's mad and savage aggression with the complex of related elements contained in the term "besotted." Gathering up the ideas the middle part of this passage expresses, the word "besot- ted" describes in one of its primary meanings the lack of a "rational soul" characteristic of man's precivilized nature as Dickens imagines it. In its other primary meaning of "stupefied with drink," it refers to the rioters' extreme drunkenness, which in its turn accelerates not only the inexor- able dissolution of their "rational souls" but also the simultaneous corro- sion of their consciousness of self. This blurring of the outlines of the self explains why the rioters bizarrely permit their own torches to burn them, just as at the Catholic chapel they were similarly "unconscious of the hurts they had received" (51).

But this abrogation of the self is not confined in the riots only to the realm of consciousness. For in the "deadly longing" which overcomes the rioters at the Warren is expressed not the weary yearning to cast off the burden of modern selfhood to which, for example, Tennyson's Lotos- Eaters give voice but rather a frenzied craving to abolish the self *literally*, to obliterate it utterly, to fling oneself onto the blazing pyre and burn oneself to vapor and ashes. In this passage, in short, Dickens suggests the existence of a kind of death-instinct; and so, when the rioters really do incinerate themselves in large numbers in a last, horrible frenzy at Langdale's Distillery, we are to understand their self-immolation as attributable, at least in part, to this impulse.

The liberation of Bedlam imagined in the Warren passage's opening sentence is one of the novel's several invocations of that institution. The most notable is Chapter 67's account of how, during the last days of the riots, the rumor that the rioters "meant to throw the Gates of Bedlam open, and let all the madmen loose" spread like wildfire throughout the metropolis. Even though the other enormities the rioters threatened must result in nothing less than "national bankruptcy and general ruin," this last rumor, Dickens says, "suggested such dreadful images to the people's minds, and was indeed an act so fraught with new and unimaginable horrors in the contemplation, that it beset them more than any loss or cruelty of which they could foresee the worst, and drove many sane men nearly mad themselves."

This seems more fear than was appropriate: would it really have been so blood-curdling to have Bedlam's lunatics grinning or glowering or raving in the public streets? But what is terrifying here is a thought, not a reality: the thought of the liberation not of Bethlehem Hospital in its everyday actuality, but rather of Bedlam as the symbolic embodiment of a primal madness whose place of banishment is, paradoxically, at the heart of the city. What is threatened, in other words, is the release of the madness which is always within ourselves, which never disappears but only goes underground, and whose dormant existence presents the danger of an epidemic return in just such a "contagion" of "infectious madness," just such a "moral plague," as swept London in the Riots of 1780 (53).

Too bad Dickens missed, in his Gordon Riot researches, the related rumor, tailor-made for him, that the rioters were going to release the lions from the Tower and so symbolically liberate the savagery as well as the madness that lurks within us.[7] But in the destruction of Newgate, the next major event of the riots, Dickens does symbolically represent the liberation of that criminal aggression chained down in every human breast. We meet at once in this episode with the familiar landmarks: the rioters' "savage faces," the "infernal christening" they perform on Newgate. We know just where we are when Dickens remarks of the mob that "[t]he whole great mass were mad." Again, the rioters succumb to such a paroxysm of aggression that they "spent their fierce rage on anything—even on the great blocks of stone." But what is new here is the quality of the mob's savagery, which at this pitch of intensity passes beyond the realm of the not civilized into that of the not human. Now the crowd "howled like wolves" and "thirsted, like wild animals, for . . . blood."

With this much of their humanity lost, Dickens believes, it is a short step to losing everything, and the rioters take that final step into the abyss in the last of *Barnaby*'s riot scenes, the burning of the Catholic-owned Langdale's Distillery (68). Opening with Hugh "savagely threatening someone," and noting "the rabble's unappeasable and maniac rage," this scene has the characteristic elements of madness, savagery, and aggression.[8] But in the main issue at Langdale's is the final consequence of this "unappeasable rage," for here the rioters fulfill their double-barrelled program of "Down with everybody, down with everything!" (The symbolic demolition of the outward structure of civilization, by the time the rioters reach Langdale's, is of course complete. What they accomplish in razing the vintner's is ruin of a yet further order.)

That night, the mob "rose like a great sea . . . in so many places at once, and with such inconceivable fury," that soon, "[o]ne after another, new fires blazed up in every quarter of the town, as though it were the intention of the insurgents to wrap the city in a circle of flames, which, contracting by degrees, should burn the whole to ashes" (67). The conflagration at Langdale's blazes at the center of this circle of fire, and there Dickens conjures up, in the image of "the reflections in every quarter of the sky, of deep, red, soaring flames, as though the last day had come and the whole universe were burning" (68), a lurid vision of the end of the world straight out of the Apocalypse. By a logical progression, these flames of the "last day"—the Day of Judgment—merge in the next paragraph into the fires of hell.

The mob has burst into the blazing distillery and broken open its casks of liquor. The leaping flames and the unwholesome smoke make up a dreadful enough scene, says Dickens—

But there was a worse spectacle than this—worse by far than fire and smoke, or even the rabble's unappeasable and maniac rage. The gutters of the street and every crack and fissure in the stones, ran with scorching spirit; which, being dammed up by busy hands, overflowed the road and pavement, and formed a great pool, in which the people dropped down dead by dozens. They lay in heaps all round this fearful pond, husbands and wives, fathers and sons, mothers and daughters, women with children in their arms and babies at their breasts, and drank until they died. While some stooped with their lips to the brink and never raised their heads again, others sprang up from their fiery draught, and danced, half in a mad triumph, and half in the agony of suffocation, until they fell, and steeped their corpses in the liquor that had killed them. Nor was even this the worst or most appalling kind of death that happened on this fatal night. From the burning cellars, . . . some men were drawn, alive, but all alight from head to foot; who, in their unendurable anguish and suffering, making for anything that had the look of water, rolled, hissing, in this hideous lake, and splashed up liquid fire which lapped in all it met with as it ran along the surface, and neither spared the living nor the dead. On this last night of the great riots—for the last it was—the wretched victims of a senseless outcry, became themselves the dust and ashes of the flames they had kindled, and strewed the public streets of London. (68)

The "hideous lake" of "liquid fire" cannot but remind us of the "burning Lake" of "liquid fire" into which Satan and his cohorts are hurled "with hideous ruin" at the beginning of *Paradise Lost*, and which is, says Milton, Hell in the midst of Chaos.[9] Here we reach the final development of Barnaby's theme of the demonic: in this infernal scene at the vintner's, the rioters complete their nullification of civilized life by immolating their own inner faculty of civilization and returning to that demonic, original personality whose free operation, Dickens insists, must lead to the general chaos that overwhelms this scene.

In the all-inclusive destruction Dickens depicts at Langdale's, it turns out that "Down with everybody!" really means *everybody*. The aggression the rioters directed against the whole of reality reaches its inexorable conclusion by swallowing them up as well. And if intoxication has all along been bringing about in them a progressive loss of self, here liquor produces a loss of self of the most literal kind, in a scene that conjures up Hogarth's "Gin Lane" and goes it one better.[10]

But more important than the allusion to Hogarth are the evocations of Shakespeare. For when Dickens says that the rioters "drank until they died"—a phrase given special emphasis by the similar alliteration of the "dropped down dead by dozens" in the preceding sentence—he is echoing a passage in *Measure for Measure* that ends "when we drink we die" and that succinctly anticipates a central premise of *Barnaby Rudge*. Lucio, meeting Claudio, who has just been arrested, asks, "Why, how now, Claudio! whence comes this restraint?" Claudio replies:

> From too much liberty, my Lucio, liberty.
> As surfeit is the father of much fast,
> So every scope by the immoderate use
> Turns to restraint. Our natures do pursue,
> Like rats that ravin down their proper bane,
> A thirsty evil; and when we drink we die.[11]

Beyond the assertion that too much exercise of liberty leads to jail lies the more fundamental proposition that liberty needs restraint because our natures, left to their free operation, pursue courses that bring harm and finally ruin upon us. Exactly that is what happens at Langdale's, where the rioters, having liberated all the impulses of their original human nature, at last themselves fall victim to the universal violence and destructiveness they have loosed. Here, at this final stage of their mass reversion to the character of natural man, is the fullest demonstration of civilization's reason for being: life without it, in Dickens's view, must be an all-devouring anarchy, tending always toward just such a holocaust as the scene at the vintner's describes.

The rioters destroy themselves: and Dickens, in concluding his account of how they do so, is thinking, I believe, of another passage from Shakespeare, a passage which describes exactly the kind of radical inner disintegration that befalls them in the course of the riots. The passage I mean—the famous speech of Ulysses on the subject of "degree" in *Troilus and Cressida*—strikes me as having been in Dickens's mind on some level all through *Barnaby*, though it is only in the last sentence of our present description that it percolates up to the surface.

> How could communities,
> Degrees in schools, and brotherhood in cities,
> Peaceful commerce from dividable shores,
> The primogenitive and due of birth,
> Prerogative of age, crowns, scepters, laurels,
> But by degree, stand in authentic place?
> Take but degree away, untune that string,
> And, hark, what discord follows! Each thing meets
> In mere oppugnancy. The bounded waters
> Should lift their bosoms higher than the shores
> And make a sop of all this solid globe.
> Strength should be lord of imbecility,
> And the rude son should strike his father dead.
> Force should be right; or rather, right and wrong,
> Between whose endless jar justice resides,
> Should lose their names, and so should justice too.
> Then everything includes itself in power,
> Power into will, will into appetite;
> And appetite, an universal wolf,
> So doubly seconded with will and power,

> Must make perforce an universal prey,
> And last eat up himself.[12]

Behind Dickens's image of the rioters becoming "themselves the dust and ashes of the flames they had kindled" lurks Shakespeare's "universal wolf" who "must make perforce an universal prey, and last eat up himself." And the reason Ulysses' speech is so much in Dickens's mind at this moment is that it describes precisely the kind of thing that is happening at Langdale's, providing an explicit statement of the unstated propositions which not only explain the meaning of this event but also are the fundamental propositions that Barnaby as a whole dramatizes.

If, says Ulysses, you were to overturn the order of society, you would produce anarchy, chaos, and finally universal destruction: you would replace the rule of right with the rule of the stronger, and, by thus enfranchising force, you would precipitate a process of change in human beings, the last stage of which would find them so wholly given up to their insatiable, wolfish aggressiveness that, having destroyed everything around them, they would implacably turn their aggression against themselves and become their own final victims. Essentially this is the argument of *Barnaby Rudge*, which seeks to demonstrate that, if you do not have civilization, with all its concomitant oppression and unhappiness, then you must have a state of brutal anarchy. And in that state, the voracious aggressiveness inherent in human nature, liberated from the restraints, both internal and external, which it is the program of civilization to oppose to it, will set about destroying everything it meets with, until it is itself swallowed up in the universal conflagration which must necessarily result— and which symbolically *does* result in the fiery consummation of Dickens's riots here at Langdale's, where *Barnaby Rudge* rests its case.[13]

8

The Riots 3: Pirates and Patriots

B ecause the city mob "has—perhaps only half-consciously— played an important part in the political evolution of the modern world, before giving way to better movements, and other group-ings of the poor," says Eric Hobsbawm, "the historian must make the attempt to understand how it worked, even though it can scarcely arouse his sympathy."[1] Recent historians have followed this advice. But they have often treated the mob outbreaks of the late eighteenth century as if, in relation to them, the Paris mob of 1789 were like *Middlemarch*'s candle, which, held up before a mirror, composes its surface's myriad, random scratches into a coherent pattern. Illuminated by the French Revolution, events like the various eighteenth-century food riots or the "Wilkes and Liberty" demonstrations or the Gordon Riots or even the Birmingham Church and King riots of 1791 seem to orient themselves and form a meaningful arrangement in its light. Thus many recent historians tend to entertain seriously the assertion of the "foremost pioneer"[2] in the study of the mob in history that, in the Gordon Riots, "behind the slogan of 'No Popery' and the other outward forms of religious fanaticism there lay a deeper social purpose: a groping desire to settle accounts with the rich, if only for a day, and to achieve some rough kind of social justice."[3] But George Rudé's assertion is based on evidence that could with equal ease be used to "prove" quite different conclusions, and one cannot help suspecting that genial faith has played the decisive role in his interpretation of the material he has so painstakingly collected.

At any rate, for understanding Dickens's interpretation of the Gordon Riots, the most helpful recent historian turns out to be Norman Cohn. For in the *Pursuit of the Millennium*,[4] even though that book is chiefly concerned with events predating the Gordon Riots by centuries, Cohn identifies a distinctive class of mass-movement whose characteristics are overwhelmingly in evidence in an important aspect of the riots not yet considered—Sim Tappertit's riotous organization, the 'Prentice Knights. Sim *does* have a program, and Dickens's point with him and his "Knights" is that, insofar as the riots had any kind of articulate agenda, it was the lunatic one embodied by these motley youths—an agenda that, though disguised as a politics, is in reality entirely opposed to the necessary conditions of political life and that, in Sim's not untypical case, is merely a direct expression of his neurotic fantasies of sexual power and paternal persecution. This program is a modern descendant of what Cohn has identified as millennialism, a set of impulses and attitudes which, whether in religious or secular guise, has throughout history regularly provided an ideology for mindless anarchists and has no less regularly declined into mindless anarchy.

Virtually by definition, millennialism is antipolitical: the wish to establish the City of God on earth displays an exhausted patience with the City of Man. Indeed, the millennial kingdom chiliastic sects seek to create is a realm which has superseded the need for government on any level, including the individual's government of himself. For the millenarian revolution proposes to rectify the human condition, abolishing man's chronic unhappiness by making absolute the freedom of each individual and sanctifying his every impulse. This revolution will bring about a world not new but, instead, identical to man's primitive condition before such fallen, corrupt institutions as the state and the organized church arose to constrict human life.

Central to the ideology of revolutionary millenarianism, Cohn shows, is "a self-exaltation that often amounted to self-deification." Such representative millenarians as the heretics of the Free Spirit, finding God in everything and everything a part of God, did not hesitate to extend these principles to themselves: they needed only to become conscious of their essential divinity, they held, "to surpass the condition of humanity and become God." From this vaguely neo-Platonic view sprang the many claims of "prodigious miracle-making powers" and the widespread delusions of total omnipotence.[5]

But what chiefly followed from such overcharged self-cherishing was a conviction of the immaculate holiness of one's own impulses coupled with a certainty that one was incapable of sin.[6] "Although the practical consequences of this belief could vary, one possible consequence was certainly antinomianism or the repudiation of moral norms." For the adepts of the Free Spirit, "the proof of salvation was to know nothing of conscience or remorse." Here, in other words, was "an affirmation of freedom so reckless and unqualified that it amounted to a total denial of every kind of restraint and limitation."[7] And thus more profoundly meaningful than he knew was the manifesto of one adept who declared, "I belong to the Liberty of Nature, and all that my nature desires I satisfy. . . . I am a natural man."[8] Little wonder that, when translated into mass action, such an urge for freedom should (as Freud predicts) direct itself, not "against particular forms and demands of civilization" but "against civilization altogether."[9] Anarchism does not come any more absolute than such an "ideal of a total emancipation of the individual from society."[10]

Millenarian movements belong to a long tradition of popular protest against the irreducible unfreedom of the civilized condition. Certainly the impulses that generated them by no means vanished when religious forms of thought, growing old, began to provide an increasingly rickety framework for their expression. They found, instead, other vehicles—Cohn argues that the adepts of the Free Spirit "could be regarded as remote precursors of Bakunin and of Nietzsche in their wilder moments," while the "blend of millenarianism and primitivism" so typical of these sects "has become one of the commoner forms of modern romanticism."[11]

Moreover, there were actual millenarian protests at the time *Barnaby Rudge* was written, which provided Dickens with unforgettable examples of the most radically antipolitical impulses masquerading as politics. There was, for instance, the amazing case of J. N. Thom, whom Dickens holds up, along with the Mormons and the antinomian Johanna Southcote, as the very personification of battiness in Chapter 18 of *American Notes*. After presenting himself, clad in Eastern attire, as "Sir William Courtenay, King of Jerusalem, Prince of Arabia, King of the Gypsies, [and] Defender of his King and Country," Thom retired for an interlude in prison and the madhouse before setting himself up in 1838 in the villages around Canterbury as the messianic leader of a millennial sect, composed of fifty or a hundred Kentish laborers. Armed with bludgeons and believing he had miraculous powers, they followed his standard of a loaf of bread carried on a pole from village to village. A constable having been sent to arrest him, Thom put him to death and withdrew to Blean Wood with some fifty followers, where he was set upon by the military and killed, along with one officer and a dozen of his own men, in a battle of extreme ferocity. Edward Thompson calls this "the last peasants' revolt";[12] more precisely, it was an outbreak of revolutionary millenarianism straight out of the Middle Ages. While Thom preached against the oppression of the poor by the rich, condemning the New Poor Law as an offense against divine law and holding out to his followers the promise of grants of land, he simultaneously and paradoxically proclaimed the advent of the Millennium, displayed the nail wounds in his hands and feet, and promised (if killed) to rise again. As his followers, concealed in the Blean Wood underbrush, awaited the approach of the soldiers, "he sounded a trumpet and said it was heard at Jerusalem, where 10,000 were ready to obey his command."[13]

Certainly *Barnaby*'s Gordon Riots are not themselves a millenarian outbreak, notwithstanding their ostensibly religious goals and the quasi-messianism of their leader. Nonetheless, with so comprehensive an hostility to civilization as their essential principle, they make much more sense seen in relation not to Thomas Paine or Karl Marx but to this other tradition—a tradition regularly associated with pogroms similar in kind (though vastly worse in degree) to the rioters' attacks upon Catholics. And the existence of such a tradition should forestall any objection that Dickens's representation of the riots can by no possibility have anything to do with historical reality but instead is made up of nothing but the ideological fictions which compose bourgeois mythology.

Sim Tappertit, the locksmith's apprentice who becomes a minor leader of the riots, displays in abundance all those self-regarding, antisocial impulses disguised as a politics that earlier centuries had precipitated the heresy of the Free Spirit. Of the characteristic self-cherishing, Sim has enough and to spare. So lofty is his opinion of himself that "in personal dignity and self-esteem" he "had swelled into a giant" (39); he carried himself about "with the air of a man who was faint with dignity" (8). For his puny little body "he entertained the highest admiration," and with his lean and meager legs, in particular, "he was enraptured to a degree amounting to enthusiasm" (4).

Nor does he find his inner qualities any less exceptional than his external man. A special power, he thinks, radiates from within him. In particular, he has majestic, shadowy ideas . . . concerning the power of his eye. Indeed he had been known to go so far as to boast that he could utterly quell and subdue the haughtiest beauty by a simple process, which he termed "eyeing her over;" but it must be added, that neither of this faculty, nor of the power he claimed to have, through the same gift, of vanquishing and heaving down dumb animals, even in a rabid state, had he ever furnished evidence which could be deemed quite satisfactory and conclusive.

It may be inferred from these premises, that in the small body of Mr. Tappertit there was locked up an ambitious and aspiring soul. As certain liquors, confined in casks too cramped in their dimensions, will ferment, and fret, and chafe in their imprisonment, so the spiritual essence or soul of Mr. Tappertit would sometimes fume within that precious cask, his body, until, with great foam and froth and splutter, it would force a vent, and carry all before it. It was his custom to remark, in reference to any one of these occasions, that his soul had got into head; and in this novel kind of intoxication many scraps and mishaps befel him. (4)

One thing this passage's second paragraph emphasizes with its extravagant sexual innuendoes is that Sim's psychic mechanisms of repression are undependable: forbidden impulses keep breaking through, their nature made clear by the wishes, both sexual and aggressive, expressed in Sim's fantasies about the power of his eye. Upon these impulses Sim dotes with the same peculiar intensity of self-adoration the millenarians of previous centuries so often showed. And he too takes such cravings for total power as irrefragable evidences of election.

"If I had been born a corsair or a pirate, a brigand, gen-teel highwayman or patriot—and they're the same thing," thought Mr. Tappertit, . . . "I should have been all right. But to drag out an ignoble existence unbeknown to mankind in general—patience! I will be famous yet. A voice within me keeps on whispering Greatness. I shall burst out one of these days, and when I do, what power can keep me down? I feel my soul getting into my head at the idea. . . ." (8)

Such fantasies, if acted out, can take a variety of forms, as Sim's list of roles suggests. His particular case can best be understood in light of Cohn's demonstration of how fantasies like the heresy of the Free Spirit tended time and again to channel themselves into outbreaks of revolutionary millenarianism. For the controlling insight at the center of *The Pursuit of the Millennium* is that the motivation behind certain kinds of mass social movements can be traced to the most radically individualistic impulses—to impulses which in their essence are emphatically antisocial.

That is what Dickens suggests in having Sim gloss over as irrelevant the question of whether he is impelled by "Private vengeance, sir, or public sentiment, or both combined" (24), and it is certainly what he means by having Sim equate patriots and pirates—roles Dickens sees as diametrically opposed, one being eminently social and the other the apotheosis of the antisocial. They can be regarded as equivalent only from the vantage point of Sim's Byronic narcissism, whose uncompromising individualism strips all roles of their social function and sees them merely in terms of their potential for self-aggrandizement.

As an example, consider Sim presenting himself in his glory during the riots to the abducted Dolly Varden, long the object of his humid fantasies:

> "You meet in me, Miss V.," said Simon, laying his hand upon his breast, "not a 'prentice, not a workman, not a slave, not the victim of your father's tyrannical behaviour, but the leader of a great people, the captain of a noble band. . . . You behold in me, not a private individual, but a public character; not a mender of locks, but a healer of the wounds of his unhappy country. Dolly V., sweet Dolly V., for how many years have I looked forward to this meeting! . . . Behold in me, your husband. Yes, beautiful Dolly—charmer—enslaver—S. Tappertit is all your own!" (59)

This highly delusional statement—whose yoking together of paranoid fantasies of persecution with equally fantastic assertions of grandeur and power suggests a familiar enough pathology—confirms our suspicion that in Sim's world view there is no room for an independent public realm, existing without reference to himself. What he expresses here in political terms and represents as a matter of social significance is, as is always the case with him, only a personal matter of the most private kind. Indeed, as Sim's "altered state of society" is (so he claims) about to spring into existence, his politics are revealed as being in large measure nothing but the erotic fantasy with which he inveterately entertains himself. One can scarcely be more of a "private individual," less of a "public character," than this; and if we keep in mind that the total system of Sim's fantasies contains, in addition to these wishes for sexual power, nothing save exceptionally violent aggressive wishes, we will hardly be surprised when, impersonating (as he thinks) a patriot, he becomes in fact a brigand.

This is Dickens's point in satirizing Sim's farcical "noble band" of 'Prentice Knights and its claim of being a high-minded political organization. For the real essence of this secret society is disclosed by its having "had its origin," as Sim explains, "in his own teeming brain, stimulated by a swelling sense of wrong and outrage" (8). What is teeming in that brain, we know, is self-adoration "amounting to enthusiasm," and the wrong and outrage Sim feels derive from his impatience with any limitation of the impulses of his "aspiring soul." It is this assertion of total freedom, entailing an utter denial of all authority, that the 'Prentice Knights embody. Thus each novice Knight swears an oath, binding him—true metropolitan artisans that they are, the 'Prentices' image of authority is the Corporation of the City of London—"to resist and obstruct the Lord Mayor, sword-bearer, and chaplain; to despise the authority of the sheriffs and to hold the court of aldermen as nought" (8). From this hostility to authority and affirmation of freedom flow the society's "general objects; which were briefly vengeance on their Tyrant Masters (of whose grievous and insupportable oppression no 'prentice could entertain a moment's doubt) and the restoration . . . of their ancient rights and holidays"—holidays when, according to Sim, apprentices had "broken people's heads by scores, defied their masters, nay, even achieved some glorious murders in the streets, which privileges had gradually been wrested from them, and in all which noble aspirations they were now restrained." Here again is the desire to restore the absolute freedom of primal aggression: the 'Prentices' "noble aspirations," identical to those of Sim's "aspiring soul," amount only to a wish to "carry all before" them.

Typically, too, the "altered state of society" (27, 39, 51) Sim and the 'Prentice Knights claim to be ushering into existence in the Gordon Riots is, they assert, not a new state of society but rather the restoration of an old one. Like so many millenarians before them, they seek to return to an imaginary state of nature, gilded with innocence, spontaneity, equality, and contentment, all lost in that long degeneration which is the history of human society. Man's primitive state, of course, is just what Dickens shows the 'Prentice Knights in process of restoring, and quite a different thing it is from any Edenic millennial vision. The "noble band"—"illustrating the wisdom of going backward" like "that sagacious fish, the crab"—wants to roll back the whole progress of human civilization. Believing that "the degrading checks imposed upon them were unquestionably attributable to the innovating spirit of the times, . . . they united therefore to resist all change, except such as would restore those good old English customs, by which they would stand or fall" (8). And to what good old English past do they look back? Their regret, as Sim says (conjuring up nothing so much as the old, conventional image of the wild man), is for the days when they "carried clubs wherewith to mace the citizens: that was his strong expression" (4).

Hence, of course, a paradox: the 'Prentice Knights appear to be both extremely reactionary and utterly revolutionary at once. Like generations of millenarians before them, they wish to overthrow the existing state of things—in order to return to a state in which man's original liberty was unabridged.[14] Here is the outer limit at which reaction and revolution turn into one another, and their very names lose their meaning, for, as Cohn has prepared us to see, we have slipped over into a realm beyond politics. The combination of diehard loyalism and extreme subversiveness contained in each 'Prentice Knight's oath to love the Constitution, as well as the "Church, the State, and everything established—but the masters" (8) embodies the paradox perfectly: in this case, the appeal to those good old English customs and institutions, and to the immemorial rights guaranteed by the past, expresses above all a denial of legitimate authority in the present. The voice that speaks here in the accents of reactionary patriotism nevertheless speaks a message that, like so many millenarian utterances of old, is one more expression of that hostility to civilization whose ultimate tendency, Dickens believes, is disclosed for all to see in the Riots of 1780.

. . .

As an interpretation of the actual events of 1780, Dickens's account cannot be dismissed lightly. But what of this novel's implicit commentary on certain political phenomena of Dickens's own time? *Barnaby*, as John Butt and Kathleen Tillotson point out, would have been a highly topical novel had it appeared at any time in the 1830s or 1840s:

It would have suggested (as most historical novels did) "new foes with an old face," for the revolution that never happened seemed always imminent. But the events of 1836–41 made the novel [which appeared in weekly parts from February 13 to November 27, 1841] almost journalistically apt. The Poor Law riots, the Chartist risings at Devizes, Birmingham, and Sheffield, the mass meetings on Kersal Moor and Kensington Common, and most pointed of all, the Newport rising of 1839 with its attempt to release Chartist prisoners—all these, with their aftermath of trials, convictions, and petitions against the punishment of death, gave special point in 1841 to "a tale of the Riots of '80."[15]

This list, by no means complete, is enough to show that there had been popular tumults aplenty immediately before the appearance of *Barnaby*, and the whole book implies a vague though wide-reaching uneasiness about the anarchic potential of working-class radicalism in general. But in the representation of the 'Prentice Knights that uneasiness finds a more specific object, for in this fictitious secret society Dickens is caricaturing the Chartist clubs and the trades unions of his own day.[16]

"The imperfections of the historical parallel [between the Gordon Riots and the Chartist demonstrations], the vital difference between agitation directed to limited and specific ends and the madness of the underworld let loose, were," Butt and Tillotson remark, "less obvious then than now."[17] Indeed, as we can see with the benefit of hindsight, the negative judgment of Chartism contained in *Barnaby Rudge*'s satire on the 'Prentice Knights is largely mistaken. But as this mistake was made not just by Dickens but by virtually the whole English middle class in the 1830s and 1840s, it is worth pausing for a moment to ask why.

First, few middle-class Englishmen of that time shared Thomas Carlyle's dialectical sense of history, which impelled him to see the destructive violence of the French Revolution as *necessary*—to believe that the old order had to be exploded and its particles whirled in the air before they could recohere into a radically new structure, so that all the revolutionary horror constituted, along with much else, a *creative* negation. (Even in *A Tale of Two Cities*, Dickens sees the Revolution's violence only as a necessary consequence of previous evils but not as an historically necessary part of the solution.) True, Carlyle bases the largest part of what he has to say in his *French Revolution* on the same complex of assumptions about human nature and its vicissitudes in civilized society that we have seen in operation in *Barnaby*; but alongside these assumptions, and existing simultaneously with them, are ideas about historical reality which allow certain specific instances of anarchy and chaos to be considered from an utterly different perspective.

These ideas were by no means incorporated into the fabric of Dickens's imagination in 1841, in spite of his probably having read *The French Revolution* by then; on the contrary, for him (as for Edmund Burke) violence was violence, anarchy was anarchy, and together they constituted a negation of civilized society that contained no promise of regeneration. Unlike Carlyle, Dickens had no notion of an alchemy in which negation might serve as the crucible of historical change. Thus when he thought of the "physical force" faction of the Chartists—and clearly that is what he has in mind when he has Sim talk of making demands on Parliament "temperately at first; then by an appeal to arms, if necessary" (4)—he could hear in their threat of violence only brute anarchism, speaking in accents so mindless as to make self-evident the Chartists' intrinsic irresponsibility and to disqualify them from the serious consideration of serious men. The Carlyle of *The French Revolution* (1837) and *Chartism* (1840) deplored and feared revolutionary violence, to be sure; but he understood it: and now that useful work has been done on the important

Carlylean influence on Dickens, this difference between the prophet and the novelist will give us a better perspective on their relationship by reminding us that the Carlyle who is most modern is not always the Carlyle who influenced Dickens.

Second, in the 'Prentice Knights' harebrained and highly reactionary "constitutional" rhetoric, and especially in their demand for the restoration of now-lost rights that prevailed in the immemorial past, Dickens has caught an authentic accent of English radicalism, whose meaning he has misconstrued. Far from being reactionary, this invocation of lost ancient liberties was a time-honored strategy for demanding altogether new political rights by claiming venerable precedents for them, in the best tradition of English constitutionalism. What Dickens jeers at as mindless reaction in his satirical representation of radicalism in *Barnaby Rudge* is in fact a version of what Christopher Hill has identified as the theory of "The Norman Yoke," which informed a central current of the radical impulse from the seventeenth century onward. This theory "took many forms," Hill explains,

> but in its main outlines it ran as follows: Before 1066 the Anglo-Saxon inhabitants of this country lived as free and equal citizens, governing themselves through representative institutions. The Norman Conquest deprived them of this liberty, and established the tyranny of an alien King and landlords. But the people did not forget the rights they had lost. They fought continuously to recover them, with varying success. Concessions (Magna Carta, for instance) were from time to time extorted from their rulers, and always the tradition of lost Anglo-Saxon freedom was a stimulus to ever more insistent demands upon the successors of the Norman usurpers.[18]

All this is about nine-tenths myth. Nonetheless, the picture painted by radical constitutionalists of a democratic, egalitarian society presided over by wise King Alfred and the Anglo-Saxon Witenagemot gave to demands for reforms such as annual parliaments and manhood suffrage an indispensable justification, and it provided also the framework for a general critique of "the landed aristocracy, political oligarchy [and] social privilege."[19] Though by the 1830s and 1840s appeals to the "historical" precedents of "our Saxon ancestors" were being gradually superseded in radical rhetoric by appeals to reason and the abstract rights of man, such invocations nevertheless remained current, even among Chartists.[20]

Nor was this myth the only backward-looking strand woven into the fabric of English radicalism. William Cobbett's retrospective nostalgia, for instance, is notorious; but, again, the historical myth he elaborated, "which assumes some medieval social compact between the Church and the gentry, on one hand, and the labourers, on the other, was employed," as Edward Thompson observes, "to justify claims to new social rights in much the same way as the theory of . . . the Norman Yoke had been used to justify the claim to new political rights"—namely, that the community should "succor the needy and the helpless, not out of charity, but as of right." And, finally, we must include "the social myth of the golden age of the village community before enclosure and before the [Napoleonic] Wars," which, current throughout the 1840s, was given " gargantuan dimensions" by the Chartist leader, Feargus O'Connor.[21]

It is easy to see how readily Dickens would have dismissed all this as the plainest irrationality, a foolish attempt to hold back a present that had in any event already arrived—an attempt as crazy as he might have considered (for instance) the machine-breaking of the Captain Swing rioters and other latter-day Luddites to stave off progress as inevitable as the rising of the sun. Moreover, in this novel Dickens has very little use for the "good old English" values, whose spokesmen in *Barnaby* are that "father of the good old English sort," Mr. Willet (30); the bloodthirsty hangman, Mr. Dennis, "who had been bred and nurtured in the good old school, and had administered the good old laws on the good old plan" (65); and the troglodyte county squire—the "genuine John Bull"—who tries to force Barnaby to sell Grip to him and who had married his most unhappy wife for "the good old English reason" of property (47). In this book Dickens believes unreservedly in the progress of civilization: the good old English times were markedly *less* civilized, *less* just, and *less* humane than the present, with all its undeniable imperfections; and for working men to vow, as the 'Prentice Knights vow, "to resist all change, except such change as would restore those good old English customs" (8)—for working men to join, however unwittingly, with the most reactionary elements in society in regretting those vanished times in which their lot in particular was so very much worse than now (as they should know but do not)—is the most perfect absurdity. Here the reader will recognize the authentic voice of middle-class Victorianism giving its most characteristic reply to the newly formulated "condition of England" question: five generations later, our faith in progress less assured, we might speak in a more diffident voice and give a more qualified answer.

In ridiculing as further evidence of mindless irrationality the 'Prentice Knights' mumbo-jumbo initiation ceremony, with its skulls, bones, candles, swords, and "dismal groaning by unseen 'prentices without" (8),

Dickens satirizes something real in the radical tradition: elaborate rituals and oaths were an indigenous part of working-class culture, and working-class associations, legal and illegal, employed them, partly to assert a respectable status which working people were afraid was being taken away from them.[22] To outsiders they were bound to look silly.

The last characteristic that led Dickens to judge Chartism and trades unionism fundamentally irrational movements is a more general matter than those already mentioned. It has to do with a certain kind of language and tone, certain images and metaphors that could be heard in English radicalism—William Blake's voice is a case in point—from the later eighteenth century at least up until the collapse of Chartism in 1848, and which was a legacy from the radicalism of the 1640s and 1650s. Because political and religious matters were so closely bound together in the Civil War, the soundest politics often found utterance in the most apparently other-worldly, religious language, and the habit of formulating political thought in the vocabulary and imagery of religious belief, so salient a feature of that epoch of English radicalism, remained a feature of the radical tradition until a surprisingly late date. M. H. Abrams, speaking of the political climate of the 1790s, observes that the "chief strength and momentum of English radicalism . . . came from the religious Nonconformists who, as true heirs of their embattled ancestors in the English Civil War, looked upon contemporary politics through the perspective of biblical prophecy." The pioneering scientist Joseph Priestley, to name one notable example, thought in such terms about politics, as Abrams reminds us.[23] Edward Thompson has shown how complex were the relations among radical politics, political messianism, revolutionary millenarianism, and religious revivalism from 1790 to 1830. Among the poor, these states of mind kept turning into each other and turning back again, from year to year, with protean fluidity. Among significant numbers of Chartists, such a peculiar tension between the rational and the mystical, the political and the millennial, was still to be found.[24]

Or take the case of the Owenites, who proclaimed a millennium that could look indistinguishable from the competing millennium trumpeted at exactly the same time by Messiah J. N. Thom, whose deranged career we reviewed earlier in this chapter. But notwithstanding their chiliastic tone and streak of sexual antinomianism, based (as usual) on an ideology of communitarianism and liberation, the Owenites of the 1830s, as we can see more clearly with the benefit of hindsight, offered a relatively reasonable critique of existing political arrangements, and they proposed an alternative mindful of the complexity of a world they recognized as being

irrevocably transformed by the industrial revolution.[25] Middle-class observers, focusing on the "tone of the ranter" which Hazlitt noticed in
Robert Owen,[26] were likely to see only the crankiness and humbug. Given
the chiliastic strain in radicalism generally—given, moreover, the array of
pseudo-political millennial sects that had most often nothing whatever to
do with rationality and responsibility—it would have been easy to dismiss all radicals (appropriating a term from the seventeenth century) as
mere antinomian "Ranters."[27]

And even more sympathetic observers usually saw only an undifferentiated collection of miscellaneous crazies, without a shred of a reasonable
political principle or plan to be found among the lot of them. Such, certainly, was the view taken by so perspicacious an observer as Carlyle.
Are the people governed? he asks in *Chartism*. Are they taught? Are they
guided? To be sure! answers Aristocracy and Church; of course they are.

Fact, in the mean while, takes his lucifer-box, sets fire to wheat-stacks; sheds an
all-too dismal light on several things. Fact searches for his third-rate potato, not
in the meekest humour, six-and-thirty weeks each year; and does not find it. Fact
passionately joins Messiah Thom of Canterbury, and has himself shot for a new
fifth-monarchy brought in by Bedlam. Fact holds his fustian-jacket *Fehmgericht* in
Glasgow City. Fact carts his Petition over London streets, begging that you would
simply have the goodness to grant him universal suffrage and "the five points,"
by way of remedy. These are not symptoms of teaching and guiding.[28]

And what are these "popular commotions and maddest bellowings" that
Carlyle indiscriminately lumps together as symptoms of how "mad and
miserable" the people are?[29] The "Captain Swing" rick-burning and
machine-breaking of 1830; the brutalized Irish sans-potato, reduced by
oppression to a virtually uncivilized condition; the 1838 outbreak of revolutionary millenarianism led by our acquaintance J. N. Thom; the strike
of the Glasgow cotton-spinners' union in 1837 ("a primary source . . .
for the follies of Simon Tappertit's 'Prentice Knights in *Barnaby Rudge*"[30]);
and Chartism itself—all these equally irrational, desperate, and pathetic
groups are merely symptoms of a wrong condition of England, and no
sensible man would consider listening to any one of them to learn how to
put that wrong condition right. Thus (and much more) Carlyle; and if so
acute an analyst formed so imperfect a judgment in 1840, it is not astonishing to find Dickens making much the same mistake, based on essentially the same assumptions, in 1841.

9

The Authority
Erected by Society for
Its Own Preservation

E arly on, we saw how the authority of the community, in the form of paternal authority, establishes a hold upon the individual, severely restricting the dark impulses of anarchic aggression ingrained in every human heart. But Dickens's representation of the restraints inseparable from the civilized condition is not confined to the merely domestic level—as how could it be? For he is acutely conscious in *Barnaby* that, as these necessary limitations of personal freedom form the very basis of the public realm, a public circumscription of aggression is a no less essential part of the foundation upon which the social order is raised.

One of the novel's key pronouncements, the following passage brings into sharp focus the public authority enforcing these fundamental restrictions. Just after describing the rioters' first real act of destruction, Dickens remarks: "Hot and drunken though they were, they had not yet broken all bounds and set all law and government at defiance. Something of their habitual deference to the authority erected by society for its own preservation yet remained among them, and had its majesty been vindicated in time"—the riots would doubtless have been nipped in the bud (51). Well, the majesty of the law was not vindicated in time, and the mob did set all law and government at defiance; but most striking about this passage is that it contains, in telegraphically condensed form, a whole political philosophy—which, unpacked, turns out to be the familiar theory of society that is so vitally important a part of *Barnaby Rudge*'s intellectual substructure. For a phrase like "the authority erected by society for its own preservation" announces the presence of that most potent and illuminating of political myths, the myth of the social contract.

In the state of nature, this myth posits, man's life was an intolerable scene of universal war. (Hobbes imagines the human condition from the very outset as a war of all against all, resulting from human nature's inborn aggressiveness, whereas Rousseau stipulates that the dismal condition "of the state of nature, where every man is at war and at the risk of his life," only gradually came into being, although it ultimately became no less universal than Hobbes's account imagines it as having been.[1]) Eager to put an end to the inconveniences of this state of war and secure "their own preservation, and . . . a more contented life"—wishing to defend themselves against "the injuries of one another" and thus provide themselves with enough security and peace "as that by their owne industrie, and by the fruites of the Earth, they may nourish themselves and live contentedly"—men joined together in mutual agreement to limit their freedom by circumscribing, in particular, their liberty of aggression.[2] But at the very moment that men thus brought society into existence, a further problem presented itself: how could any man be certain that others, when put to the test, would observe the covenant all had solemnly entered into?

To meet this difficulty, still another agency came into existence simultaneously with the creation of society, an agency Hobbes and Rousseau call the *sovereign*, though Rousseau in some contexts calls it by its modern name of the *state*. For, because "Covenants, without the sword, are but Words, and of no strength to secure a man at all," it was necessary to guarantee that men would honor the social contract by erecting "a common Power to keep them all in awe"—a power that would, if necessary, coerce them by means of physical force to abide by their agreement, punishing or indeed slaying them if they would not.[3] Rousseau sums up the institution of this "common Power" in his most celebrated paradox:

Hence, in order that the social pact shall not be an empty formula, it is tacitly implied in that commitment—which alone can give force to all others—that whoever refuses to obey the general will shall be constrained to do so by the whole body, which means nothing other than that he shall be forced to be free. . . .[4]

Or, in Hobbes's more phlegmatic formulation, "Where there is no common Power, there is no Law; where no Law, no Injustice."[5] To this "common Power" underlying "all law and government" Dickens refers by the phrase "the authority erected by society for its own preservation." And of course in *Barnaby* he, like Rousseau, understands this system to be "really nothing other than the conditions on which civil society exists."[6]

So crucial is the theme of institutionalized social authority to Dickens's conception of *Barnaby* that the novel as first projected in 1836 bore the name of the character Dickens presents as the very embodiment of that authority. And though the title *Gabriel Vardon, the Locksmith of London* was soon superseded by *Barnaby Rudge, a Tale of the Riots of 'Eighty*—though, in other words, the emphasis shifted to the principles diametrically opposed to social authority—the Locksmith of London nevertheless remained one of the heroes of the novel, to the extent that it may be said to have heroes.[7]

Gabriel Varden makes his living from society's need to keep things "bottled up and corked down" (11), the locks he makes being literal instruments of restriction, by means of which we secure ourselves against others by locking them out or, in extreme cases, locking them up. As Hobbes reminds those reluctant to acknowledge man's natural aggressiveness:

It may seem strange to some man, that has not well weighed these things; that Nature should thus dissociate, and render men apt to invade, and destroy one another: and he may therefore . . . desire perhaps to have the same confirmed by Experience. Let him therefore consider with himselfe, when taking a journey, he armes himselfe, and seeks to go well accompanied; when going to sleep, he locks his dores; when even in his house he locks his chests; and this when he knows there bee Lawes, and publike Officers, armed, to revenge all injuries shall bee done him; what opinion he has of his fellow Citizens, when he locks his dores; and of his children, and servants, when he locks his chests. Does he not there as much accuse mankind by his actions, as I do by my words?[8]

Indeed he does: for the existence of locks attests to a clear recognition of the powerful tendency in every man to "invade, and destroy" others, and it attests, at the same time, to society's determination to restrain this tendency by setting up barriers against it and confining it within bounds.

A look in at Gabriel at his anvil provides a better idea of the relationship Dickens imagines between locks and "the authority erected by society for its own preservation." It shows, too, how Dickens's faithful adherence to the political theory underlying *Barnaby* betrays him occasionally into representing social authority as a more unproblematic reality than, as is clear from the other parts of the novel, he knows it really is.

From the workshop of the Golden Key, there issued forth a tinkling sound, so merry and good-humoured, that it suggested the idea of some one working blithely, and made quite pleasant music. . . .

Tink, tink, tink—clear as a silver bell, . . . as though it said, "I don't care; nothing puts me out; I am resolved to be happy." . . .

Who but the locksmith could have made such music! A gleam of sun shining through the unsashed window . . . fell full upon him, as though attracted by his sunny heart. . . . The very locks that hung around had something jovial in their rust, and seemed like gouty gentlemen of hearty natures, disposed to joke on their infirmities. There was nothing surly or severe in the whole scene. It seemed impossible that any one of the innumerable keys could fit a churlish strong-box or a prison-door. Cellars of beer and wine, rooms where there were fires, books, gossip, and cheering laughter—these were their proper sphere of action. Places of distrust, and cruelty, and restraint, they would have left quadruple-locked forever.

Tink, tink, tink. (41)

The prose rings false as it tries to slide over conflict and contradiction with forced heartiness, acknowledging truths even while appearing to deny them. Declaring how impossible it "seemed" that any of Varden's keys could fit "churlish" strong-boxes or prison doors, Dickens is of course confessing that the opposite is the case, for locks and keys have in their essence to do with "distrust, and cruelty, and restraint." Even if Varden's keys (as Dickens tries to make believe for a moment) opened only wine cellars or rooms like the Maypole bar or Lord Mansfield's library, surely those locks, like all locks, have the straightforward purpose of securing something from invasion. Dickens knows just as well as Hobbes why we lock our doors and our chests.

But locks, this passage reminds us, have a function still more "surly" than securing strong-boxes. They also lock up jails, a circumstance Dickens makes doubly sure we will notice by reinforcing his reference to the

"prison-door" with his mention two sentences later of "[p]laces of distrust, and cruelty, and restraint"—in other words, prisons. And here we
have entered the realm of that coercive force which guarantees the social
contract. For the two instruments with which society ultimately assures
"its own preservation" are, precisely, the prison and the gallows. The laws
have teeth: if you do not observe them, the state can make you pay with
your liberty or your life. As for Gabriel Varden: what makes him not just
a locksmith of London but " *The* Locksmith of London" is that he, as Dickens later emphasizes, made *the lock on Newgate* (63), the chief prison of the
realm.

The profound, painful problem confronting Dickens in his imagination of Varden is this: being presented as the very personification of social
authority, the representative of that power which secures society's existence, the locksmith embodies what for Dickens in *Barnaby* is the greatest
good and the highest value. (And thus it is no accident that this stout artisan with his Toby mug looks like John Bull, the mythical personification of the unpretentious, commonsensical strength and social solidarity
of "free-born Englishmen.") Yet because Dickens recognizes, as Hobbes
observed, "that it is Men, and Arms, not Words, and Promises, that make
the Force and Power of the Laws"[9]—because, that is, the social authority
he so greatly values is inextricably bound up with force and violence, as
he knows—he cannot help feeling ethically uneasy about the quantum of
terror with which the essential means to so positive an end are unalterably
charged.[10]

Were Dickens systematically to think this problem through to its ultimate consequences—were he a philosopher instead of a novelist—the
logic inherent in his own premises would lead him toward the conclusions
Max Weber reached in his speech of 1918 on "Politics as a Vocation."[11]
Taking it for granted that the primary function of the state is the guaran-
teeing of the laws by coercive power, Weber throws Dickens's problem
into sharper focus by zeroing in on the special ethical difficulties posed by
the necessity of coercive power to man's collective life. So inextricably is
the state bound up with violence, in Weber's view, that "one can define the
modern state sociologically only in terms of the specific *means* peculiar to
it, as to every political association, namely, the use of physical force." A
state, then, is "a human community that (successfully) claims the *monop-
oly of the legitimate use of physical force* within a given territory." Now, if
this be the case, anyone who undertakes to act a part in man's political life
"must be willing to pay the price of using morally dubious means or at
least dangerous ones." So morally dubious are these means, indeed, that

they are unchristian. "For if it is said, in line with the acosmic ethic of love, 'Resist not him that is evil with force,' for the politician the reverse proposition holds, 'thou *shalt* resist evil by force,' or else you are responsible for the evil winning out." Moreover, what makes these means so dangerous is that if you use them, you must face "the possibility or even the probability of evil ramifications." This is an old, old insight: "the early Christians knew full well the world is governed by demons and that he who lets himself in for politics, that is, for power and force as means, contracts with diabolical powers and for his actions it is *not* true that good can follow only from good and evil only from evil, but that often the opposite is true." [12] Your actions, aiming to compass a laudable end, may nevertheless have evil consequences, for which, if your life is to rise to the level of ethical significance, you must accept the responsibility.

Were there no evil to resist with force, then the ethic of turning the other cheek—the ethic of the Sermon on the Mount—would be a practicable as well as a holy one; but the whole existence of society is based on nothing other than the resisting of evil with force. Yet, even so, by what possible *right* can one take it upon oneself to act in violation of the absolute imperatives of the Christian ethic?

At the heart of Weber's speech lies the insight that, in considering the relations between ethics and politics, we enter a realm in which "ultimate *Weltanschauungen* clash, world views among which in the end one has to make a choice." [13] The confrontation Weber explicitly identifies is between two mutually contradictory ethical systems—respectively labeled the "ethic of ultimate ends" and the "ethic of responsibility"—both of which claim to be absolute. The content of these ethical systems need not concern us here; for our present purposes what is important is that behind this conflict lies another, more fundamental conflict between mutually opposed realms of value—a conflict of which the opposition between the "ethic of ultimate ends" and the "ethic of responsibility" is only a subcategory. This more fundamental conflict, which Weber makes only partly explicit but whose existence clearly is the primary assumption on which his essay is based, is the opposition between (on the one hand) those ethical systems that locate the ultimate source of value in the human community and (on the other hand) those ethical systems, such as Christianity, whose ultimate source of value is in some sense other-worldly—between, in the eloquent language of Isaiah Berlin,

Stoic, or Christian or Kantian or even some types of utilitarian ethics, where the source and criterion of value are the word of God, or eternal reason, or some

inner sense or knowledge of good and evil, of right and wrong, voices which
speak directly to individual consciousness with absolute authority . . .

and (on the other hand)

an equally time-honoured ethics, that of the Greek *polis*, of which Aristotle provided the clearest exposition. Since men are beings made by nature to live in communities, their communal purposes are the ultimate values from which the rest
are derived, or with which their ends as individuals are identified. Politics—the
art of living in a *polis*—is not an activity which can be dispensed with by those
who prefer private life: it is not like seafaring or sculpture which those who do
not wish to do so need not undertake.

There is irreconcilable opposition, in other words, between Christian
ethics and "another system, another moral universe—the world of Peri-
cles or of Scipio, . . . a society geared to ends just as ultimate as the
Christian faith, a society in which men fight and are ready to die for
(public) ends which they pursue for their own sakes." This is not a conflict between "a realm of means (called politics) as opposed to a realm of
ends (called morals)." It is instead a conflict between two moralities—two
"alternative realm[s] of ends." [14]
    Returning, after this rather fancy excursus, to plain Gabriel Varden in
his workshop, we can see that what Dickens faces at this moment in the
novel is truly a dilemma. At the very time he is in process of establishing
Gabriel as his representative of public authority, he half-covertly confesses that this authority is founded on force and violence; and he uneasily
senses that the very existence of social authority, because of its insep-
arability from violence, presupposes a constant infringement of Christianity's most fundamental precepts. And this is not all. For in this scene,
Dickens, who throughout *Barnaby* has been imagining the civilized condition as man's highest good, is uncomfortably close to the recognition
not just that the *means* specific to man's communal life require constant
violation of Christian principles, but also that the end in whose service
these means are employed constitutes a realm of value no less ultimate
than Christianity. "The genius or demon of politics lives in an inner tension with the god of love, as well as with the Christian God as expressed
by the church," Max Weber observed. "This tension can at any time lead
to an irreconcilable conflict." [15] Of course this conflict, when recognized,
has often enough in history been rationalized away (most notably by Saint
Augustine, for example, or by Calvin) by asserting that such guilty means

are appropriate to man's fallen state in a fallen world: what can one expect in so tainted a realm as the City of Man? But Dickens's commitment to the City of Man will not permit him this equivocation. He faces what he can see of this conflict as manfully as he can. There is certainly falsification here—the "jolly locks" are reminiscent of the Cheeryble ledgers in *Nicholas Nickleby*. But what is false at this moment is chiefly Dickens's tone, not his thought.

One might think that Gabriel's trade as a locksmith and his position as one of that class of "masters" about whom the 'Prentice Knights are always complaining would be enough to establish him unequivocally as *Barnaby Rudge*'s personification of public authority. But it is not enough for Dickens, who, as soon as he is finished describing the "jolly locks," goes on to tell us that Varden is also "a serjeant in the Royal East London Volunteers." In fact, he is standing at his anvil in his militia uniform, because he is about to take part in practice maneuvers, joining the other Volunteers in displaying "their military prowess to the utmost in these warlike shows" (42).

Gabriel, harumphs the astringent Mrs. Varden, was foolish ever to have volunteered for the militia. The locksmith protests against her attitude:

". . . I mean, how strange it is of you to run down volunteering, when it's done to defend you and all the other women, and our own fireside and everybody else's, in case of need."

"It's unchristian," cried Mrs. Varden, shaking her head.

"Unchristian!" said the locksmith. "Why, what the devil— . . . what on earth do you call it unchristian for? Which would be most unchristian, Martha—to sit quietly down and let our houses be sacked by a foreign army, or to turn out like men and drive 'em off? Shouldn't I be a nice sort of a Christian, if I crept into a corner of my own chimney and looked on while a parcel of whiskered savages bore off Dolly—or you—? . . . Well, that would be the state of things directly. Even Miggs would go. Some black tambourine-player, with a great turban on, would be bearing *her* off. . . ." (41)

The first of Dickens's unquestioned assumptions in this very funny passage is that men really do have a strong tendency "to invade, and destroy one another," seeing in their neighbor "someone who tempts them to satisfy their aggressiveness on him, . . . to use him sexually without his consent, to seize his possessions, to humiliate him, to cause him pain, to torture and to kill him." [16] It is the function of society, this passage also takes for granted, to protect us against such dangers from within or without—as Gabriel Varden does, making locks while dressed in his militia uniform.

If, like Mrs. Varden, you are an extremist about your Christianity, then of course to resist evil with force is "unchristian." But if Dickens, in so gingerly associating Varden with prisons, sees for a moment a conflict between the imperatives of civilized life and certain fundamental Christian precepts which he values, he has no such problem when the legitimate violence of the state is to be directed against foreign invaders, and *savage* ones at that. Scruples here would be misplaced—would be unmanly— would be mere fanaticism. Thus, while the jocular tone, and the vision of the inflexible Miggs carried off "kicking and scratching" by "a pagan negro," go a long way toward deflating the seriousness of the issues this passage raises, Dickens is setting the tone and content at variance here not because he would prefer not to have to face what his insight insistently shows him to be true (as was the case in the passage describing Gabriel at his anvil), but rather because he wants to play down certain grim realities, which, however, he is quite capable of gazing at with perfect steadiness and equanimity. Hence, too, the festive atmosphere of the militia maneuvers themselves in Chapter 42: Dickens knows what stern facts lie at the heart of all this, but his concern at this moment is to present public authority in as bright and rosy a light as possible.

Now, if we want to know how public authority should respond when people "set all law and government at defiance" and threaten to annihilate "all that [is] good and peaceful in society" (45)—if, in other words, we want to see how authority should perform the function it was called into existence to perform—we have only to watch Gabriel Varden in action, for Dickens's representation of him as the embodiment of such authority has a practical as well as a theoretical aspect. Gabriel, we saw, declares himself ready to stand and fight to protect his home against a foreign army. Well, when the Gordon Riots raged, it was, says Dickens, "as if the city were invaded by a foreign army" (50), and the rioters do indeed carry away Gabriel's daughter, on whom they have sexual designs. And then in the midst of the riots, the mob comes to kidnap Varden himself, to force him to pick the lock on Newgate, which he has made. True to his word, he tries to stand and fight, to resist evil with force: he holds them off at gunpoint. But because Miggs announces to the crowd that she has "poured a mug of table-beer right down the barrel" of his weapon, his resistance— almost the first offered to the rioters in their headlong career—is quickly overcome (63). Forcibly hurried away to the prison walls, Gabriel—again dressed in his militia uniform—resists still again, categorically refusing to do the mob's bidding and calling upon the governor of the prison, who is watching the whole scene from the roof of his house, to "[b]ear witness for me . . . that I refuse to do it; and that I will not do it, come what may of my refusal. If any violence is done to me, please remember this" (64).

"Is there no way of helping you?" the governor asks.

"None, Mr. Akerman," Gabriel replies, "You'll do your duty, and I'll do mine."

But, urges the governor, there are extenuating circumstances. If you are forced to comply with lawlessness at peril of your life, then, perhaps, you have "ample excuse for yielding." Gabriel, however—"an old man, quite alone," in the midst of the "furious multitude who beset and hemmed him in, on every side"—repeats that he will *not* yield, and cries to the prison governor to "Keep 'em out, in King George's name."

He had never loved his life so well as then, but nothing could move him. The savage faces that glared at him, look where he would; the cries of those who thirsted, like wild animals, for his blood; the sight of men pressing forward, and trampling down their fellows, as they strove to reach him, and struck at him above the heads of other men, with axes and with iron bars; all failed to daunt him. He looked from man to man, and face to face, and still, with quickened breath and lessening colour, cried firmly, "I will not!"

Here Dickens is using the locksmith in two related but distinct capacities. Insofar as Gabriel personifies the public, institutionalized social authority of the state, Dickens demonstrates through him his belief that no extenuating circumstances can excuse the state from resisting such an assault. Yet Gabriel is not imagined just as the personification of an institution but also as a flesh-and-blood individual citizen, plentifully endowed with the civic virtues; and, in that capacity, he demonstrates to us the kind of civil courage required even from a "private" individual, who always faces the possibility of having to give his life to preserve the community.

·   ·   ·

Gabriel shows us that social authority *must* resist such evil; but, as he is only one individual man, his resistance to the mob must be essentially passive, whereas the resistance the state is called upon to offer must be active, supressing anarchy with the violence it has legitimately at its disposal. This is just what the duly constituted public officers failed to do in the Gordon Riots, and Dickens contemptuously takes them to task in *Barnaby* for their shameful pusillanimity, so very different from Gabriel's civil courage. Dickens would certainly have agreed with Thomas Hol-

croft's imputation that the magistrates were for a time "disgracefully stu-
pified" with "consternation." [17] Indeed, *Barnaby Rudge* presents the chief
magistrate of London—the Lord Mayor himself (who in real life, inci-
dentally, had risen to prominence on the success of his profitable whore-
houses)—as the very personification of cowardly moral impotence.
Begged by Mr. Langdale the distiller, whose house has been " threatened
with destruction," to provide him with "the benefit of the laws" by sending a force to protect his property, this gentleman refused to act, notwithstanding the vintner's reminding him that "the chief magistrate of the city
can prevent people's houses from having any need to be rebuilt, if the
chief magistrate's a man, and not a dummy." But this Lord Mayor *is* a
dummy, unmindful alike of his power and his duty. "I'm sure I don't
know what's to be done, . . ." he whimpers. "Oh dear me, what a thing
it is to be a public character!" (61).

In Dickens's mind there is no doubt at all "what's to be done": the riots
would never have reached such an extreme of chaos had the "authority
erected by society for its own preservation" been "vindicated in time."
The mob could have been stopped in its tracks at the very beginning of
the disturbances.

Fifty resolute men might have turned them at any moment; a single company of
soldiers could have scattered them like dust; but no man interposed, no authority
restrained them, and, except by the terrified persons who fled from their approach, they were as little heeded as if they were pursuing their lawful occupa-
tions with the utmost sobriety and good conduct. (52)

The soldiers themselves were perfectly ready to do their duty. All that
was required, a bluff, honest sergeant tells Joe Willet, is "the needful authority, and half-a-dozen rounds of ball cartridge" (58). But, the sergeant
bitterly complains, "the needful authority" was just what the civil magistrates refused to give. As a contemporary observer (with staunch Tory
sympathies) remarked, "The Nero of the Mansion-house is said to have
calmly smoked his pipe while Rome was burning." [18]

In other words, what permitted the Gordon Riots to reach such an extreme of ferocity and helped make them what Dickens's contemporary,
G. L. Craik, believed to be "the most dreadful riots London ever saw," [19]
was the resounding failure of public authority to perform precisely the
one specific function it was called into existence to perform. This, according to *Barnaby Rudge*'s political theory, is a blatantly obvious conclusion. If you subscribe to this theory, you start with the unsavory impulses
at the heart of human nature, which it is civilization's primary function to

repress. You know that civilization does not extinguish these impulses but only banishes them underground, standing guard over them while always recognizing their inherent tendency to burst out from their subterranean bondage. Then, following this same logic, you recognize, first, that men have an ineradicable propensity to return to the condition from which civilization seeks to deliver them; second, that it is the *unremitting* pressure of civilization that prevents them from doing so; and, third, that if people begin collectively to give themselves over to their primitive impulses—as, in the nature of things, is bound to happen from time to time—and if the appropriate officers of "the authority erected by society for its own preservation" fail to offer the necessary resistance, then the first regression will lead to a further and a further, until at last citizens will grow feral in just such a wholesale way as they do in the Gordon Riots.[20]

A man who believes this theory does not find himself perplexed when faced with a mob outbreak like this; he knows at once that the strongest measures on the part of the civil authorities are required without loss of time. Dickens, who would hardly be sympathetic to the *laissez-faire* principles of a utilitarian Useful Knowledge Diffusionist like Craik, is nevertheless perfectly in accord with him in condemning the protracted indecisiveness of the civil authorities during so many of those dreadful June days of 1780. In Craik's view, "passions more dangerous to society than those which instigated these furious and reckless rioters cannot be named or imagined. They were such as could not be allowed to rage uncontrolled without all society being quickly torn in pieces." "These men were, in fact, openly making war upon society." In such a case, when observers

express a silly or affected horror at the adoption of energetic measures against a mob at the commencement of its career of outrage, they are in reality objecting to the only humane course to be followed. The tumult must be met and suppressed at one stage or another; if not resisted with decision at first, it will spread and become more terrible every moment; not only will the devastation committed by the rioters be prodigiously augmented, but their numbers will rapidly grow more formidable, their phrenzy more inflamed, their courage more bold, reckless, and desperate, and their strength in every way more obstinate and difficult to be subdued. Yet, after all, subdued they must be. . . . The military execution, which earlier applied, would have cost but a few lives, is now a protracted and widespread carnage.[21]

Exactly this is Dickens's view of the case. The Government waited until the very last moment, waited until it was absolutely "driven to the exercise of the extreme prerogatives of the Crown": only when it was almost too late did the authorities take decisive action by "giving to the military, discretionary and unlimited power in the suppression of the riots" (66). But by that time, of course, things had reached such a pass that it looked "as though the last day had come and the whole universe were burning" (68); and, after the troops had gone to work in earnest, it was found when the smoke had cleared (according to a note Dickens pencilled into the margin of his copy of Holcroft's *Narrative*) that there were "Seven hundred shot besides wounded."[22] Had action been taken sooner, there need have been none.

.　　.　　.

Failure to perform its proper role in a moment of need is not the only malfunction to which institutionalized social authority is liable in *Barnaby*. For the stupefied Lord Mayor's completing counterpart—his brother, the country magistrate, whose single appearance in the novel (47) is as vivid as the nightmare that wakes you up—makes manifest the no less alarming danger presented by public authority's improper and excessive operation. Certainly this latter example makes it hard to disagree with Gabriel Varden's contention that "all good things perverted to evil purposes, are worse than those which are naturally bad" (51).

It will be remembered that John Willet, in his oppression of his son Joe, conducted himself "in his small way with as much high mightiness and majesty, as the most glorious tyrant that ever had his statue reared in the public ways, of ancient or of modern times." Public officers, this passage reminds us, do indeed become "tyrants" often enough; and they are always surrounded by men who will urge them on "to the abuse of power (when they need urging, which is not often)" (30).

Our country magistrate needs no such urging. Mrs. Rudge and Barnaby, fleeing from their rural refuge after Stagg and Mr. Rudge have discovered it, have the misfortune on their journey of attracting this functionary's notice, whose first impulse, the moment he lays eyes on them, is to have them whipped and jailed as beggars and vagrants. Being informed by Mrs. Rudge "that her son was of weak mind," he thunders,

"I don't believe it. . . . It's an excuse not to work. There's nothing like flogging to cure that disorder. I'd make a difference in him in ten minutes, I'll be bound."

"Heaven had made none in more than twice ten years, sir," said the widow mildly.

"Then why don't you shut him up? We pay enough for county institutions, damn 'em. But thou'd rather drag him about to excite charity—of course. Ay, I know thee."

At length deciding he wants to buy Grip, though his wife suggests that perhaps Mrs. Rudge and Barnaby "prefer to keep him," the magistrate snorts in disbelief,

Prefer to keep him! . . . These people, who go tramping about the country, a pilfering and vagabondizing on all hands, prefer to keep a bird, when a landed proprietor and a justice asks his price! . . . If my clerk was here, I'd set ye [Mrs. Rudge and Barnaby] in the stocks, I would, or lay ye in jail for prowling up and down, on the look-out for petty larcenies. (47)

This same magistrate turns up by chance in court at Barnaby's trial, along "with other country justices, into whose very dense heads curiosity had penetrated" (as Mr. Chester reports); and it is he who seals Barnaby's doom by volunteering the testimony that Barnaby "had, to his knowledge, wandered about the country with a vagabond parent, avowing revolutionary and rebellious sentiments" (75).

Perhaps it should be a source of comfort in a world of flux and change that the self-important insolence of office brayed itself forth generations ago in the identical tones in which it brays itself forth today. In any event, watching this public official in action we are emphatically reminded that, while in the best of all possible worlds the citizens would be sovereign and the will of the sovereign could not but be identical with the will of the people, in the world Dickens is describing, it is not true that the governors are identical with the governed. Nor are men ruled entirely by laws but, as Hobbes insisted, "by them he fears, and beleeves can kill or hurt him when he obeyeth not." No one "beleeves the Law can hurt him; that is, Words, and Paper, without the Hands, and Swords of Men." [23] We are reminded, in other words, that when human beings created society they created as well a system of men dominating men—a system which, to be sure, guarantees the social contract, but which, in conferring on some men legitimate power over their fellows, provides its own opportunities for oppression and tyranny of many varieties, grand and petty alike.

This bullying magistrate, "a landed proprietor and a justice," reminds us how the division of society into rulers and ruled has so regularly taken the form of the oppression by the rich and powerful of the poor and weak. The angry incredulity with which he meets Mrs. Rudge's declaration that he cannot buy Grip reminds us that if society, as was so often claimed from the seventeenth century onward by critics and apologists alike, was a vast engine for the preservation of property, the property in question was that of the rich not the poor. It is at least conceivable, Dickens encourages us to remark in protest against this man's swollen insolence, that the poor did not get to be poor out of an unceasing search for "an excuse not to work" but rather are casualties of the predations of the rich, who in any event have taken it upon themselves to treat poverty as a crime and poor people as criminals. Thus the poor cannot be "travellers" but only "vagrants and vagabonds," forbidden "to roam about this place" (47), because their purpose can only be thievery, unless of course they are looking "to excite charity," to which, it goes without saying, they are not entitled. And should they hint that they have certain rights, not to be abridged even by "a landed proprietor and a justice"—why, these are nothing but "revolutionary and rebellious sentiments," for which hanging is an appropriate remedy.

The portrait Dickens sketches of this country justice suggests how readily public authority, in the hands of benighted men, may become an instrument of oppression.

Now, this gentleman had various endearing appellations among his intimate friends. By some he was called "a country gentleman of the true school," by some "a fine old country gentleman," by some "a sporting gentleman," by some "a thorough-bred Englishman," by some "a genuine John Bull;" but they all agreed . . . that it was a pity there were not more like him, and that because there were not, the country was going to rack and ruin every day. He was in the commission of the peace, and could write his name almost legibly; but his greatest qualifications were, that he was more severe with poachers, was a better shot, a harder rider, had better horses, kept better dogs, could eat more solid food, drink more strong wine, go to bed every night more drunk and get up every morning more sober, than any man in the county. . . . He had no seat in Parliament himself, but he was extremely patriotic, and usually drove his voters to the poll with his own hands. He was warmly attached to the church, and never appointed to the living in his gift any but a three-bottle man and a first-rate fox-hunter. He mistrusted the honesty of all poor people who could read and write, and had a secret jealousy of his own wife . . . for possessing those accomplishments in a greater degree than himself. In short, Barnaby being an idiot, and Grip a creature of mere brute instinct, it would be very hard to say what this gentleman was. (47)

This judgment is unequivocal enough: if this is what is meant by "a thorough-bred Englishman" or "a fine old country gentleman," then, as Mrs. Rudge reflects, "possibly the terms were sometimes misappropriated, not to say disgraced" (47).

Dickens draws a portrait here not just of an individual but of a class, against which he bitterly railed in his political squib of 1841 called "The Fine Old English Gentleman, to be said or sung at all conservative dinners."[24] These backwoods Tory squires are the representatives of public authority in districts from one end of the realm to the other, and in their coarse hands public authority turns brutal. As the glimpse of this country justice driving "his" voters to the polls reminds us, they preside over a corrupt electoral system (reformed in 1832, of course) which disgraces what should be the most august social institution in the land. By filling the pulpits with hard-drinking sportsmen, they have blunted the moral force of society's primary ethical institution. This segment of the ruling class sees its main function as Preserving its Game, as Carlyle jeered in *Chartism*; and men who exercise the authority of the state to enforce laws as unjust and nonsensical as the game laws will also favor severity in punishing offenders while opposing the diffusion of education, by which alone their numbers might be diminished. Invincibly ignorant, barbaric in his pastimes, our country justice resembles, in his stable knowledge and his gross appetites, no one so much as Hugh the satyr: in him, in other words, we glimpse the possibility of a social authority so debased as to be in certain respects little better than the savage counterprinciple it is supposed to civilize. Such a degradation in Dickens's view is by no means inevitable but rather an aberration to be censured with utmost vigor. Yet it is an aberration to be met with often enough; and Dickens—who did not need a Matthew Arnold to tell him about ruling-class barbarians—also knew that rulers like this will rule in an inhumane and barbarous way.

Now, this country magistrate is hardly the sole "functionary of the law" in *Barnaby* who embodies the improper, excessive use of public authority. We have only to remind ourselves that, in tying up the loose ends in the novel's last chapter, Dickens disposes of the *pogromshchik* Gashford by enrolling him as one of the "wretched underlings" in "the honourable corps of spies and eaves-droppers employed by the Government"—and employed often enough, as Dickens goes out of his way to mention is Gashford's case, in that network of *domestic* spies, informers, and *agents-provocateurs* which formed an even worse blot than usual on the conduct of English politics between 1780 and 1830, exactly the period of Gashford's service. As Dickens elsewhere jeered, in the age of Pitt

> every English peasant had his good old English spies,
> To tempt his starving discontent with fine old English lies,
> Then call the good old Yeomanry to stop his peevish cries,
> In the fine old English Tory times;
> Soon may they come again![25]

Or consider Miggs, who after the riots "turned very sharp and sour" and became the "female turnkey for the County Bridewell," which office "she held until her decease, more than thirty years afterwards, remaining single all that time." And how does this rigid lady (whom, it will be remembered, sexual frustration has made angry and resentful in the extreme) exercise her constitutional office? It was observed of her

that while she was inflexible and grim to all her female flock, she was particularly so to those who could establish any claim to beauty: and it was often remarked as a proof of her indomitable virtue and severe chastity, that to such as had been frail she showed no mercy; always falling upon them on the slightest occasion, or on no occasion at all, with the fullest measure of her wrath.

Miggs transforms the legitimate authority of the state into an instrument of her own aggressiveness, sharpened by envy to the keenest of edges. Precisely such an abuse of power is a constant temptation, not only because in such circumstances it is easy to satisfy one's own aggression, but also because such an indulgence is often mistaken, even by the person guilty of it, for zealous virtue. "Private vengeance," as we found with Sim Tappertit (and will find with Dennis the hangman), is not hard to disguise as "public sentiment" (24)—hence we find in the history of public authority numberless grim accounts of what "man has . . . done to man in the horrible caprice of power and cruelty" (65). Nor is this the only way Miggs suggests the danger of authority improperly used, for her special harshness to those of her charges who are manifestly sexual reminds us that social authority on the public scale may be as life-denying as it has a tendency to be on the domestic scale, seeking not merely to restrain the natural impulses but to oppose them implacably.

But Miggs, Gashford, and even the country justice are triflers compared to Dennis the hangman, far and away the worst of *Barnaby's* sordid, brutal "constitutional" officers. In Dennis—at once the embodiment of public authority and pure, ferocious aggression—Dickens confronts us starkly with how literally "the authority erected by society for its own preservation" is grounded on the same violence from which it is intended to preserve us. He asks us to consider, in disquieting detail, the deadly potentialities of a medicine which is to this extent identical to the malady it is supposed to cure, and which, moreover, though effective when administered with circumspection, keeps getting prescribed in massive and lethal doses.

Dickens depicts Dennis—who, you remember, shouts the novel's slogan of universal aggressiveness, "Down with everybody, down with everything!" (38)—as, almost literally, a monster of aggression:

a squat, thickset personage, with a low retreating forehead, a coarse shock head of hair, and eyes so small and near together, that his broken nose alone seemed to prevent their meeting and fusing into one of the usual size. A dingy handkerchief twisted like a cord about his neck, left its great veins exposed to view, and they were swoln and starting, as though with gulping down strong passions, malice, and ill-will. (37)

This ape-like creature seems ready to burst with aggression, and the detail about his eyes puts us in mind of those one-eyed ogres in fairy tales, or of that colossus of violence, the one-eyed Polyphemus, who like his brother cyclopes "devoured human beings and cared naught for Zeus."[26] Moreover, in the "knotted stick" he always carries, "the knob of which was carved into a rough likeness of his own vile face," he and his weapon, which he shakes "with a ferocious air" and which suggests the wild man's or ogre's traditional club, become extensions of each other in a highly menacing interfusion.

For his violent vocation, Dennis has "a true professional relish." He literally loves to hang people or to "work them off," as he terms it, and when he sees a neck well suited "for stretching," he ogles it "with a horrible kind of admiration, such as that with which a cannibal might regard his intimate friend, when hungry" (38). He cannot keep himself from fondling Hugh's handsome throat (39), and during the sack of the Maypole he has to be restrained from "working off" Mr. Willet, which he urges would "be better for all parties" and "would read uncommon well in the newspapers" (54). He takes great pride in "the helegant bits of work" he "has turned off," boasting that he does his job "with a neatness and dex-terity, never known afore." When Sim, trying to guess his trade, asks, "Was you 'prenticed to it?" Dennis replies, with more profound truthfulness than he intends, "No. Natural genius. . . . No 'prenticing. It comes by natur'" (39). Assuredly it does, for "natur'" contains just such violent aggression as it is Dennis's legitimate function to exercise.

The hangman is proud not only that he is "a constitutional officer that works for my living, and does my work creditable," but also that his work is "sound, Protestant, constitutional, English work," which no man alive can doubt—"Nor dead neither" (37). Indeed, quite as fervid a lover of the Constitution as the 'Prentice Knights, and even more dedicated a constitutional theorist than Sim Tappertit—who interprets "that

same Constitution (which was kept in a strong-box somewhere, but
where exactly he could not find out, or he would have endeavoured to
procure a copy of it)" as a guarantee of an Englishman's freedom of aggression (8)—Dennis professes a lunatic political philosophy, whose outrageous humor derives from the fact that it is a grotesque, macabre parody of the fundamental theoretical assumptions on which *Barnaby Rudge*
as a whole is based.

For example: explaining his reasons for supporting the Protestant Association, Dennis remarks, "If these Papists gets into power, and begins
to boil and roast instead of hang, what becomes of my work! If they touch
my work that's a part of so many laws, what becomes of the laws in general, what becomes of the religion, what becomes of the country!" (37).
Now Dickens, we know, is well aware that the social contract is ultimately
guaranteed by the violence at the disposal of the state; society in this sense
does depend upon force. But for Dennis, hanging—not just any variety
of force available to the state (such as imprisonment) but rather the most
extreme form of the power that authenticates the laws, and not just any
kind of capital punishment but only sound Protestant hanging—*is* the
constitution. The gallows, in his bloodthirsty mind, are not just an instrument of the constitution: they are the *whole* constitution. Dennis,
therefore, joins the rioters, "take[s] up arms and resort[s] to deeds of violence, with the great main object of preserving the Old Bailey in all its
purity, and the gallows in all its pristine usefulness and moral grandeur"
(70); and he later turns against his associates when they insist upon releas-
ing, along with all the other Newgate inmates, also the four prisoners
condemned to be hanged by him in his professional capacity. "Don't you
respect the law—the constitootion—nothing?" (65) he demands of
Hugh, as the centaur determinedly leads the rioters into the condemned
cells. But because, by refusing to "leave these here four men to me" (65),
Hugh has failed to "respect the soundest constitootional principles, you
know," and has "wiolated the wery frame-work of society" (69), Dennis
vindicates the gallows' "moral grandeur" by betraying his late comrade to
the soldiers.

Having thus turned his coat, however, he wonders if he has not made a
mistake when, a moment later, he sees the soldiers shoot an escaping
rioter, who, if captured alive, would surely have been sentenced to hang:

Look at this man. Do you call *this* constitootional? Do you see him shot through
and through instead of being worked off like a Briton? Damme, if I know which
party to side with. You're as bad as the other. What's to become of the country if

the military power's to go a superseding the ciwilians in this way? Where's this
poor fellow-creetur's rights as a citizen, that he didn't have *me* in his last moments!
I was here. I was willing. I was ready. These are nice times, brother, to have the
dead crying out against us in this way, and sleep comfortably in our beds arter-
wards; wery nice! (69)

To his prejudiced eye, it is as if capital punishment were the sole function
of the state, and a citizen's prime political right his right to be hanged.

Insofar as capital punishment is the ultimate sanction of "the authority
erected by society for its own preservation," the execution of men who
have broken the social treaty is, in a profoundly somber sense, a thoroughly social circumstance. But of course capital punishment affirms society by an act of negation; like any exercise of the legitimate violence at
the disposal of the state, it delineates the realm of the social by showing
what the social is not. In Dennis's mind, this complex reality undergoes a
series of distortions, resolving itself at last into a zany conviction that
hanging is an eminently *sociable* activity, a positive celebration of society,
one of those great public festivals in which the whole of man's social existence is reconsecrated. Thus it is right that he, the hangman, representing
the fraternity of all mankind, should call everybody (as he does indiscriminately) "brother"; and it is fitting that he, officiating at this rite,
should boast with genial self-congratulation, "I rather like company. I
was formed for society, I was" (74). The last sentence, with its rather
ghoulish double meaning, epitomizes Dennis's dizzy parody of Dickens's
political theory: the hangman, in that he administers the state's legitimate
violence, performs, as Dickens and Dennis would agree, an essential social function; therefore (as Dennis alone concludes) I, the hangman, am
an exceptionally sociable man.

As for the hanged, how should they feel? Well, Dennis evidently gives
no credence to that familiar notion, lucidly expressed by Rousseau, that a
condemned criminal is put to death "less as a citizen than as an enemy"
who is "no longer a member of the state."[27] On the contrary: in his view
hanging is so quintessentially sociable that it is sociable even for the
hanged. In this spirit, and "with the air of a pastor in familiar conversation with his flock," Dennis advises the four condemned men in Newgate
not to strain their voices, for

you'll only be hoarse when you come to the speeches,—which is a pity. What I
say in respect to the speeches always is, "Give it mouth." That's my maxim. Give
it mouth. . . . I've heard a eloquence on them boards—you know what boards I

mean—and have heerd a degree of mouth given to them speeches, that they was as clear as a bell, and as good as a play. . . . And always, when a thing of this nature's to come off, what I stand up for, is, a proper frame of mind. Let's have a proper frame of mind, and we can go through with it, creditable—pleasant—sociable. (65)

Dennis's conjunction of hanging and art gives Dickens's parody of his own most basic assumptions in *Barnaby Rudge* one further, outrageous twist. The most profound of *Barnaby*'s central insights is that it is in the nature of civilization to retailor human nature—to transform the nature of the self and, in so doing, to confer upon it its full humanity. For Dickens as for Rousseau the program of civilization is "to transform each individual, who by himself is entirely complete and solitary, into a part of a much greater whole, from which the same individual will then receive, in a sense, his life and his being," gaining thereby "a moral and communal existence."[28] It is true that the violence at the disposal of the state plays its part in this extraordinary transformation—but how does all this come out in Dennis's political philosophy? Well, according to him, *hanging* is the great transformation civilization works on human nature, which, to be sure, it transforms pretty radically. "You're a kind of artist, I suppose—eh!" asks Sim Tappertit, still trying to guess Dennis's profession. "Yes," Dennis replies; "Yes—I may call myself a artist—a fancy workman—art improves natur'—that's my motto" (39).

If in his presentation of Gabriel Varden Dickens strove to play down the harsh reality latent in "the authority erected by society for its own preservation," no such diffidence restrains him in painting the hangman, in whom the violence that is the irreducible kernel of state authority is made manifest in all its ugly actuality, clearly revealing what makes Dickens so uneasy. For when "this functionary of the law" (65) vows that "'In support of the great Protestant principle of having plenty of [hanging], I'll,' and here he beat his club upon the ground, 'burn, fight, kill—do anything you bid me, so that it's bold and devilish—though the end of it was, that I got hung myself'" (37)—and when, indeed, the hangman becomes, along with the wild man and the idiot, one of the principal leaders of the riots—the point Dickens is dramatizing is that the violence authenticating "all law and all government" is identical to the violence from which "the authority erected by society for its own preservation" was instituted to preserve us, and if social authority is stripped down to this its ultimate instrument it becomes as brutal as the brutality it was instituted to humanize.[29]

What makes Dennis so scary is that his crazy views are not really so idiosyncratic. In fact, at the time of the riots, Dickens reports, it was virtually a universally accepted principle that "the symbol of [the law's] dignity,—stamped upon every page of the criminal statute-book, was the gallows . . ." (76); and *Barnaby Rudge* presents Dennis as not substantially exaggerating the truth

[w]hen he remembered the great estimation in which his office was held, and the constant demand for his services; when he bethought himself, how the Statu[t]e Book regarded him as a kind of Universal Medicine applicable to men, women, and children, of every age and variety of criminal constitution; and how high he stood, in his official capacity, in the favour of the Crown, and both Houses of Parliament, the Mint, the Bank of England, and the Judges of the land; when he recollected that whatever ministry was in or out, he remained their particular pet and panacea, and that for his sake England stood single and conspicuous among the civilized nations of the earth. (74)

He is by no means alone in believing that, "That being the law and practice of England, is the glory of England" (37). Such, indeed, is the accepted wisdom of "the good old school" in which he, like the country magistrate, "had been bred and nurtured" (65); and John Willet, another distinguished graduate of that same school, has likewise learned there the prescribed lesson that "it's a blessed thing to think how many people are hung in batches every six weeks. . . , as showing how wide awake our government is" (11). Matters had not quite reached the extreme implied by Mr. Chester's notion that "insane creatures make such very odd and embarrassing remarks, that they really ought to be hanged, for the comfort of society" (75); but clearly a society that has, according to Dennis, fifty or so "hanging laws" (37), mandating the death penalty (as Dickens reported in 1846)[30] for one hundred and sixty crimes, has come uncomfortably close to embodying Dennis's theory that the gallows is the constitution.

Through John Willet in particular, "who grew so despotic and so great, that his thirst for conquest knew no bounds" (30), Dickens demonstrates how in the personal realm social authority tends toward excess, demanding a renunciation of freedom so far in excess of the necessary limitation of impulse as to be life-denying. The example of Dennis, and the world's willingness to regard him as a Universal Medicine, suggests an analogous tendency in the public realm. There, social authority can reduce itself to the violence on which it is founded—which, like violence in general, tends to grow with what it feeds on, until at last it threatens the very citizens it was instituted to protect.

Such, certainly, was the fate that befell Mary Jones, "a young woman of nineteen who come up to Tyburn with a infant at her breast," as Dennis reports,

and was worked off for taking a piece of cloth off the counter of a shop in Ludgate-hill, and putting it down again when the shopman see her; and who had never done any harm before, and only tried to do that, in consequence of her husband having been pressed three weeks previous, and she being left to beg, with two young children—as was proved upon the trial. Ha ha! (37)

Here, truly, the end is eaten up by the means. In order to maintain that great instrument of legitimate coercive force, the Royal Navy, the state has forcibly coerced Mr. Jones to leave his wife and children. This turns out to be his wife's death sentence: deprived of her means of support and choosing not to let her children starve, she in desperation almost commits a theft, for which she is hanged—not imprisoned or transported, but hanged—as a criminal, something she assuredly is not. And why, ultimately, has Mr. Jones been conscripted? To protect, as we know from Gabriel Varden's speech on the militia, his hearth, his wife, and his children—all now lost. And lost along with Mary Jones, as goes without saying, are also justice and right, devoured by that coercive force erected to safeguard them.[31]

Now, if your response to the need of people to be governed is simply to provide a gallows, you will have brutal society. Capital punishment, so horrifying an exercise of violence and cruelty, is brutalizing to the whole community, and the excess with which it was dealt out in the later eighteenth century multiplied that evil many times over. That it brutalizes its victims goes without saying: describing how the arrival of the moment of their execution had reduced Hugh to "the dogged desperation of a savage at the stake" and Dennis to "such an extreme of abject cowardice that it was humiliating to see him," Dickens remarks that "these were the two commonest states of mind in persons brought to their pass" (76). And "the frequent exhibition of this last dread punishment, of Death" also "hardens the minds of those who deal it out, and makes them, though they be amiable men in other respects, indifferent to, or unconscious of, their great responsibility" (76). If amiable men are thus hardened, brutal men are made more brutal: Forster judges that Dennis has "become the mass of moral filth he is" through "constant contact with the filthiest instrument of law and state."[32] Such brutalization breeds an increasingly brutal administration of justice.

Along with the functionaries of the law, the general populace is made callous by "the incessant execution of men and women, comparatively innocent, [which] disgraced every part of the country" at this time.[33] This "last dreadful and repulsive penalty" makes life seem cheap, and so, far from being an effective deterrent to criminals, it has on the contrary "never turned a man inclined to evil, and has hardened thousands who were half inclined to good" (65). As for the law-abiding, the knowledge that so many of those violently struck down on "these human shambles" have like Mary Jones committed the paltriest of offenses and are the "weakest, meanest, and most miserable" of the guilty rather than the most dangerous—all this tends rather "to awaken pity for the sufferers, than respect for [the] law" (77). Indeed, Dickens's belief that a willingness to use the law's ultimate means as its usual means was subversive of society's highest ends led him to the position, stated just over four years after the completion of *Barnaby*, of "advocating the total abolition of the Punishment of Death, as a general principle, for the advantage of society, for the prevention of crime, and without the least reference to, or tenderness for any individual malefactor whomsoever."[34] It is not that the state has no right to take life, but at a certain stage in the progress of civilization it is counterproductive to exercise that right.

Brutalization attributable to "the obscene presence" (77) of the gallows helped bring the Gordon Riots to pass, according to Dickens, for the "vast throng" of rioters was, at the early stages of the disturbances, "composed for the most part of the very scum and refuse of London, whose growth was fostered by bad criminal laws, bad prison regulations, and the worst conceivable police" (49). This part of the mob was of course not *created* by such conditions—*Barnaby Rudge*'s theory of human nature makes such a judgment impossible—but certainly the darker propensities built into man's precivilized character are inflamed no less than they are restrained by a social authority that is by turns excessive and inadequate: that acts, when it does act, with the ugly aggressiveness prescribed by its "bad criminal laws," but which usually fails to act, because its "worst conceivable police" is virtually no police at all, providing little impediment to the commission of crime and threatening but little chance of apprehension to the resourceful criminal.

But the theory that the gallows is the constitution results in a still worse sin of omission on the part of public authority, portending still more corrosive consequences to the social fabric. "You've had law," says Dennis, reproving the four condemned men in Newgate, who are clamoring to be rescued by the rioters; "laws have been made a' purpose for you; a wery handsome prison's been made a' purpose for you; a parson's kept a' purpose for you; a constitootional officer's appointed a' purpose for you; carts is maintained a' purpose for you—and yet you're not contented!" (65). In other words, what more could a citizen possibly ask from society beyond these thoughtful arrangements for working him off in case of need?

He could ask not to be brought to such a pass. He could say, how much better to have prevented him from being a criminal, thus obviating the need to punish him. How? He could answer, as the whole of *Barnaby Rudge* goes to show, that men observe the restraints of civilized social life in response not so much to external control as to inner assent, in response to having identified their individual purposes with those of a community and having thus taken its authority into themselves. He might say that a transformation of human nature has to be worked in each man to make him a civilized member of society, a transformation affected by something other than the coercive force of the state, which on the contrary is only the ultimate means society uses to keep already civilized men from succumbing to those antisocial impulses built into their nature.

He might urge that if society wants to make men into citizens—who obey laws—it has to humanize them, to which the necessary first step is to *teach* them. But that step the good old English school had prevented English society from taking. The hangman, for instance, hates reading and writing,

those two arts being (as Mr. Dennis swore) the greatest possible curse a civilized community could know, and militating more against the professional emoluments and usefulness of the great constitutional office he had the honour to hold, than any adverse circumstances that could present themselves to his imagination. (38)

And a slightly less biased constitutional officer, the country justice of our acquaintance, has similar feelings about literacy—his own accomplishments in that direction being meager. Mistrusting "the honesty of all poor people who could read and write," he hysterically accuses Mrs. Rudge of having "been to school," violently refusing to accept her excuse that "there was no harm in it" and using that fact instead to confirm his opinion that she is an "old rebel" (47). And so our condemned man might conclude by complaining, as Dickens complained in *Nicholas Nick-*

leby, that "ignorance was punished and never taught," and that "the world rolled on from year to year, alike careless and indifferent, and no man seeking to remedy or redress it."[35]

Dennis's constitootional theory finds a domestic counterpart in a sentiment of Mr. Chester's. Meditating on his discovery, made just before Hugh is to be hanged, that this wild man is his bastard son, Chester confesses that it is

[e]xtremely distressing to be the parent of such an uncouth creature! Still, I gave him very good advice: I told him he would certainly be hanged: I could have done no more if I had known of our relationship; and there are a great many fathers who have never done as much for *their* natural children. (75)

But the infallible way to become the parent of such an uncouth creature is to provide, like Chester, nothing whatever beyond the threat of the gallows. This is a truth Dickens has Hugh himself emphasize in his final speech, when, in the name of "all its victims, past, present, and to come," he curses "that black tree, of which I am the ripened fruit" (77). Indeed, he is the fruit of the gallows in two separate senses. An adult version of the infant at Mary Jones's breast—his mother, too, was a young, handsome woman hanged for a relatively trivial first offense—he was condemned by the gallows to grow up utterly abandoned. Nor was one single effort made by society to civilize this neglected creature, who is the ripe fruit of the gallows also in that he is the last, completest demonstration of the ultimate consequences of the good old English theory that the only really essential social institution is the scaffold.

In other words, if you have a brutal society, which provides vast numbers of its citizens with nothing but a noose (or even this or that variety of treadmill of the latest and most ingenious design), you will produce a society teeming—not with political revolutionaries, struggling to institute a brave new order freed from the injustices under which they themselves suffered—but rather with savages like Hugh. If society does not undertake to fulfill its duty of civilizing and humanizing its citizens, then whole classes of them will remain brutes. And in a society content to leave some in mere savagery and many more in an only half-civilized condition, how inconceivable would it be—should someone shout Down with everybody! down with everything!—to see the war of all against all blaze up from its ashes and burn with its old, aboriginal fury?

Part Three

"The Republic of My Imagination"

The primaeval forest still occupies a considerable portion of the ground, and hangs in solemn grandeur from the cliffs. . . . Often a mountain torrent comes pouring its silver tribute to the stream, and were there occasionally a ruined abbey, or feudal castle, to mix the romance of real life with that of nature, the Ohio would be perfect.
       (Frances Trollope, *Domestic Manners of the Americans*)

Man must begin, know this, where Nature ends;
Nature and man can never be fast friends.
       (Matthew Arnold, "To an Independent Preacher Who
Preached That We Should Be 'In Harmony with Nature'")

10

American Notes

By the time he had finished *Barnaby Rudge*, Dickens had imaginatively worked out a complex political theory—unsystematic but nevertheless coherent—and it was this theory he took with him to America less than six weeks after the last number of *Barnaby* appeared. What he went to see was neither monuments nor scenery but rather a new and remarkable society engaged in a profoundly interesting experiment in government. He went, in other words, with a primarily *political* interest, such as impelled Western visitors to the Soviet Union in the 1920s and early 1930s or impels them today to China, and his imagination was filled not so much with any clear idea about what he would find in the land of the future as with a generous curiosity, a sympathetic predisposition toward it, based on the thoroughgoing anti-Toryism expressed, for instance, in his caustic version of "The Fine Old English Gentleman" or in his famous pronouncement about "how radical I am getting!"[1]

His quick disillusionment with America, however, is no less famous. Just a month after his arrival he wrote Forster: "I tremble for a radical coming here, unless he is a radical on principle, by reason and reflection, and from the sense of right. I fear that if he were anything else, he would return home a tory. . . . I do fear that the heaviest blow ever dealt at liberty will be dealt by this country, in the failure of its example to the earth."

With the passage of another month he reported: "I *am* disappointed. This is not the Republic I came to see. This is not the Republic of my imagination. I infinitely prefer a liberal monarchy—even with its sickening accompaniments . . .—to such a government as this." Ten days later he confessed himself "a Lover of Freedom, disappointed—That's all."[2]

Outside the *Letters*, the record of this disillusionment is to be found not in one book but in two, and what I hope to suggest in the following discussion of *American Notes* and certain major aspects of *Martin Chuzzlewit* is that Dickens found America shocking not so much because he was unprepared for what he saw there but rather because, unexpected though those sights may have been, he was nevertheless well prepared to interpret them in a very definite way. Having sailed for the New World preoccupied with the political theories whose formulation he had only just accomplished, he found the primary meaning of his five-month American experience in its powerful confirmation of precisely those beliefs about human nature and the nature of society which form the imaginative center of *Barnaby Rudge*.

What major aspects of Dickens's political theory did his American trip corroborate? *American Notes* suggests at least four. The first of these is the notion, central to *Barnaby* and fundamental to Dickens's political imagination, that it is in the nature of society to transform the inner nature of man, conferring on him in the process the full measure of his humanity. Two American institutions in particular, the Perkins Institution for the Blind in Boston and Pennsylvania's Eastern Penitentiary, demonstrate this proposition, the one from a positive and the other from a negative point of view; and the importance Dickens attaches to this demonstration accounts for what at first glance appears to be the excessively long description of these two diametrically opposed establishments, whose essential features, moreover (to compound our initial sense of the *disproportionate* emphasis Dickens places on them in a book supposedly about specifically American phenomena), are not dependent on their American-ness.

The account of the Perkins Institution focuses on the celebrated case of Laura Bridgman, a young pupil there, who, under the tutelage of the Institution's notable director, Dr. Samuel Gridley Howe, was the first blind, deaf, and dumb person successfully to be educated. It is clear that Dickens associated Laura with Barnaby Rudge and Maypole Hugh, for, if he presented the two fictional characters as imaginative representations of his theory of precivilized human nature, in Laura he saw living, flesh-and-blood proof of important parts of that theory. He could easily make such an association, of course, based on the once-commonplace sentiment—voiced by Daniel Defoe, for example, or by Lord Monboddo—

that the deaf and dumb "are nearly in the condition in which we suppose men to have been in the natural state," for they lack that "use of speech" which more than anything else emblematizes (and facilitates) the host of external and internal differences distinguishing civil man from his solitary, brutish ancestor.[3] Indeed, in his representation of the idiot Barnaby Rudge and his talking raven as inseparable companions, each capable in his way of an unsettling travesty of rational discourse, we have already seen Dickens ruminating upon two of the notions which gave birth to this idea—on the one hand, the Aristotelian view that "the power of reasoned speech" is what sets man apart from the beasts, and, on the other hand, the judgment that natural man, lacking that power, is a creature not yet fully or definitively human.[4] This whole complex of ideas explains why philosophers of human nature came to include the deaf and dumb among the acceptable though imperfect laboratory substitutes for unprocurable "wolf-children" and to cite deaf-mutes, in their isolation of mind and spirit, as concrete, experimental confirmation of various theories about the precivilized nature of man.

It is in this light that Dickens views Laura Bridgman with so much interest, and her blindness intensifies these same associations for him, not only because it increases the extremity of her isolation, and not only because it associates her with the "natural" Barnaby Rudge's "blindness of the intellect,"[5] but also because it prevents her, even after she has learned to communicate in the finger alphabet of the deaf, from acquiring fully a trait that Rousseau and Diderot, to name two examples out of many, had singled out as especially characteristic of the transformations wrought on the original nature of man by the pressure of civilization.

It is strange to watch the faces of the blind, and see how free they are from all concealment of what is passing in their thoughts [Dickens remarks in introducing Laura]; observing which, a man with eyes may blush to contemplate the mask he wears. Allowing for one shade of anxious expression which is never absent from their countenances, and the like of which we may readily detect in our own faces if we try to feel our way in the dark, every idea, as it rises within them, is expressed with the lightning's speed, and nature's truth. If the company at a rout, or drawing-room at court, could only for one time be as unconscious of the eyes upon them as blind men and women are, what secrets would come out, and what a worker of hypocrisy this sight, the loss of which we so much pity, would appear to be! (3)

Civilized man, driven by the pride, the love of praise, the need to interest others in himself that he acquires when he leaves his self-sufficient, original state for the condition of mutual dependence that characterizes social

life, comes perforce to live largely outside himself, in the eyes of his fellows, where, as Rousseau says, it becomes necessary to appear to be other
than what one in fact is: "[t]o be and to seem to be bec[o]me two altogether different things."[6] The civilized condition requires all of us to
compromise our authenticity, to conceal ourselves behind a mask of hypocrisy, to "assume a position" (as Rameau's Nephew says), and to feel (at
least from time to time) the shame that is the inseparable obverse face of
our vanity intensified by shame at our own falsity and duplicity. The
blind no doubt live as much in the breath of others as those who can see,
but they do not live in the *eyes* of others: less aware than we of the gaze of
others constantly upon them, they develop much less of a hardened,
Chesterfieldian shell than the rest of us bear, and in this respect they preserve, in the (to us) sometimes grotesque artlessness of their faces and the
degree of inner artlessness those faces express, at least a part of "nature's
truth" and nature's original unselfconscious inner undividedness.

What then can be discovered about "nature's truth" insofar as Laura's
case discloses it? Chiefly, I think, Dickens saw in Laura living verification
of his intuition—explored in *Barnaby Rudge* with no less uneasiness than
fascination and therefore expressed in that novel in only the most guarded
terms—that the rational soul which signalizes man's full humanity is part
of his original endowment only as a potentiality, requiring immersion in
civilized social life to awaken and nourish it. Dickens chose a negative
strategy for establishing this idea in *Barnaby*: natural men do *not* have
souls; the civilization of civilized men, as the case of Mr. Chester demonstrates, is *not* a matter of mere externals. From these negatives, the positive conclusions we have drawn—that civilization is an *internal* quality,
that through the process of socialization civilized man gains a new, mental
faculty or dimension, which confers upon him his esential humanity and
which is precisely that "soul" that Dickens's representative natural men
lack—seem amply justified. But any reservations we may have had about
identifying these as Dickens's conclusions—reservations raised by Dickens's own misgivings about them in *Barnaby* and his circumspection in
suggesting them there—are set to rest by the frankness with which he
voices them in *American Notes*.

Consider, for example, his first description of Laura:

I sat down in another room, before a girl, blind, deaf, and dumb; destitute of
smell; and nearly so, of taste: before a fair young creature with every human faculty, and hope, and power of goodness and affection, inclosed within her delicate
frame, and but one outward sense—the sense of touch. There she was, before me;

built up, as it were, in a marble cell, impervious to any ray of light, or particle of sound; with her poor white hand peeping through a chink in the wall, beckoning to some good man for help, that an Immortal soul might be awakened. (3)

All the distinctively human powers and prerogatives which constitute the "Immortal soul" are latent within her, but they cannot be expected to unfold themselves spontaneously. Only if she can be brought into the human community can her specifically human essence be realized.[7]

Were she left in her isolation, with all that Dickens means by the "Immortal soul" remaining undeveloped in her, her condition would be wretched indeed, for "[t]hose who cannot be enlightened by reason, can only be controlled by force; and this, coupled with her great privations, must soon have reduced her to a worse condition than that of the beasts that perish" (3). Such, of course, was the fate of the "baby savage" in *The Haunted Man*—that urban wolf-child, who, tumbling up in uncivilized neglect in the midst of London, is "a creature who might live to take the outward form of a man, but who, within, would live and perish a mere beast." Like Laura before Dr. Howe rescues her, the "baby savage" exemplifies at least half of Aristotle's dictum that "[t]he man who is isolated—who is unable to share in the benefits of political association, or has no need to share because he is already self-sufficient—is no part of the polis, and must therefore be either a beast or a god."[8] And just as the "baby savage," having never received a "humanising touch," is said to have "been abandoned to a *worse* condition than the beasts" (emphasis added), so too, says Dickens, has such a fate threatened Laura: for the bestiality that fulfills the nature of the beasts that perish is by no means the appropriate state for a creature whose perfection, when achieved, is said to be imperishable.

From the lowest limits of humanity—from this bestial or even subbestial condition—Dr. Howe and his assistant deliver Laura by bringing her into connection with her fellows. With infinite patience, they teach her to associate words spelled out in labels of raised letters with the objects those words denote, which, in an imitative, uncomprehending way, she laboriously learns. At length, however, she is shown how to make up the labels herself. Dr. Howe, in his case notes (which Dickens quotes extensively in this chapter of *American Notes*), reports the results:

Hitherto, the process had been mechanical, and the success about as great as teaching a very knowing dog a variety of tricks. . . . [B]ut now the truth began to flash upon her: her intellect began to work: she perceived that here was a way by which she could make up a sign of any thing that was in her own mind, and show it to another mind; and at once her countenance lighted up with a human expression: it was no longer a dog, or parrot: it was an immortal spirit, eagerly seizing upon a new link of union with other spirits! (3)

By making her capable of participation in society, Dr. Howe believes he has humanized her, in the literal sense of the word; and with this conclusion, *American Notes* makes clear, Dickens is in complete agreement. Indeed, so much does Dr. Howe take for granted that the human *is* the social that his conception of the "immortal spirit" which is man's human essence has a social element at its center: at the moment Laura awakens as an "immortal spirit," her first impulse is (*of course*, Dr. Howe assumes) to seek "union with other spirits."

Of the passages from Dr. Howe's case notes that Dickens thought interesting or telling enough to include verbatim in *American Notes*, one more deserves our attention, for it confirms still another of the intuitions of *Barnaby Rudge*. Dr. Howe reports that Laura, when left alone, often

amuses herself by imaginary dialogues, or by recalling past impressions; she counts with her fingers, or spells out names of things which she has recently learned, in the manual alphabet of the deaf mutes. In this lonely self-communion she seems to reason, reflect, and argue: if she spell a word wrong with the fingers of her right hand, she instantly strikes it with her left, as her teacher does, in sign of disapprobation; if right, then she pats herself upon the head, and looks pleased. She sometimes purposely spells a word wrong with the left hand, looks roguish for a moment and laughs, and then with the right hand strikes the left, as if to correct it. (3)

What more graphic evidence can there be for the assumption, implicit all through *Barnaby Rudge*, that the social self is a transformed and complicated self in large part because in civilization our close social relations get internalized and become institutionalized within our minds? And here too is confirmation of an intuition much more darkly grasped in *Barnaby* that these internalized relations have everything to do with our *conscience*.

However much philosophers of human nature might have longed to shut away an infant and let it grow up in solitude, they nevertheless resigned themselves to doing without the invaluable data such an experiment would undoubtedly provide. But from 1830, a somewhat modified version of this experiment was actually being conducted near Philadelphia, Pennsylvania, by a quite different set of men and on adult subjects rather than on children. Not unexpectedly, Dickens went to examine the results, and what he saw on his visit to Pennsylvania's Eastern Penitentiary was a situation exactly the reverse of that he found at the Perkins Institution, the one as deplorable as the other had been laudable.

This celebrated prison is "conducted on a plan peculiar to the state of Pennsylvania," Dickens reports. "The system here, is rigid, strict, and hopeless solitary confinement."

Over the head and face of every prisoner who comes into this melancholy house, a black hood is drawn; and in this dark shroud, an emblem of the curtain dropped between him and the living world, he is led to the cell from which he never again comes forth, until his whole term of imprisonment has expired. He never hears of wife or children; home or friends; the life or death of any single creature. He sees the prison-officers, but with that exception he never looks upon a human countenance, or hears a human voice. He is a man buried alive; to be dug out in the slow round of years; and in the mean time dead to everything but torturing anxieties and horrible despair. (7)

However "kind, humane, and meant for reformation" the Separate System (as penologists of the day called it) might be in its intention, in its actual effects, Dickens judges, it is flagrantly "cruel and wrong." Clearly, he argues, those who devised this system of prison discipline and those who administer it, benevolent though they be, nevertheless "do not know what it is that they are doing." For this "dreadful punishment" achieves a degree of torture "which no man has a right to inflict upon his fellow-creature." Indeed, Dickens continues,

I hold this slow and daily tampering with the mysteries of the brain, to be immeasurably worse than any torture of the body: and because its ghastly signs and tokens are not so palpable to the eye and sense of touch as scars upon the flesh; because its wounds are not upon the surface, and it extorts few cries that human ears can hear; therefore I the more denounce it, as a secret punishment which slumbering humanity is not roused up to stay. (7)

In fact, so profoundly moved was Dickens by all that he saw in this prison that he declared to David Colden, "I never in my life was more affected by anything which was not strictly my own grief, than I was by this sight. It will live in my recollection always." And a few days later he wrote to Forster, "I never shall be able to dismiss from my mind, the impressions of that day."[9]

It was the "tampering with the mysteries of the brain" that so appalled him: hopeless isolation was insidiously working in its victims a massive, internal transformation of the most terrible kind. Such a regime brought about not reformation but disintegration—as anyone might have predicted, for of course such a regime has always produced results more or less of this kind. Of the "many instances on record, of men who have chosen, or have been condemned, to lives of perfect solitude," there is scarce "one, even among sages of strong and vigorous intellect, where its effect has not become apparent, in some disordered train of thought, or some gloomy hallucination." Indeed, "nothing wholesome or good has ever had its growth in such unnatural solitude, and . . . even a dog or any of the more intelligent among beasts, would pine, and mope, and rust away, beneath its influence." Dickens notices that the solitary prisoners even have had their very senses impaired: every man who has served a long term seems to have grown deaf. In every conceivable way the convicts are "dejected, heartbroken, wretched"; they have become "helpless, crushed, and broken" men: and, gazing at the "wan and unearthly" prisoner who held in his arms one of the pet rabbits he was allowed to keep in his cell, Dickens remarks, "I thought it would have been very hard to say in what respect the man was the nobler animal of the two."

One reflects that although Robinson Crusoe bore up magnificently under his epic ordeal, he was after all a fictional character, not a man. Alexander Selkirk, whose real-life abandonment on the island of Juan Fernandez appears to have been chief among the several stranded-mariner accounts influencing Defoe's conception, was evidently not so lucky, having (according to one legend) "slipped back into animalism and lost the use of speech." [10] "Man is thus nothing by himself," the naturalist Cornelius de Pauw concluded from Selkirk's example; "he owes what he is to society; the greatest Metaphysician, the greatest philosopher, if he were abandoned for ten years on the Isle of Fernandez, would come back transformed into a brute, dumb and imbecile, and would know nothing in the whole of nature." [11]

Less categorical than de Pauw, Dickens at any rate believes that men, being thus deprived of participation in social life, become profoundly defective, losing their noblest human qualities. He sees it in the Solitary Prisoners' faces, each one of which wears the expression of "that strained attention which we see upon the faces of the blind and deaf, mingled with a kind of horror, as though they had all been secretly terrified." These prisoners, in other words, wear the face of Laura Bridgman—whose habitual "anxious expression" of countenance Dickens has already mentioned—combined, by a remarkable coincidence, with a characteristic expression of the idiot Barnaby Rudge, who bears a look ("never absent for a moment") "to which an instant of intense and most unutterable horror only could have given birth,"[12] and who is related to Laura Bridgman in that both in their separate ways represent for Dickens precivilized human nature. Moreover, like Laura "built up in [her] marble cell," these prisoners, in their "long separation from human life," are men who are "buried alive," their lives "wasted in that stone coffin." Dickens looks at them, he tells Forster, "with the same awe as I should have looked at men who had been buried alive, and dug up again."[13] Buried alive like Laura; as if blind and deaf like Laura: if bringing Laura Bridgman into society can awaken in her an Immortal soul and stir into activity her slumbering humanity, being isolated from the communal life can transform the Solitary Prisoners into a sad detachment of Laura Bridgmans. "Better to have hanged him in the beginning," says Dickens of an utterly broken and unmanned long-term prisoner about to be released from the Penitentiary, "than bring him to this pass, and send him forth to mingle with his kind, who are his kind no more."[14]

.   .   .

Both the second and third aspects of Dickens's political theory that his American travels confirmed are borne out by what he most dislikes in American society—by the peculiar American theory and practice of freedom, which seem to him to be producing a society deficient in certain (for him) essential characteristics of any society. As a result, American society appears to him imperfectly capable of performing society's fundamental humanizing function, whose far-reaching effects the evidence of Laura Bridgman and the Solitary Prisoners so graphically illustrates.

Man, says the anthropologist Clifford Geertz, "is an animal suspended in webs of significance he himself has spun"; and Dickens, too, as *Nickleby* and especially *Barnaby* so forcefully attest, shares the belief that men collectively create the meaning of their lives in and through their mutual relations.[15] Yet American society perversely seemed to be sabotaging this enterprise; and observing that negation and its results fixed Dickens even more firmly in his belief—the second of those ratified by his American experiences—that social life, with its whole panoply of rituals, celebrations, and myths, provides the only context in which individual human lives can achieve significance.

What particularly strengthened Dickens in this view was the spectacle of the Americans trying to free themselves from the prevailing European ideal of social intercourse that centers on the value of courtesy and its related code of sociability and good manners. Manners, as Hobbes had pronounced, are not limited to "Decency of behaviour; as how one should salute another, or how a man should wash his mouth, or pick his teeth before company, and such other points of the *Small Moralls*"; more important, they include "those qualities of man-kind, that concern their living together in Peace, and Unity."[16] So Dickens saw the matter, too; and he recognized with horror that the Americans, in "reject[ing] the graces of life as undeserving of attention" (18), in dismissing the ideal of courtesy as mere outward "prejudice" and the practice of politeness as a "conventional absurdity" that "compromised their independence" (9), were in fact discarding what *Nicholas Nickleby* called the "polite forms and ceremonies which must be observed in civilised life, or mankind relapse into their original barbarism." And these forms and ceremonies, as *Barnaby Rudge* makes especially clear, are precisely the celebrations and reaffirmations of that communal life from which men derive their sense of the meaningfulness and dignity of their existence. In other words, the musty cobwebs of custom that Americans are so resolutely sweeping away (those "mere human conventions" to which Hillis Miller accords, as we saw, so little value) are really the "webs of significance" of Geertz's apt image.

The dismal dinners that he shared with his fellow passengers on board American steamboats brought this deplorable cultural trend most sharply into focus for Dickens. Bolted in silence and with astonishing rapidity, these meals were, he says, mere "animal observances," stripped of any "sociality"—"as if breakfasts, dinners, and suppers, were necessities of nature never to be coupled with recreation or enjoyment" (11). Therefore, he reports,

I really dreaded the coming of the hour that summoned us to table; and was as glad to escape from it again, as if it had been a penance or a punishment. Healthy cheerfulness and good spirits forming a part of the banquet, I could soak my crusts in the fountain with Le Sage's strolling player, and revel in their glad enjoyment: but sitting down with so many fellow-animals to ward off thirst and hunger as a business; to empty, each creature, his Yahoo's trough as quickly as he can, and then slink sullenly away; to have these social sacraments stripped of everything but the mere greedy satisfaction of the natural cravings; goes so against the grain with me, that I seriously believe the recollection of these funeral feasts will be a waking nightmare to me all my life. (12)

In other words, everything that *Barnaby Rudge*'s Maypole Inn does to humanize life, to establish a realm of human value and meaning rooted in communal existence, is deliberately *not* done in America. As a result of this determined neglect of all those rituals and observances so feelingly dramatized in *Nickleby* and *Barnaby* and summed up in this passage by the by no means fanciful term "social *sacraments*," Americans are debasing and impoverishing human life. They are dispossessing man's life of that dimension of sacredness that *Barnaby* imagined as one of its signal accomplishments, and they are markedly depriving it of what makes it, in Dickens's view, more dignified and more valuable than the mere animal existence that the language of our passage represents as particularly furtive and squalid. Dickens, one feels, is not being hyperbolic in predicting that these gloomy "funeral feasts" will haunt him, like the ghost of Hamlet's father, for the rest of his life, for they epitomize for him the American subversion of the values he most deeply cherishes. *If life is not about this,* America makes him keep asking of his own beliefs, *what is it about?* The dismaying answer America seems to provide is a rustling in the straw.

Dickens's visit to the community of the Shakers moved him to similar reflections. This sect of extreme religious enthusiasts conceives of man's earthly existence as "but a narrow path towards the grave," beyond whose bourne the real meaning of human life is to be found; and thus, like their fellow Americans, but for quite different reasons, they too reject the fully socialized life as frivolous and unreal (15). They too, driven by their gloomy, life-denying Puritanism, resolutely set their faces against the observance of the social sacraments; and in spite of their high protestations, Dickens for this reason classes them among the worst of "the enemies of Heaven and Earth, who turn the water at the marriage feasts of this poor world, not into wine, but gall."

The Shakers, moreover, brought into sharper focus for Dickens another tendency in American culture, closely related to this widespread assault on the social sacraments. For that "bad spirit" which "would strip life of its healthful graces" Dickens recognizes as identical to "that odious spirit which, if it could have had full scope and sway upon the earth, must have blasted and made barren the imaginations of the greatest men, and left them, in their power of raising up enduring images before their fellow creatures yet unborn, no better than the beasts." This is the spirit, in other words, that would wither the imaginative, myth-making life of man—the life of culture—which alone clothes the shivering nakedness of "this poor world" of human doing and suffering with its fabric of redeeming significance.

His acute apprehension of the American threat to invention and imagination, one feels, accounts for Dickens's insistence throughout *American*

Notes that his own imagination is working just fine: he can still imagine the meaning in moonbeams he fancied as a child (16); he calls up such varied and surprising images on shipboard that they "far exceeded, as it seemed to me, all power of mine to conjure up the absent" (2); he imagines in the stumps of trees "a Grecian urn . . . a woman weeping at a tomb . . . a crouching negro . . . a horse . . . a hunch-back throwing off his cloak and stepping forth into the light" (14). For clearly Dickens felt personally menaced by this corrosive tendency in the American spirit, which not only (I imagine) threatened his defenses against the nihilism that yawns under all us dwellers in "this poor world," but which also threatened his special genius and his special social function as a novelist— and the world's most popular novelist, at that. "Macready," Dickens gasped after two months on American soil, "if I had been born here, and had written my books in this country,—producing them with no stamp of approval from any other land—it is my solemn belief that I should have lived and died, poor, unnoticed, and 'a black sheep'—to boot. I was never more convinced of anything than I am of that." [17]

What else, after all, could be the fate of a novelist in a

state of things which broadly divides society into two classes—whereof one, the great mass, asserts a spurious independence, most miserably dependent for its mean existence on the disregard of humanizing conventionalities of manner and social custom, so that the coarser a man is, the more distinctly it shall appeal to his taste; while the other, disgusted with the low standard thus set up and made adaptable to everything, takes refuge among the graces and refinements it can bring to bear on private life, and leaves the public weal to such fortune as may betide it in the press and uproar of a general scramble? [18]

In this remarkable description of how one form of radical individualism in America gives birth to another individualism more refined but not necessarily less radical, Dickens prophetically summarizes much of the history of nineteenth-century American literature: it is as if he clairvoyantly foresees the inevitable appearance in America of a writer like Henry James. [19]

"Among the works of man which human life is rightly employed in perfecting and beautifying, the first in importance surely is man himself," declares John Stuart Mill in *On Liberty*; and the epigraph from Alexander von Humboldt on the book's first page identifies as the work's "leading principle" a belief in "the absolute and essential importance of human development in its richest diversity." [20] Dickens's astonishing fertility in peopling his novels with figures so arrestingly individual that we have had to invent the term "Dickens characters" to describe them and their real-life counterparts is evidence enough that these are sentiments after his heart too; and these sentiments find active expression in *American Notes* when Dickens so enthusiastically describes the accomplished Lowell factory girls in Chapter 4, for example, or when he praises the Perkins Institution for choosing not to make its pupils wear uniforms and thus allowing each child to appear "in his or her own proper character, with its individuality unimpaired" (3). But, on the whole, Dickens judged that precisely the opposite result was being achieved in America, thanks to the repudiation of the social sacraments that he found so disturbing. "The people are all alike," he affirms of his fellow steamboat passengers, taking them as representative of Americans in general (outside the major cities, that is). "There is no diversity of character. They travel about on the same errands, say and do the same things in exactly the same manner, and follow in the same dull cheerless round. . . . [T]here is scarcely a man who is in anything different from his neighbour" (11). Indeed, "at every new town I came to," Dickens reports of his travels in the interior, "I seemed to meet the very same people whom I had left behind me, at the last" (18).

In other words, not only did the texture of human life seem to be becoming thinner in America, to be losing some of its density of meaning, but human individuality was apparently being attenuated, too, as part of the same general process of impoverishment. For, if social life is (as Dickens believes) the medium in which each individual's humanity germinates and takes root, it is also the medium which nourishes and sustains the development of individual selfhood; and thus the specific richness of the communal life of this or that particular society will affect its ability to promote the growth of individual character. The aridity of American society makes it drearily barren in this respect, Dickens judges. Like some vast Solitary Prison, America denies men participation in a fertile communal life, and as a result it characteristically produces stunted, undeveloped selves, whose individuality never blooms. Thus, from another point of view, America seems to resemble the primitive equality of the state of nature, from which no individual can be differentiated, for all men are identical atoms. This is but one of the senses in which neglect of the "polite forms and ceremonies" reduces men to "their original barbarism."

"Healthy cheerfulness and good spirits forming a part of the banquet, I could soak my crusts in the fountain with Le Sage's strolling player, and revel in their glad enjoyment," says Dickens, to contrast his own values with those of the Americans, who view dinners as "sitting down with so many fellow-animals to ward off thirst and hunger as business." For Dickens, that is—in some moods at least—spiritual deprivation seems even worse than material deprivation. But in "that vast counting-house which lies beyond the Atlantic" (3), such a judgment would be inconceivable: so devoted are Americans to the merely material, to what *Nickleby* calls "mere utilitarianism," that for them even eating dinner is a *business.* And here *American Notes* crystallizes the Carlylean insight that central trends in modern life were bringing about a society that was really not a society at all "but rather, cloaked under due laws-of-war, named 'fair competition' and so forth, it is a mutual hostility."[21] For America seemed to Dickens to have taken to an unprecedented extreme the ethos of capitalist individualism that was so potent and worrisome a force in English life, too. In America it became abundantly clear that this ideology—the prevailing social theory of the modern world, after all—produced as its ultimate tendency a social system more nearly resembling the primeval war of all against all than a grand incorporation of civilized human beings. What else could be expected, after all, from an ideology which with complacence and satisfaction described society as a collection of separate, equal, and mutually repellant atoms?

"[A]ll kinds of deficient and impolitic usages, are referred to the national love of trade," Dickens reports, and what he has in mind as the chief impolitic usages are precisely the various American subversions of the social sacraments and shared myths. For example:

The love of trade is assigned as a reason for that comfortless custom, so very prevalent in country towns, of married persons living in hotels, having no fireside of their own, and seldom meeting from early morning until late at night, but at the hasty public meals. The love of trade is a reason why the literature of America is to remain for ever unprotected: "For we are a trading people, and don't care for poetry," . . . while healthful amusements, cheerful means of recreation, and wholesome fancies, must fade before the stern utilitarian joys of trade. (18)

Here, in other words, is a social ethos that undermines social relations on the most fundamental level of family life, while, on the level of society as a whole, it blights the common culture—of which literature (with its dependence on "wholesome fancies") is a prime constituent—and thus despoils the ground from which men collectively generate human meaning. No wonder Dickens judges that "It would be well . . . for the American people as a whole, if they loved the Real less, and the Ideal somewhat more" (18). And no wonder he was so relieved to be homeward bound on an English ship, among "as cheerful and snug a party . . . as ever came to the resolution of being mutually agreeable, on land or water." What a pleasure to find himself eating shipboard dinners of "extraordinary length" among a

select association . . . , to whose distinguished president modesty forbids me to make any further allusion, which, being a very hilarious and jovial institution, was (prejudice apart) in high favour with the rest of the community, and particularly with a black steward, who lived for three weeks in a broad grin at the marvellous humour of these incorporated worthies. (16)

For this is celebrating the social sacraments with a vengeance, and in the "association," the "institution," the "community" that is thereby "incorporated," so consummately social a creature as Dickens feels once more truly at home.

.   .   .

For the fundamental insight of Dickens's political theory—his profound conviction that aggression is an inseparable component of human nature, and that therefore men need to be restrained by law and government from doing to each other the awful things their built-in aggressiveness impels them to do—one can of course find confirmation all the time. A glance at history provides scores of examples, and if we in our era would begin our catalogue with Auschwitz, Dickens's contemporaries would point for example to the Reign of Terror and might cite realities like this from Carlyle's great *French Revolution*:

"At Meudon," says Montgaillard with considerable calmness, "there was a Tannery of Human Skins; such of the Guillotined as seemed worth flaying: of which perfectly good wash-leather was made"; for breeches, and other uses. The skin of the men, he remarks, was superior in toughness (*consistance*) and quality to shamoy; that of the women was good for almost nothing, being so soft in texture!—History looking back over Cannibalism . . . will perhaps find no terrestrial Cannibalism of a sort, on the whole, so detestable. . . . Alas, then, is man's civilisation only a wrappage, through which the savage nature of him can still burst, infernal as ever? Nature still makes him: and has an Infernal in her as well as a Celestial.[22]

The newspapers, introspection, metropolitan life—all these likewise lend support to such a view. But Dickens, on his visit to the American South, found confirmation of it made unusually dramatic by its unusually massive scale. For there he saw that men are capable of seeking so utterly to subdue and dominate their fellow men as to enslave them by the thousands—not metaphorically but literally, though it often boggles the mind that this was an American *institution* almost within living memory—and the brief glance Dickens took before turning his face away in disgust from a system that placed one class of men in the absolute power of another reinforced his pessimistic sense of just what it is men will do to their fellow creatures if they are free to follow their own impulses.

Indeed, the *idea* of freedom embraced by many American slave owners ominously warns that if men are left free to do what they like, what they will like to do will be highly dismaying. For these are people who, "when they speak of Freedom, mean the Freedom to oppress their kind, and to be savage, merciless, and cruel" (17), and who, in "the Pursuit of Happiness," insist on their "Inalienable Right . . . to take the field after *their* Happiness, equipped with cat and cartwhip, stocks, and iron collar, and to shout their view halloa! (always in praise of Liberty), to the music of clanking chains and bloody stripes" (8). Like Wackford Squeers, whose absolute freedom depends on the absolute enslavement of his pupils—or like the powerful rich men in Rousseau's *Second Discourse*, who "prize the things they enjoy only insofar as the others are deprived of them" and "would cease to be happy if the people ceased to be miserable"—these are people "whose inalienable rights can only have their growth in negro wrongs" (17).[23]

Just take a look into any Southern newspaper, says Dickens, where you will find column after column of advertisements like these:

Ran away, the negro Manuel. Much marked with irons.

. . .

Ran away, a negro woman and two children; a few days before she went off, I burnt her with a hot iron, on the left side of her face. I tried to make the letter M.

. . .

One hundred dollars reward, for a negro fellow, Pompey, 40 years old. He is branded on the left jaw.

. . .

Was committed to jail, a negro man. Says his name is Josiah. His back very much scarred by the whip; and branded on the thigh and hips in three or four places, thus (J M). The rim of his right ear has been bit or cut off.

. . .

Ran away, my man Fountain. Has holes in his ears, a scar on the right side of his forehead, has been shot in the hind parts of his legs, and is marked on the back with the whip. (17)[24]

To the list of these everyday mutilations of Negroes by their masters ought to be added "the common practice of violently punching out their teeth," Dickens interjects. "To make them wear iron collars by day and night, and to worry them with dogs, are practices almost too ordinary to deserve mention." Often enough, too, one hears of "husbands obliged at the word of command to flog their wives; women, indecently compelled to hold up their own garments that men might lay the heavier stripes upon their legs, driven and harried by brutal overseers in their time of travail, and becoming mothers on the field of toil, under the very lash itself." The sexual abuse and humiliation suggested here are not the only sexual violations inflicted upon slaves, as we might expect: the "noble patriot" (modelled on Thomas Moore's caricature of Jefferson[25]) "who dreamed of Freedom in a slave's embrace, and waking sold her offspring and his own in public markets,"[26] points to a whole other area of sexual tyranny, less sadistic but not always less violent. For pure sadism, of course, who can surpass those freeborn citizens who, unpunished by the laws, "burned a slave alive at a slow fire in the city of St. Louis" (17)?

Yet what impressed on Dickens most deeply the enormity of violence being relentlessly inflicted upon this victimized race was the sight of the slaves themselves.

To those who are happily unaccustomed to them, the countenances in the streets and labouring places, too, are shocking. All men who know that there are laws against instructing slaves, of which the pains and penalties greatly exceed in their amount the fines imposed on those who maim and torture them, must be prepared to find their faces very low in the scale of intellectual expression. But the darkness—not of skin, but mind—which meets the stranger's eye at every turn; the brutalizing and blotting out of all the fairer characters traced by Nature's hand; immeasurably outdo his worst belief. That travelled creation of the great satirist's brain, who fresh from living among horses, peered from a high casement down upon his own kind with trembling horror, was scarcely more repelled and daunted by the sight, than those who look upon some of these faces for the first time must surely be. (9)

Like Laura Bridgman and the Solitary Prisoners, the slaves too provided Dickens with tangible confirmation of central aspects of his theory of original human nature. Men really do have it within them to be *this* brutish, Dickens sees as he watches these "biped beasts of burden slinking past," and—much like Swift and Conrad after their glimpse of the beastliness within human nature—he turns away from this glance into the heart of darkness muttering, The horror! The horror!

But, more important, the faces of the slaves provided another, more oblique, glance into this same heart of darkness. For the slaves are brutish because they have been *forcibly* deprived of the means of realizing their full humanity. They are brutish because they have been brutalized; and that this has happened to them—that it is written upon their faces for all to see—makes sickeningly manifest to Dickens the scale of the violence their fellow men have committed against them by enslaving them, by terrorizing, maiming, and torturing them, by condemning them to such grievous darkness of mind. To produce such a terrible effect, in other words, a hellish cause must be at work.

Some historians have argued that the slave owners were nothing but rational entrepreneurs, carrying out an exaggerated form of the characteristic capitalist program of profiting through exploitation of the labor of others. And, these historians add, why should an ethos that sees everything as a commodity refrain from buying and selling human beings too? It may be violent and immoral, but it is not irrational. Dickens, however, does not view the slave owners in this light—no more than he would view as a mere earnest businessman such a figure as Wackford Squeers, a monster of aggression, whose willingness to exploit his pupils so radically is part and parcel of his monumental sadism. In this context does Dickens place the American slave owners: these "freeborn outlaws," whose social relations with each other by no means "bear the impress of civilisation and refinement" or suggest men in any way "accustomed to restrain their passions"—whose "brutal, sanguinary, and violent" habits are those of a "brutal savage"—these men form for Dickens a nation of Squeerses, and he interprets what they are doing to the slaves not in economic terms but rather in terms of the psychology of aggression (17).

Thus he contemptuously dismisses the economic argument that one class of slave owners puts forth as evidence that slaves are not systematically mistreated by masters. After all, these men urbanely point out, slaves represent a large capital investment—they are a slave owner's capital plant. Therefore, can it possibly "be a general practice to treat them inhumanly, when it would impair their value, and would be obviously against the interests of their masters"? Such a thing would be irrational—and therefore unthinkable.

Is it in the interest of any man [Dickens replies] to steal, to game, to waste his health and mental faculties by drunkenness, to lie, forswear himself, indulge hatred, seek desperate revenge, or do murder? No. All these are roads to ruin. And why, then, do men tread them? Because such inclinations are among the vicious qualities of mankind. Blot out, ye friends of slavery, from the catalogue of human passions, brutal lust, cruelty, and the abuse of irresponsible power (of all earthly temptations the most difficult to be resisted), and when ye have done so, and not before, we will inquire whether it be the interest of a master to lash and maim the slaves, over whose lives and limbs he has an absolute controul. (17)

A convinced anti-Utilitarian, Dickens rejects out of hand the contention that rational self-interest is the primary human motivation. Far from it, he believes; on the contrary, human motives are various and unpredictable, and prominent among them are the often irrational impulses inherent in human nature, including such dark urges of aggression as Dickens lists here among the "vicious qualities of mankind." As Dickens exasperatedly informed a "hard, bad-looking," and very bellicose slave owner, "cruelty, and the abuse of irresponsible power, [are] two of the bad passions of human nature, with the gratification of which, considerations of interest or of ruin [have] nothing whatever to do." [27] And it is the active existence of these "bad passions of human nature" that the faces of the slaves—the devastated victims of such "vicious qualities"—emphatically prove.

.   .   .

If rational self-interest really were the primary human motivation, and if Adam Smith were right that the ceaseless striving of individuals to achieve their private ends is led by the guidance of an invisible hand miraculously to advance the general interest at the same time, then rational self-interest might by itself serve as virtually the only necessary agency of social control. But for Dickens, with no such faith in the operation either of human rationality or of an invisible hand, froward mankind needs the restraint of law and government. Yet on his visit to America Dickens repeatedly felt himself in a nation essentially without laws. On the most banal level, he observes that one cannot count on the passenger steamboats departing on time: they are not hours but weeks late—"for if the law were to bind down a free and independent citizen to keep his word with the public, what would become of the liberty of the subject" (10)? More serious is the epidemic level of personal violence. Duels, savage murders, bloody revenges are matters of course. Not unusual is the American who threatened to follow back to England the British officer who eloped with his niece "'and shoot him down in the street wherever he found him.'" Such are hardly the customs of a civilized country, and Dickens testily remarks that, should the murderous American make good his threat in England "or gratif[y] any other little whim of the like nature, he would find himself one morning prematurely throttled at the Old Bailey" (14).

But if America applies the principle of *laissez-faire* not just to economic matters but to everything and carries it to such an extreme that all law and government threatens (as it seems) to evaporate, most other modern nations are less plagued with insufficient government than with an excess of one part of it, an hypertrophy of the legitimate force and violence which safeguard the social contract. Dickens derided the ideology out of which such a distorted state of affairs develops in *Barnaby Rudge*'s Mr. Dennis, and *American Notes* explicitly returns to the whole issue in its mention of "those good old customs of the good old times which made England, even so recently as in the reign of the Third King George, in respect of her criminal code and her prison regulations, one of the most bloody-minded and barbarous countries on the earth" (3). Such a governmental theory and practice, as *Barnaby Rudge* suggested, necessarily result in a savage society; and Dickens's experience of America reinforced still further his already powerful belief that a people requires of its rulers the provision of much more than merely "the authority erected by society for its own preservation."

The reinforcement America provided came from Dickens's seeing in Boston and its environs what admirable results ensue when the "State is a parent to its people; [and] has a parental care and watch over all poor children, women labouring of child, sick persons, and captives."[28] For this little corner of America—a corner not visited by *Martin Chuzzlewit*, so as not to dilute the concentrated acerbity of that novel's anti-American philippic—maintained an impressive array of publicly supported institutions or charities that substantially embodied Dickens's idea of what a nation's rulers should be doing for the ruled. Much of the credit for this happy state of affairs must be given to still another estimable institution—Harvard College, which has educated most members of the Boston area's propertied classes, imbuing them with a wide range of "humanising tastes and desires," while wholesomely dispelling "vanity and prejudice." No wonder Dickens was so greatly pleased "to observe the almost imperceptible, but not less certain effect, wrought by this institution among the small community of Boston" (3).

In Boston's exemplary public institutions—the workhouse, the insane asylum, the reform school, the Perkins Institution—

the unfortunate or degenerate citizens of the State are carefully instructed in their duties both to God and man; are surrounded by all reasonable means of comfort and happiness that their condition will admit of; are appealed to, as members of the great human family, however afflicted, indigent, or fallen; are ruled by the strong Heart, and not by the strong (though immeasurably weaker) Hand. (3)

Organized along these lines, the House of Reformation for Juvenile Offenders, for example, is the very model of what so basic a social institution should be.

The design and object of this Institution is to reclaim the youthful criminal by firm but kind and judicious treatment; to make his prison a place of purification and improvement, not of demoralisation and corruption; to impress upon him that there is but one path, and that one sober industry, which can ever lead him to happiness; to teach him how it may be trodden if his footsteps have never yet been led that way; and to lure him back to it if they have strayed: in a word, to snatch him from destruction, and restore him to society a penitent and useful member. (3)

Here, to be sure, the "authority erected by society for its own preservation" is working with appropriate firmness—this is after all a jail—but to the firmness is superadded "kind and judicious treatment" as well. For what ensures that people will be "useful members" of society, who tread the path of "sober industry," is not merely the dependable operation of official terror, however necessary that may be. An internal source of social control is certainly as necessary as the external: citizens are made not by terror but by teaching. And so, attached to the reformatory (which, unusually, really does reform) is another institution, "an asylum for neglected and indigent boys who have committed no crime, but who in the ordinary course of things would very soon be purged of that distinction if they were not taken from the hungry streets and sent here," where they are "exceedingly well taught, and not better taught than fed." Were there institutions like this in England, children like the baby savage in *The Haunted Man* would be spared the fate of full-grown savagery.

The relatively greater reliance placed on the strong Heart as opposed to the strong (though immeasurably weaker) Hand—on internal as opposed to external control—is one of the features of these Boston institutions that most warmly kindled Dickens's admiration, and over and over again he registers his strong conviction that the heart is not only stronger in these matters but also better. Take, for example, the State Hospital for the Insane, "conducted on those enlightened principles of conciliation and kindness," and guided by the precept that one should "[e]vince a desire to show some confidence, and repose some trust, even in mad people," who, notwithstanding their defects, are still recognizably human beings, responsive to a human appeal. And so, with the kind and judicious resident physician seated in their midst,

Every patient in this asylum sits down to dinner every day with a knife and fork. . . . At every meal, moral influence alone restrains the more violent among them from cutting the throats of the rest; but the effect of that influence is reduced to an absolute certainty, and is found, even as a means of restraint, to say nothing of it as a means of cure, a hundred times more efficacious than all the strait-waistcoats, fetters, and handcuffs, that ignorance, prejudice, and cruelty have manufactured since the creation of the world.

An appeal from the strong Heart to an answering heart not only restrains the violence even of people of such damaged humanity as these: what is more important, it also *cures* them. People whose "irritability . . . would otherwise be expended on their own flesh, clothes, and furniture" not only are kept from doing violence by these means; they are also made "cheerful, tranquil, and healthy," and (more important still) they enjoy the human luxury of feeling "a decent self-respect" (3).

The same human spirit prevails at the Boston workhouse. "It is not assumed and taken for granted that being there [the paupers] must be evil-disposed and wicked people, before whose vicious eyes it is necessary to flourish threats and harsh restraints." Instead, the "mild appeal" to conduct themselves with quiet discretion which meets them "at the very threshold," coupled with the plain but comfortable arrangements made for them, "bespeaks an amount of consideration for those who are reduced to seek a shelter there, which puts them at once upon their gratitude and good behaviour" and gives them "a motive for exertion and becoming pride." This is very different from English workhouses, in which "a certain amount of weazen life may mope, and pine, and shiver, all day long"; and the favorable judgment Dickens forms of these Boston institutions ultimately derives from a belief that *American Notes* most explicitly formulates in its account of Laura Bridgman. "Those who cannot be enlightened by reason, can only be controlled by force," Dickens remarks in describing Laura's plight; and he goes on to explain that, had her state made necessary the application of force in the absence of reason, it "must soon have reduced her to a worse condition than that of the beasts that perish." To some form of social control or other she *must* be subjected—this Dickens takes for granted. But he is acutely aware how sharply the varieties of social control differ from each other: the strong Hand tames, no doubt, but the strong Heart civilizes: the one promotes order, while the other fosters humanity as well. Precisely these are the considerations Dickens has in mind when he recommends the example of such an institution as the Boston reformatory from "every point of view, and with reference to every consideration of humanity and social policy." The *utility* of reliance, whenever possible, on the strong Heart is beyond dispute; equally indisputable and perhaps even more important is its *justice*.

Dickens believes these Boston institutions to be "as nearly perfect, as the most considerate wisdom, benevolence, and humanity, can make them," but his point in describing them is not merely to show how individual establishments of such a kind ought to be run. For the most significant feature of these institutions is "that they are either supported by the State or assisted by the State; or . . . that they act in concert with it, and are emphatically the people's." After registering his wholehearted endorsement of such a governmental policy, Dickens goes on to explain in more specific terms what in his view constitutes both its utility and its justice.

I cannot but think, with a view to the principle and its tendency to elevate or depress the character of the industrious classes, that a Public Charity is immeasurably better than a Private Foundation. . . . In our own country, where it has not, until within these latter days, been a very popular fashion with governments to display any extraordinary regard for the great mass of the people or to recognise their existence as improvable creatures, private charities, unexampled in the history of the earth, have arisen, to do an incalculable amount of good among the destitute and afflicted. But the government of the country, having neither act nor part in them, is not in the receipt of any portion of the gratitude they inspire; and, offering very little shelter or relief beyond that which is to be found in the workhouse and the jail, has come, not unnaturally, to be looked upon by the poor rather as a stern master, quick to correct and punish, than a kind protector, merciful and vigilant in their hour of need.

Dickens judges it mistaken to think simply that "one [is] caught, trapped into" socially acceptable behavior, "pinned by the leg instead of going into it of one's own accord and glorying in the act" (to adapt Mr. Lillyvick's defense of marriage, that "highest and most estimable of social

ties"²⁹). Constrained though one no doubt is, one does not act in socially
useful ways only out of fear of punishment, but also because one identifies one's individual purposes with the collective purpose, which one has
internalized. This internalization, as we know, Dickens takes to be much
the strongest agency of social control, though to call it by that name does
not properly emphasize the degree of freedom and consent involved in
this acceptance of limitation. And so a government that succeeds in making itself felt as a "kind protector" need fear public disorder far less than a
government seen by its subjects only as a "stern master." Citizens do not
make revolutions against governments that inspire "gratitude."

But the utility of this governmental policy, however great, is finally a
matter of less importance to Dickens than its justice. For government policy has everything to do with determining whether "the character of the
industrious classes" will be "elevate[d]" or "depress[ed]." The specific
gravity of the social medium in which people are immersed, Dickens believes, affects the level of selfhood they can reach: the full humanity
which exists as a potential within us all only finds realization through
substantial participation in a sustaining communal life. Thus, while the
"great mass of the people" emphatically are "improvable creatures," the
question of whether or not they actually will acquire all the improvement
of which human nature is capable cannot be answered with such absolute
certainty, for so much depends on whether the rulers allow the ruled the
social means necessary for full human development. It is in this way that
fundamental governmental policy deeply affects the degree to which men
can be men.

This responsibility falls not just on the government but on the governing classes as a whole. In England, however, Dickens fears, a lamentably
large proportion of that class—and especially of its Manchester contingent—recognizes no such responsibility but instead subscribes with
varying degrees of urgency to Mr. Dennis's constitootional theory, holding that all a society owes to the great mass of the people is the jail or the
Poor Law Bastille or the gallows in case of need. Diametrically opposed
to this pervasive English attitude is the spirit that prevails twenty-five or
so miles north of Boston, in the flourishing American factory town of
Lowell, Massachusetts: and here Dickens saw just how radically "the
character of the industrious classes" can be affected by the policy of the
propertied class toward them.

The condition of the working class in Lowell in 1842 is utterly the reverse of the condition of the working class in England at around the same
time, as described (for example) so graphically by Friedrich Engels. The

American workers (almost all of whom are women) are well-dressed, clean, and healthy. Their workrooms—tidy, airy, comfortable—are "as well ordered as themselves": potted plants, even, have been arranged to shade and ornament the factory windows. The workers' boardinghouses, supervised by the mill owners, are models of respectability, and an excellent hospital, whose fees are moderate, receives the girls with "gentleness and consideration" in case of need. Nearly a thousand girls have money in the bank, the average account totalling around a hundred dollars. Without exception, these girls have "the manners and deportment of young women: not of degraded brutes of burden" (4). And they are accomplished young women, at that:

Firstly, there is a joint-stock piano in a great many of the boarding-houses. Secondly, nearly all these young ladies subscribe to circulating libraries. Thirdly, they have got up among themselves a periodical called THE LOWELL OFFERING, "A repository of original articles, written exclusively by females actively employed in the mills,"—which is duly printed, published, and sold. . . .

Need one add that such "young *ladies*," much to Dickens's delight, display a sufficiency of that becoming "pride" that is "a worthy element of self-respect" (4)?

To all this, says Dickens, large numbers of well-to-do Englishmen "will exclaim, with one voice, 'How very preposterous! . . . These things are above their station.'" In rebuttal, he in turn "would beg to ask what their station is. It is their station to work," he replies. "And they *do* work. They labour in these mills, upon an average, twelve hours a day, which is unquestionably work, and pretty tight work too." This being the case, can it really be maintained that "it is above their station to indulge in such amusements, on any terms?" If we do go on maintaining that, are we not guilty of a fundamental misconception: "Are we quite sure that we in England have not formed our ideas of the 'station' of working people, from accustoming ourselves to the contemplation of that class as they are, and not as they might be?" In England these are two very different things; and in recommending the enlightened policy of the Lowell magnates to his English readers (in particular, to his propertied readers), in reporting what luminously dramatic results can be achieved when a class that in England are mere "degraded brutes of burden" are in Lowell creatures of achieved, even polished, humanity—Dickens emphasizes once more how momentous are the considerations facing a governing class as it decides whether "the character of the industrious classes" will be, or will remain, elevated or degraded. "For myself," he says, summing up his endorsement of the pianos, the circulating libraries, the *Lowell Offering*, and the circumstances that make these things possible,

I know no station in which, the occupation of to-day cheerfully done and the occupation of to-morrow cheerfully looked to, any one of these pursuits is not most humanising and laudable. I know no station which is rendered more endurable to the person in it, or more safe to the person out of it, by having ignorance for its associate. I know no station which has a right to monopolise the means of mutual instruction, improvement, and rational entertainment; or which has ever continued to be a station very long, after seeking to do so.

This is first and foremost a question of *right*: no ruling class has a right to debar the great mass of the people from these "humanising and laudable" activities which attest to the presence of man as Man. No ruling class has a right to withhold the means—material, social, spiritual—of raising life above the merely brutish and savage, like that country justice in *Barnaby Rudge*, who thinks it an act of presumption tantamount to rebellion for a poor person like Mrs. Rudge to obtain a scrap of education. Society is not merely a machine to keep the humbler classes in their "station" but exists to provide a realm of human value in which the full humanity that is man's specific prerogative can find realization. By no possibility can any ruling class have a right—since it has a choice in the matter—to create a class of helots, of "degraded brutes of burden," as brutish and degraded from the standard of achieved human excellence as the American slaves or Maypole Hugh or the baby savages in *The Haunted Man* and *A Christmas Carol*.

But such a course of action is no less foolish than it is wrong; for, as Dickens darkly warns here (giving voice to a fear quite general in the decade of the 1840s), a governing class that does debar the populace from the means of humanization, that thereby assures the existence of a class of Maypole Hughs in society's midst, makes conditions ripe for an outbreak of mad and savage disturbances like the Gordon Riots—anarchic upheavals that might end by sweeping away the classes whose injustice and folly had suffered such barbarism to prevail.

What specific steps the English propertied classes should take Dickens does not say; and it is true that "[m]any of the circumstances whose strong influence has been at work for years in our manufacturing towns have not arisen here" in America. But the example of Lowell proves that somehow or other so good a result *can* be brought about, and Dickens "earnestly adjure[s]" his English readers, at the end of his chapter on the Lowell factories, to resolve to do something about "those great haunts of desperate misery," the English manufacturing centers, "to purge them of their suffering and danger"—and quickly, for "precious Time is rushing by" (4).

Here readers of Dickens find themselves on very familiar ground: this is the liberal, reforming voice recognized as characteristically Dickensian by critics from his own time to the present. This is the "nineteenth-century liberal" George Orwell describes in his great essay: the Dickens with that "generously angry" expression on his face,[30] who laid such urgent emphasis on educating the great mass of the people; who strenuously supported Ragged Schools; who condemned "the frightful neglect by the State of those whom it punishes so constantly, and whom it might, as easily and less expensively, instruct and save";[31] who did not wonder that so many of the poor could not even "guess at any social duty, being so discarded by all social teachers but the gaoler and the hangman"; and who endorsed with wholehearted approval the injunction of Sir Thomas More's *Utopia*: "Let the State prevent vices, and take away the occasions for offences by well ordering its subjects, and not by suffering wickedness to increase, afterward to be punished."[32] This is the Dickens who spoke publicly in support of such causes as administrative reform, sanitary reform, and the Hospital for Sick Children, and who gladly consented to address enormous audiences at the Manchester Atheneum, the Liverpool Mechanics' Institution, the Leeds Mechanics' Institution, the Birmingham Polytechnic Institution, each time praising unstintedly the efforts these establishments were making to educate the working classes. The excoriator of Bumbledom and its workhouses, the eloquent defender of the Sunday amusements of the working man, this is the Dickens who, driven by one of his deepest impulses, strove so manfully to take the roofs off the houses and dens of the poor, in the magnanimous belief that if only that which lay within could be *seen* it would be ameliorated.

As often as one rehearses this familiar litany, it never fails to stir the heart. But here we can discern, with exceptional distinctness, that within the familiar liberal spirit is contained a conviction that, if less familiar, is no less essentially Dickensian. For deep within what we call Dickens's "liberal reformism"—like the dense, elemental core at the center of the revolving earth—lies the political theory this book has undertaken to bring to light. Lacking any patience with the notion that men are essentially pacific, benevolent creatures and that wickedness and evil in human actions are to be explained by saying that oppressive social conditions have warped this or that originally well-disposed evil-doer and made him bad, Dickens's liberalism, on the contrary, grows out of the belief that since men, plentifully endowed by nature with instincts of violence and aggression, get tamed and humanized in society, then society's civilizing work ought to be done as well and as fully as possible. And if society's civilizing function is not limited solely to the interdiction of human aggression but also includes the fostering of that full humanity which nature gives men only as a potentiality not an achieved actuality, then society's civilizing means cannot be confined to the legitimate force and violence at the disposal of the state—to the "strong Hand"—but must also incorporate the "strong Heart," with its reliance on education, on trust and forbearance, on the full inclusiveness of the community of men, on the human appeal that calls into being a human response. And all these liberal means are the more to be recommended because they are also immeasurably the best means of social control, by far more dependable for accomplishing society's necessary function of ensuring public order than any threat or application of force. Dickens's liberal reformism, in other words, is firmly based on, indeed is part and parcel of, what we in our day (especially here in America) would identify as an essentially conservative political philosophy: it is based on the belief that "[c]ivilisation is the humanisation of man in society" (as Matthew Arnold formulated it [33]) and that it is thanks to the transforming power of society, not to the original goodness and rationality of man's unmodified human nature, that human life is anything other than solitary, poor, nasty, brutish, and short.

11

Martin Chuzzlewit in Context

W hat's the good of Shakespeare?" cries an inconsequential character in *Martin Chuzzlewit*. "There's a lot of feet in Shakespeare's verse, but there an't any legs worth mentioning. . . . Juliet, Desdemona, Lady Macbeth . . . might as well have no legs at all, for anything the audience know about it. . . . What's the legitimate object of the drama . . . ? Human nature. What are legs? Human nature. Then let us have plenty of leg pieces. . . !" (28).

Everyone no doubt has an obsession—and Dickens's in *Martin Chuzzlewit* is that great question of human nature that for him is formulated with more precision, complexity, and import than could begin to be imagined by *Chuzzlewit*'s leg-fancying theatergoer. And in this novel Dickens's preoccupation with the original nature of man is inextricably linked to the question of what is the true character of that larger nature of which human nature forms only a constituent part. In *Chuzzlewit* the word "nature" or the phrase "human nature" seems to occur almost on every page. Characters in the novel, like the leg-fancier above, over and over again make speeches about human nature—theorizing about what it is, avowing their faith in it, commending or condemning this or that action as a credit or a disgrace to it. And they are constantly making judgments about what is "natural," too, as if nothing were easier to determine: Dr. Jobling is hardly the only character in this novel who believes that "We know a few secrets of nature in our profession, sir. Of course we do" (27).

One of the commonplaces of criticism holds that the first chapter of a typical Dickens novel contains in embryo most if not all of the book's major themes. It is certainly true that Chapter 1 of *Martin Chuzzlewit* poses this central question about man's nature without loss of time. What was the origin of the great human family? this rather ponderously humorous chapter asks: what was the character of the ancestor from whom we men of these latter days have sprung? Our pedigree of course derives from Adam and Eve, answers the very first paragraph, conventionally enough; but the next paragraph's reminder that "there was, in the oldest family of which we have any record, a murderer and a vagabond" quickly qualifies the opening evocation of man's Edenic innocence and nature's Edenic beneficence. If mankind's original character, fresh from the hand of God, was wholly good, it nevertheless before long suffered the fatal taint of original sin—a taint whose full magnitude was soon enough disclosed by Cain's murder of his brother and whose legacy of violence and aggression, as Chapter 1 goes on to comment, has figured centrally in the subsequent history of our race.

This preoccupation with aggression is by now a familiar feature of Dickens's imagination of human nature. But it is the chapter's last paragraph, substituting the anthropological for the theological, that most precisely foreshadows the theory of human nature informing *Martin Chuzzlewit*. This paragraph makes an elaborate, convoluted joke, whose now obscure references, imperfectly capable of stirring modern readers to laughter, are well worth tracking down before going on to discuss what *Martin Chuzzlewit* tells us about how Dickens's American journey graphically confirmed for him the essential aspects of his political theory. For these references shine light not only forward into *Martin Chuzzlewit* but also backward onto certain matters already considered. Understanding them fully, moreover, will resolve into clearer focus this novel's important and hitherto incompletely understood opening chapter while also enlarging our sense of the myriad, unexpected ways the complex tradition of European thought about human nature and the nature of society could have reached Dickens.

Whimsically considering "the foundation and increase of the human family," Dickens says that he will content himself with remarking:

Firstly, that it may be safely asserted and yet without implying any direct participation in the Monboddo doctrine touching the probability of the human race
having once been monkeys, that men do play very strange and extraordinary
tricks. Secondly, and yet without trenching on the Blumenbach theory as to the
descendants of Adam having a vast number of qualities which belong more particularly to swine than to any other class of animals in the creation, that some men
certainly are remarkable for taking uncommon good care of themselves.

I wonder how many readers have regarded this passage, as I did, as another example of Dickens's unbounded talent for inventing names at once
likely and unlikely. And yet these are real people Dickens refers to—famous people in their day—and the doctrines Dickens mentions here form
part of a notable debate in the early history of anthropology, a debate
that, as it has everything to do with the primary concerns of *Martin
Chuzzlewit*, merits the close attention of the novel's students.

Lord Monboddo, that representative Scottish moralist, who was the
associate of such Edinburgh notables as David Hume, Adam Smith, and
Lord Kames, we have met in these pages before as Rousseau's chief British
disciple. Born as James Burnett in 1714, he studied Greek philosophy before going on to take a law degree. His career as an advocate in Edinburgh was brilliant, and in 1767 he was raised to the judiciary, being made
an ordinary lord of session and assuming the title Lord Monboddo, from
the name of his birthplace in Kincardineshire. Respected throughout his
career as "both a profound lawyer and an upright judge," he refused
higher judicial advancement to preserve leisure enough for the philosophical studies which have assured him a secure if modest place in the history
of ideas. His two major works are *Of the Origin and Progress of Language* (6
vols., 1773–92), remarkable for its evolutionary theories and for what
Monboddo's friend, James Boswell, called its "strange speculation about
the primitive state of human nature," and *Antient Metaphysics* (6 vols.,
1779–99), a defense of Greek philosophy. So enthusiastic a classicist was
he, indeed—and an enthusiastic cultivator of the *mens sana in corpore sano*,
too—that, as "a carriage was not in use among the ancients, he considered it to be an engine of effeminacy and idleness." He therefore made his
annual journeys to London on horseback, attended by a single servant,
until he was over eighty years old. He died in 1799.[1]

Dickens's joke about "the probability of the human race having once
been monkeys" refers to Monboddo's notorious theory, set forth at
length in *Of the Origin and Progress of Language*, that the Orang Outang,
"an animal of the human form, inside as well as outside," possessing

"human intelligence" and the "sentiments and affections peculiar to our species, such as the sense of modesty, of honour, and of justice," in fact actually "belongs to our species."[2] This is a view also voiced by Rousseau—although he had the discretion to muffle it in a footnote[3]—and like Rousseau ("that singular genius, which this age has produced"), Monboddo considers the question only as part of a larger argument about the extraordinary evolution undergone by man, who "was originally a wild savage animal, till he was tamed, and, as I may say, *humanized*, by civility and arts." Man has come to be the fully human creature he now is only through the long-protracted, collective effort of forming and improving civil society. Thus, while it is true enough that "man in his natural state is the WORK OF GOD," nevertheless, "as we now see him, he may be said, properly enough, to be *the work of man*." Indeed, even the "rational soul" which is human nature's "chief prerogative" is "our own acquisition, and the fruit of industry, like any art or science, not the gift of nature"—a view noted in our discussion of *Barnaby Rudge*'s notion of the soul. So, considering man as he now is in the civilized and polished nations of the world, "we shall find, that our nature is chiefly constituted of acquired habits, and that we are much more creatures of custom and art than of nature. It is a common saying"—voiced in *Martin Chuzzlewit* by Mr. Pecksniff (19)—"that habit (meaning custom) is a second nature. I add, that it is more powerful than the first, and in a great measure destroys and absorbs the original nature: For it is the capital and distinguishing characteristic of our species, that we can *make* ourselves, as it were, over again, so that the *original* nature in us can hardly be seen; and it is with the greatest difficulty that we can distinguish it from the acquired." Thus we may conclude that it is "the greatest praise of man, that, from the savage state, in which the Orang Outang lives, he should, by his own sagacity and industry, have arrived at the state in which we now see him."[4]

In the Orang Outang, then (to return to the monkeys of Dickens's joke), Monboddo, like Rousseau, sees the embodiment of our species in a very early stage of its development—though not in the very first stage, for the Orang Outangs have already made some progress in the arts of life: "they use sticks for weapons; they live in society; they make huts of branches of trees, and they carry off negroe girls, of whom they make slaves, and use them both for work and pleasure." And in fact (he argues), our consanguinity with the Orang Outangs is far from incredible when we consider the report made by an officer of a Dutch ship in the Gulf of Bengal, who came upon a race of men "with tails like those of cats"—a report Linnaeus says, in a letter to Monboddo, that he too is inclined to believe—and when we recall that Mr. Barber, a mathematics teacher in Inverness, "had a tail, about half a foot long; which he carefully concealed during his life; but was discovered after his death, which happened about twenty years ago." No wonder Dr. Johnson lost patience with Monboddo, whom recently he and Boswell had very pleasantly visited during their tour of the Hebrides. "It is a pity," said the Doctor, "to see Lord Monboddo publish such notions as he has done; a man of sense, and of so much elegant learning. . . . Other people have strange notions, but they conceal them. If they have tails, they hide them; but Monboddo is as jealous of his tail as a squirrel."[5]

However scientifically prophetic Monboddo's evolutionary theories may appear from our own post-Darwinian perspective, he himself remains not a scientist but wholly an Enlightenment *savant*. In Johann Friedrich Blumenbach, however, we have a figure of a much more recognizably modern stamp. Born in 1752, he received his M.D. at Göttingen in 1775 and by 1778 had become full professor of medicine at that university and curator of its Natural History Cabinet. His skill as a lecturer was legendary—Samuel Taylor Coleridge went to Göttingen to hear two of his courses—and he produced a flood of notable students, including Humboldt. His chief distinction is that he was the founding father of scientific anthropology and in addition the founder of the science of comparative anatomy in Germany. His dissertation *On the Natural Varieties of Mankind* (1775) became world-famous, and his textbook on physiology, long the standard work on that subject, was translated into English by the fashionable London physician, mesmerist, and phrenologist, John Elliotson, who of course was for many years one of Dickens's "most intimate and valued friends,"[6] as well as his family doctor and godfather to his son Walter. Blumenbach died in 1840, not quite three years before Dickens began work on *Martin Chuzzlewit*, and (as was unusual for foreigners) the death of this "celebrated natural philosopher and professor" was reported in the English newspapers.[7]

Dickens's citation of Blumenbach's "theory" that men have "a vast number of qualities that belong more particularly to swine than to any other class of animals in the creation" refers to a comparison Blumenbach makes on at least two occasions to illustrate two of his most characteristic views. Anxious to demonstrate the fundamental unity of mankind, the membership of all men in a single basic species, Blumenbach strove to refute the views of those "persons who have most earnestly protested against their own noble selves being placed in a natural system in one common species with Negroes and Hottentots," while at the same time he was obliged to rebut extremists on the other side, such as "the renowned philosopher and downright caprice-monger Lord Monboddo," who have had no compunction in declaring themselves and the orangutan to be creatures of one and the same species."[8] Thus in his slightly whimsical paper "On Human and Porcine Races"[9] Blumenbach argues that, to settle once and for all this vexed question in science and assure ourselves that the several varieties of mankind form only one species, we ought (among other things) to consider certain other animals. For man is not the only creature differentiated into numerous varieties, and though it is indeed hard to imagine that a Senegalese Negro and a German Adonis belong to the same species, nevertheless the differences between them are by no means more sharp than the differences separating the several varieties of a thousand other species.

Let us take for example the case of the pig, he says—an example chosen because there are numerous and remarkable similarities between pigs and men. Their internal anatomy is almost identical, for instance; the taste of their flesh is so much the same (as Galen and others report) that the bad practices of an infamous innkeeper would never have come to light had a piece of a human finger not been discovered in what the menu advertised as a pork dish; leather tanned from human skin is indistinguishable from tanned pigskin; and, most important, the overall internal economy of both creatures is extraordinarily similar. Both animals are completely domesticated, both are omnivorous, both are spread over the whole globe and exposed to the same extremes of climate, style of life, and diet, and both get similar diseases, which other animals do not get. Also, Blumenbach continues, the pig is an especially appropriate example in this context, because no naturalist has ever doubted that *all* domesticated pigs are descended from the wild boar and belong to the same species. Now, there are no differences found among the several varieties of men—in stature, in color, in hair, or in skull shape—which cannot be found in the same proportions among the several varieties of pigs. Thus if we may believe that all pigs belong to the same species, there is no reason for us to doubt that all men do too.

If Blumenbach makes the comparison between men and swine central to his exposition in this instance, he invokes it again some years later to illustrate still another of his most deeply held views about the original nature of mankind. In discussing, in his *Contributions to Natural History*, the tendency of all species of living things to "degenerate"—that is, to differentiate themselves into "every sort of variety" under the pressure of environmental changes—Blumenbach remarks that *domestic* animals show this tendency in an especially marked way and that its effects are particularly notable in hogs and in men, above all other animals. After mentioning many of the same similarities already cited in "On Human and Porcine Races," he goes on to say that the special, highly advantageous adaptability of both pigs and men is no doubt ultimately to be explained by the "exceptional compactness"—shared by no other animal—of their respective mucous membranes, that tissue being "the first and most important factory of the formative force." Now, if the effects of "degeneration" are best visible in the *domestic* animals, it is no wonder that man (surpassing even the hog) is adaptable and differentiated beyond all creatures, since his is the most profoundly domestic of all animal species, qualitatively as well as quantitatively.

[The] difference between him and other domestic animals is only this, that they are not so completely born to domestication as he is, having been created by nature immediately a domestic animal. The exact original wild condition of most of the domestic animals is known. But no one knows the exact original wild condition of man.

Why? "There is none"—man has *always* been a tame and social creature.[10]

This last opinion brought Blumenbach into spirited public disagreement with Lord Monboddo: Dickens's yoking these two men together in *Martin Chuzzlewit* is not arbitrary or accidental, I believe, but instead reflects his interest in their revival of a famous debate hotly argued many years before—the debate about whether, in Peter the Wild Boy, learned Europe at last had found a living example of true natural man. This celebrated character fascinated Dickens enough to be mentioned by him not only in *Martin Chuzzlewit* (7) but in many other places as well—Peter seems, indeed, to form part of the permanent furniture of his imagination—and the debate over the Wild Boy's nature, as will at once be clear, bears centrally upon *Chuzzlewit's* intense concern with the question of human nature. Discovered running up and down in the fields near Hamelin in 1724, quite naked and apparently wild, this swarthy boy was captured by the townspeople and was found on further examination to be between twelve and fifteen years old, brutish, and without human speech. By order of King George, he was sent eventually to England in 1762, where he was given as a present to Princess Caroline and confided to the care of Dr. Arbuthnot, the former royal physician and the close friend of Pope, Swift, Gay, and Congreve.

Was this really an authentic specimen of man in the state of nature?

Swift went to see him as soon as possible and thought not. Linnaeus took the opposite view, in which his fellow naturalists Buffon and de Pauw, and also Rousseau, later concurred. Defoe for his part was not sure. The boy might very well be only an "Ideot," he allows, fraudulently presented as "the very Creature which the learned World have, for many Years past, pretended to wish for, *viz.* one that has been kept entirely from human Society." Yet on the whole, he concludes, it seems best at least tentatively to accept the *Juvenis Hanoveranus* for the "Object of MERE uninformed NATURE" that he seems to be—like the "wild Man" Orson in the old tale.

The chief singularity of this "Image or Exemplification . . . of *Meer Nature*," Defoe reports, is that while he is "a Thing in human Shape," nevertheless he may be said to be "in some sense, *as it were*, without a *Soul*; for . . . Not to be, and not to be in Exercise, is much the same." And thus this example of Meer Nature teaches one lesson above all others—a lesson very well learned by the creator of the soulless Barnaby Rudge, perhaps in part directly from so influential a teacher of his childhood as Defoe:

The Soul is plac'd in the Body like a rough Diamond, which requires the Wheel and Knife, and all the other Arts of the Cutter, to shape it, and polish it. . . . If Art be deficient, Nature can do no more; it has plac'd the capacity in the Jewel; but till the Rough be remov'd, the Diamond never shews itself. . . . '[T]is given to us to work upon ourselves, and if we do not think it worth while to bestow the Trouble, we must not expect the Blessing.

In Peter, then (as in the deaf and dumb, adds Defoe, bringing Laura Bridgman at once to the minds of Dickens readers), we see what "a plain coarse Piece of Work is a Man in the meer Condition he is born in, just coming out of Nature's Hand." This being the case, it clearly follows that

polishing the Soul of Man [by education] is an Act of the highest Consequence, and the chief Thing that distinguishes him, and enables him to distinguish himself from a Brute; for, if I may venture my own Opinion, . . . an untaught Man, a Creature in human Shape, but intirely neglected and uninstructed, is ten thousand times more miserable than a Brute.[11]

Without question these views belong to the same tradition of thought that also includes Dickens: such sentiments could come straight out of *A Christmas Carol* or *The Haunted Man* or *Barnaby Rudge* or the description of Laura Bridgman in *American Notes.* Lord Monboddo, too, is firmly within this tradition; and, in raising once again the whole issue of Peter the Wild Boy's true nature a half-century after the original controversy had raged, Monboddo draws much the same lesson from Peter's example as had Defoe. Peter, Monboddo was sure, provided irrefutable, living proof of the theories he himself held most dear.

Monboddo had asserted in the first volume of *The Origin and Progress of Language* (p. 187) that the Wild Boy was unquestionably not a mere idiot. In 1782, having read all available accounts of the case, the Judge decided to investigate the question more closely. Since Peter was still living, though by now well advanced in years, Monboddo paid a call on him at the farm near Berkhamstead where he was kept on a pension paid by the King, and he heard the short, healthy, bearded old man sing the couple of songs he knew and rehearse his whole pathetic vocabulary—consisting of the words "Pe-ter" and "King George." This visit, supplemented by the further inquiries made for Monboddo by a young Oxford friend, triumphantly vindicated his original judgment. Without question, he reports in *Antient Metaphysics*, this creature—truly an "extraordinary phenomenon; more extraordinary, I think, than the new planet [Uranus], or than if we were to discover 30,000 more fixed Stars"—really is "a living example of the state of Nature," and his existence conclusively proves that "my State of Nature is not an imaginary State . . . but a real State, upon which we may safely found our philosophy of *Man*." What Peter's example shows, above all, is that man in a state of nature is a mere brutish animal and that what we civilized men chiefly admire as the most definitively *human* of our characteristics come not from nature but from what Defoe would call "Art"—from, in other words, the transforming pressure on us of human culture and human society, by which our whole nature has been radically retailored. What we see in Peter's own life history, then, is "a brief chronicle or abstract of the history of the progress of human nature, from the mere animal to the first stage of civilised life"—and this, needless to say, is the most crucial step in "the progress of Man from the mere Animal to the Intellectual Creature." [12]

In 1811, Blumenbach systematically reviewed the literature on Peter the Wild Boy's history, from his discovery in 1724 to the moment when "he ended his vegetatory existence as a kind of very old child, in Feb. 1785." Most of the details in Blumenbach's report were contained also in Monboddo's; we hear of Peter's having to accustom himself to clothes and to an omnivorous diet; of his relish for onions, fire, gin, and music; of his lifelong indifference to money and women; of his strength and robustness, his keen sensitivity to changes in the season and the weather, his gentle and tractable disposition. But the several new details Blumenbach cites lead him to an utterly different conclusion. That Peter's thighs were whiter than his calves when he was discovered suggests he had formerly gone clothed in short trousers; the report of his unusually thickened tongue suggests a birth defect: and all in all the conclusion is inescapable that "this pretended ideal of pure human nature, to which later sophists have elevated the wild Peter, was altogether nothing more than a dumb imbecile idiot," who moreover was very likely that cast-out retarded child of a recently remarried widower named Krüger. But of course none of the various "wild children" who have from time to time been discovered can by any possibility "serve as a specimen of the original Man of Nature," for there is no such thing. Having been from the very first a tame and social creature, man simply has no wild form to which he can revert. That is why the various examples of *Homo sapiens ferus* listed in Linnaeus's catalogue are so entirely unlike one another:

Only in this were they like each other, that contrary to the instinct of nature, they lived alone, separated from the society of men, wandering about here and there; a condition, whose opposition to what is natural has been already compared by Voltaire to that of a lost solitary bee.[13]

Thus if the first chapter of *Chuzzlewit* begins by asking what is the origin of the human family, it ends by alluding to key theories proposing answers to that question—which, for all their radical disagreement with each other, share a fundamental assumption, also shared by Dickens and irradiating the whole of *Chuzzlewit*: Monboddo and Blumenbach alike endorse the view that man's specific humanity is inseparable from his life in society, and thus the authentically human creature is by definition a social creature. But Dickens's complex joke contains still one more theory about original human nature, a theory already encountered at the very beginning of *Chuzzlewit*'s first chapter. In affirming that "it may be safely asserted, and yet without implying any direct participation in the Monboddo doctrine touching the probability of the human race having once been monkeys, that men do play very strange and extraordinary tricks," Dickens (who had improved his already extensive inwardness with Shakespeare by avidly rereading him during his American travels) is, I think, relying on his reader's familiarity with an especially memorable passage in *Measure for Measure*, also quoted in *A Christmas Carol*. It is Isabella who says:

> But man, proud man,
> Dress'd in a little brief authority,
> Most ignorant of what he's most assur'd—
> His glassy essence—like an angry ape
> Plays such fantastic tricks before high heaven
> As makes the angels weep; who, with our spleens,
> Would all themselves laugh mortal.[14]

Man's essence is "glassy" in that the immortal soul which is the definitive human attribute mirrors God, like a looking-glass: created in His image, we exhibit a reflection of His divinity. No fact about human nature can be more certain—God Himself assures us of it. But if this is the most important quality of human nature, it is nevertheless not the only one: the mention of man's mortality which closes Isabella's sentence reminds us of the effects of the original sin that brought death and evil into the human world, transforming and complicating man's nature, leaving it problematic and divided, bestial as well as godlike. And Isabella's statement hints at yet another related theory about man's nature, explaining its essential duality by man's place in the great chain of being. As the anatomist Edward Tyson expressed it in his book on the natural history of apes, "*Man* is part a *Brute*, part an *Angel*; and is that *Link* in the *Creation*, that joyns them both together."[15]

.   .   .

Martin Chuzzlewit, then, as its first chapter rather reconditely announces, is centrally concerned with original human nature and its relation to society, questions which, of course, closely link it to *Nickleby* and *Barnaby*. Yet it differs from these novels in the degree of self-consciousness and explicitness it brings to the handling of these fundamental themes of political philosophy, so central to Dickens's novelistic imagination. By itself, the experience of writing *Barnaby* might fully account for the mastery Dickens shows here; but *Chuzzlewit* makes clear that an additional factor is contributing to his self-assured control, for it demonstrates that the journey to America massively confirmed for him his political theory's most basic tenets by giving him, as he evidently thought, a direct glimpse into the state of nature itself.

That the state of nature is in full swing in the New World is an idea as old as the first European discoveries. The world across the Atlantic long remained for the European imagination not simply a geographical fact but also the embodiment of the various myths and theories about the first ages of nature and man. Hobbes, for example, anticipating objections that "there was never such a time, nor condition of warre" as his state of nature, concedes that it may not ever have prevailed over the whole earth, but that it is certainly flourishing at the present moment "in many places of *America*," where "the savage people . . . have no government at all; and live at this day in that brutish manner, as I said before." [16] And, thinking of the condition not only of the inhabitants of America but also of the "wild Common of Nature" to be seen there, Locke made his famous observation that "in the beginning all the World was *America*." [17] Then, too, it was near the mouth of the Orinoco that the greatest fictional explorer of the state of nature was wrecked and cast away, and Dickens, not content with mentioning Robinson three times in *Chuzzlewit* (5, 21, 36), also cites those Crusoe imitations, Philip Quarll (in *The Hermit*, 1727) and *Peter Wilkins* (1751), in acknowledgment, I believe, of his own deep indebtedness to his first textbook of political theory, as Defoe's great novel may be said to be. It is a novel, he remarks (with his own childhood in mind), that "impressed one solitary foot-print on the shore of boyish memory, whereof the tread of generations should not stir the lightest grain of sand" (5).

The Garden of Eden and the Golden Age of the ancients were the first myths of the primitive state of the world that Europeans projected upon the newly discovered lands. [18] Thus "the first popularizer of America and its myth," the humanist Peter Martyr, affirmed that the indigenous inhabitants "seem to lyve in the goulden worlde of the which owlde wryters speake so much: wherein men lyved simplye and innocentlye without inforcement of lawes, without quarrelling Iudges and libelles, contente onely to satisfie nature, without further vexation of knowledge of thinges to come." [19] Other writers were struck not only by the prelapsarian quality of men's relations with each other but also with the paradisial condition of nature itself. Two explorers on an expedition to North Carolina sponsored by Sir Walter Raleigh, for example, after noting that the inhabitants "lived after the manner of the Golden Age," went on to remark that the "earth bringeth forth all things in abundance as in the first creation, without toil or labor." [20] This too was the Edenic aspect of the New World Michael Drayton had in mind when he characterized Virginia as "Earth's onely paradise," [21] and of course the reports about America were what Shakespeare had in mind when Gonzalo in *The Tempest* imagines a place where "All things in common Nature should produce / Without sweat or endeavour. . . ." [22]

Dickens opens *Martin Chuzzlewit* in the Garden of Eden, and, as part of a general preoccupation with the myth of Eden that pervades this novel, he makes much of the venerable notion of America as Paradise—

quite ostentatiously so, for he represents at the very heart of America a
settlement called "Eden," characterized as "a terrestrial Paradise, upon
the showing of its proprietors" (33). But so decisively in *Chuzzlewit* does
he reject this idea of America that he may be said to fling it down and
dance upon it. He rejects not merely the American mythology's Edenic
conception of man but also its Edenic conception of nature, for what he
saw in his American travels, while it strengthened his radical skepticism
about the original innocence of human nature, also categorically confirmed his long-standing sense of a darkly destructive principle at the
center of nature, too.

Moreover, his powerful descriptions of nature in America are making a
political point, in response to what he recognized as the political use to
which the Eden myth could be put. For ideas about the nature of nature
are more often than not political ideas: they bear centrally (though usually implicitly) on the question of where the evil in human affairs comes
from. If one sees in nature a scene where "every prospect pleases, and
only man is vile," then man's vileness—in the forms, especially, of crime
and oppression—appears not as part of the natural scheme but rather as
an accretion deriving from some accidental, external cause acting to over-
whelm the goodness which is no less intrinsic to man's nature than to
nature as a whole. And the accidental cause producing that artificial evil is
(as this political version of the pastoral so regularly goes on to stipulate)
either the unnatural institution of private property or the whole, organized unnatural framework of society itself, here imagined as a mere
structure of domination and submission, serving only the interest of the
powerful and rich and ruinously corrupting human life as a whole to secure so wantonly unjust an aim.

With this entire fabric of ideas Dickens, as we know, has scant patience;
and his glimpse in America on his voyage up the Mississippi of raw, uncultivated, purely natural nature—a sight invisible in England, where
every inch of ground has been transformed and retransformed by human
artifice—showed him unequivocally that the notion of nature as man's
generous, watchful, and loving nurse, which is an inseparable component
of the political ideology just sketched out, is simply false. Nature in a
state of nature is nothing of the kind; it is the very opposite of Paradise.

So Martin Chuzzlewit found, much to his cost, on his ill-starred expedition to the "settlement" of Eden on the Mississippi. His steamboat
journey upriver into the prehistoric state of nature is very like Marlow's
later journey "in the night of first ages" toward Mr. Kurtz: Dickens, exactly like Conrad, imagines it as a voyage to the Heart of Darkness. And
indeed Conrad, in the use he makes in his remarkable novella of what one

feels certain he in part learned from *Chuzzlewit*, is perhaps that novel's most profound critic. Conrad's travellers, toiling up the river on their steamer, glided past their surroundings "like phantoms, wondering and secretly appalled." To them, the "earth seemed unearthly," because they had never before seen it in its purely natural state. "We are accustomed to look upon the shackled form of a conquered monster," says Marlow, speaking of the world of nature as Europeans know it, hedged and ditched, cultivated with crops and gardens, garrisoned with manors, churches, cottages; "but there [in the Congo]—there you could look at a thing monstrous and free." For the untamed natural world—the "prehistoric earth," Marlow calls it—*is* a savage monster, seeking whom it may devour. That in his eyes it "wore the aspect of an unknown planet" is an index of how vast a transformation man has wrought in domesticating it. Thus, says Marlow, "We could have fancied ourselves the first of men taking possession of an accursed inheritance, to be subdued at the cost of profound anguish and excessive toil." Such indeed was the first man's hard fate after his own sin turned nature harsh to him, and such the burden and achievement of his posterity.

Like Conrad's travellers, Martin Chuzzlewit and Mark Tapley penetrate into the heart of mere nature like phantoms gliding down to Hades. The very trees look like the suffering damned as illustrated by Henry Fuseli or William Blake.

On they toiled through great solitudes, where the trees upon the banks grew thick and close; and floated in the stream; and held up shrivelled arms from out the river's depths; and slid down from the margin of the land: half growing, half decaying, in the miry water. On through the weary day and melancholy night: beneath the burning sun, and in the mist and vapour of the evening: on, until return appeared impossible, and restoration to their home a miserable dream. . . . [I]t might have been old Charon's boat, conveying melancholy shades to judgment. (23)

The grand language is Tennysonian, reverberating especially with echoes of "The Lotos Eaters," a poem that also laments the excessive toil with which the ill-used race of men are condemned (by indifferent and unfeeling gods) to wrest their thin subsistence from a harsh and niggardly earth.

As they . . . came more and more towards their journey's end, the monotonous desolation of the scene increased to that degree, that for any redeeming feature it

presented to their eyes, they might have entered, in the body, on the grim do-
mains of Giant Despair. A flat morass, bestrewn with fallen timber; a marsh on
which the good growth of the earth seemed to have been wrecked and cast away,
that from its decomposing ashes vile and ugly things might rise; where the very
trees took the aspect of huge weeds, begotten of the slime from which they
sprung, by the hot sun that burnt them up; where fatal maladies, seeking whom
they might infect, came forth, at night, in misty shapes, and creeping out upon
the water, hunted them like spectres until day; where even the blessed sun, shining down on festering elements of corruption and disease, became a horror; this
was the realm of Hope through which they moved.

At last they stopped. At Eden too. The waters of the Deluge might have left it
but a week before: so choked with slime and matted growth was the hideous
swamp which bore that name. (23)

This is the veritable youth of the world and the prime of nature—this
inchoate and, above all, deadly squalor. Fit only for "a Alligator, in a state
of natur'," it does not foster man but slays him (33).

Paradise? Quite the reverse, Dickens insists. Far from being the Celestial City of *The Pilgrim's Progress*, this is only the dismal domain of
Bunyan's Doubting Castle, whose lord is the sadistic Giant Despair. All
that is Edenic about this "Walley of Eden," Mark Tapley dryly notes, is
that "there's lots of serpents there" (21). Indeed, says Dickens, it is loathsome and malignant without "any redeeming feature": and for emphasis
he invokes the magical, redemptive language of another great literary exploration (also influenced by America) of the state of nature and natural
man—Shakespeare's *Tempest*—accentuating by contrast the utter unre-
generacy of this scene of raw original nature. If in *The Tempest* the young
prince, "Weeping again the King my father's wrack" upon the shores of a
wild, uncultivated island, was comforted by a spirit assuring him, in music that "crept by me upon the waters," that his father's decomposing
corpse was being transformed by the sea into something rich and strange
like coral and pearls, in this passage in *Chuzzlewit* it is "the good growth
of the earth" that has been "wrecked and cast away, that from its decomposing ashes" not coral and pearls but "vile and ugly things might rise";
and it is not Ariel and his music that creep out upon the waters but rather
fatal maladies, in misty shapes like specters, hunting down the living.[23]

By the 1840s, viewing America as the embodiment of so grim a conception of the original condition of nature was in fact a long-established
commonplace, having received authoritative, "scientific" formulation
from the great eighteenth-century naturalist, Buffon. Why are the ani-

mals of the New World so inferior to those of the Old, Buffon asked, and why do all European animals brought to America (with the exception of the pig) get progressively smaller, weaker, less appetizing? Why is America crawling with unimaginable quantities of enormous snakes, lizards, toads, and insects? Why is it that "everything languishes, decays, stifles," and that the "air and the earth, weighed down by the moist and poisonous vapors, cannot purify themselves nor profit from the influence of the star of life"? Without question, all this is due to "the raw state of nature" in America, whose lands emerged from the Flood much later than the continents of the Old World and thus remain unformed and sodden. That is why nature in America is at one and the same time both newborn and decaying. Such a view of American nature, and such a view of the raw state of nature in general, is perfectly consistent with Dickens's own; and Dickens, who had a set of Buffon's works in his library, no doubt had this theory in mind when imagining Eden on the Mississippi as newly emerged from the waters of the Deluge and also when describing, as Martin Chuzzlewit's very first sight in America, a steamboat "which, with its machinery on deck, looked, as it worked its long slim legs, like some enormously magnified insect or antediluvian monster" (15).[24]

In this just-born world, "beneath this ungenerous sky and in this empty land," Buffon reports that nature treats man "less as a mother than a stepmother," and in this view Dickens wholeheartedly concurs.[25] Contrary to what the early reports seemed to promise, raw nature as Dickens saw it does not smile beneficently on man as on Adam in the Garden of Eden. Indeed to the image of the Edenic Adam, Dickens in *Chuzzlewit* keeps opposing the figure of the fallen Adam, as a reminder that nature provides only what subsistence man toilsomely extracts by the sweat of his brow. In the same vein, when Dickens reports that the midwife Mrs. Gamp "had been up all the previous night, in attendance upon a ceremony to which the usage of gossips has given that name which expresses, in two syllables, the curse pronounced upon Adam," his play on the word "labor" takes note of still another way in which nature imposes toil and pain upon accursed humanity as a condition of its fallen existence (19). Such, too, is the point of Dickens's sweetly melancholy description of a lovely English springtime twilight, when

the smell of earth newly-upturned—first breath of hope to the first labourer, after his garden withered—was fragrant in the evening breeze. It was a time when most men cherish good resolves, and sorrow for the wasted past: when most men, looking on the shadows as they gather, think of that evening which must close on all, and that to-morrow which has none beyond. (20)

This is a benign evocation of the fallen Adam, in its assumption that nature normally grants man his reward for the toil to which he has been condemned. But the smell of the freshly plowed field reminds Dickens of a new-made grave, and it leaves him musing on the thought that for fallen mankind the one great debt of nature is death.

And alas, even the sweat of one's brow is not by itself enough to wring a living from the ungenerous natural world. It also takes skill, developed by long-protracted collective effort, to turn nature to human use. How painful, then, to see the settlers in "Eden"—those "[f]armers who had never seen a plough; woodmen who had never used an axe"—who had brought with them from Europe just such pastoral ideas about nature's loving kindness as Dickens is repudiating in *Chuzzlewit* (22). They "appeared to have wandered there with the idea that husbandry was the natural gift of all mankind." Faced with the reality, they helped each other in their pathetic attempts at farming as best they could; but, subject to the sentence pronounced on Adam and his posterity, "they worked as hopelessly and sadly as a gang of convicts in a penal settlement" (33).

In the *Christmas Carol*, written simultaneously with *Chuzzlewit*, Dickens brings on stage, in the Ghost of Christmas Present, a classical nature deity. Crowned with a wreath and pouring forth the most hospitable profusion, the Ghost is a descendant of the river gods of the ancients and indeed he is the Victorian successor to the Father Thames who intones the grand apostrophe to Peace and Plenty in Pope's "Windsor-Forest." But this is a truly Dickensian nature god, for his bounty includes not only the pure productions of nature but also many such productions of human art as sausages, plum-puddings, twelfth-cakes, and "seething bowls of punch": one feels his habitual haunt would be not so much a woodland sacred grove as the bar of the Maypole Inn. But if this makes the Ghost a somewhat unconventional nature deity, *Martin Chuzzlewit* produces a nature deity who breaks every bound of orthodoxy: for in the fat, bibulous, and snuffy person of Mrs. Gamp the nurse-midwife, Dickens presents an outrageous travesty of a nature goddess, a travesty which moreover is a wild and brilliant satire of the idea of nature the kindly nurse that is being so strenuously rejected in this novel.

Mrs. Gamp stored all her household matters in a little cupboard by the fire-place; beginning below the surface (as in nature) with the coals, and mounting gradually upwards to the spirits, which, from motives of delicacy, she kept in a tea-pot. The chimney-piece was ornamented with a small almanack, marked here and there in Mrs. Gamp's own hand, with a memorandum of the date at which some lady was expected to fall due. (49)

Mrs. Gamp's shabby room is a burlesque mirror of nature, parodically reflecting its structure and its cycles; and indeed the "divers pippins carved in timber" on her enormous tent-bedstead, which at unexpected intervals tumble down on her visitors, are both a mocking emblem of the pastoral fantasy of nature's bounty and a comic evocation of the fatal apple that put an end to man's harmonious integration into a benignant nature. As both a sick-nurse and a midwife, Mrs. Gamp presides over the two great natural mysteries that delimit human life, and, with the unshakable indifference of nature itself, she goes "to a lying-in or a laying-out with equal zest and relish" (19). For her, the great cardinal principle is continual change—"More changes too, to come, afore we've done with changes" (25).

Lying, irresponsible, careless, dirty—like *Chuzzlewit's* world of nature—she is also irresistibly fascinating in her endlessly fecund inventiveness, her irrepressible energy, her boozy professions of friendship, concern, and dependability, which are ingratiating in spite of their utter falsity and unexpectedly endearing even while they are exasperating in the extreme. Speaking, if not in the high, at least in the low heroic style, she delivers a message that is, alas, only partly comprehensible. Insofar as she makes any sense at all, what she has to say is that nature is not the Garden of Eden: while she wishes, like the rest of us, that "this tearful walley would be changed into a flowerin' guardian," she knows that we really live not in what Mark Tapley calls the "Walley of Eden" (which is anyway crawling with "twining serpiants") but rather in this "Piljian's Projiss of a mortal wale" (46, 21, 49, 25). The fallen world we live in, indeed, is the "walley of the shadder"; it is a wale of tears; and of each of us it may be said, "He was born into a wale; and he lived in a wale; and he must take the consequences of sech a sitiwation" (29, 49).

But beyond this truth, and beyond Mrs. Gamp's injunction to bear up no matter what, nature has little wisdom to impart. "Nature never did betray / The heart that loved her," Wordsworth sanguinely promises. "Bless the babe, and save the mother, is my motter," says Mrs. Gamp, proleptically turning *The Prelude's* most famous passage upside-down, but "Don't try no impogician with the Nuss" (40). "First follow NATURE," Pope urges; but what can one make of such wisdom as this from NATURE?: "seek not to proticipate, but take 'em as they come and as they go" (40). For "sech is life. Vich likeways is the hend of all things!" (29).

·   ·   ·

Providentially warned that old Martin Chuzzlewit will momentarily appear at the door on a surprise visit, Mr. Pecksniff seizes the time to strike a favorite attitude before answering his relative's knock.

Mr. Pecksniff, gently warbling a rustic stave, put on his garden hat, seized a spade, and opened the street-door: calmly appearing on the threshold, as if he thought he had, from his vineyard, heard a modest rap, but was not quite certain. . . .

   "Mr. Chuzzlewit! Can I believe my eyes! . . . Pray, my dear sir, walk in. You find me in my garden-dress. You will excuse it, I know. It is an ancient pursuit, gardening. Primitive, my dear sir; for, if I am not mistaken, Adam was the first of our calling. *My* Eve, I grieve to say, is no more, sir; but"—here he pointed to his spade, and shook his head, as if he were not cheerful without an effort—"but I do a little bit of Adam still." (24)

So beneficent is nature as presented in this outrageous little georgic that Adam appears as a gardener not a laborer, growing flowers for delight rather than bread by the sweat of his brow, and the chief occupation of Patriarchs like Pecksniff is sitting in righteous ease beneath their generously laden vines and fig trees. To put such a pastoral conceit into the mouth of an unmitigated scoundrel like this is to discredit it as thoroughly as Dickens undermines the idea of infallible parental instinct in *Nickleby* by making Messrs. Squeers and Snawley its champions, and Mr. Pecksniff's sentimental image of nature is the less plausible in that it follows immediately the chapter describing young Martin's nightmarish journey to the dark heart of nature that is "Eden." But the notion of kindly nature is not the only element of the pastoral idea being exploded here, for, by allowing the flagitious Pecksniff to present himself as the embodiment of Edenic innocence, Dickens similarly mocks the notion of the radical goodness of *human* nature which is the pastoral idea's other essential component. In this passage as throughout the novel, Pecksniff is, as Steven Marcus observes, "a monumental parody of the ideal of pastoral innocence": the little bit of Adam he does is the Old Adam—and not such a little bit of it, at that.[26]

   As with Pecksniff, so with his silly and self-righteous daughters, whose demeanor, Dickens derisively reports, is "worthy of the Pastoral age." The younger girl in particular, possessed of a "child-like vivacity" (though she is certainly no child), is "artless . . . fresh and guileless." She is all "wildness" and "simplicity and innocence." Her appearance strikes the same note, what with her loose and natural hairdo—no combs or frizzling for her—and her simple, naive dress, which calls attention to her "moderately buxom . . . and quite womanly" shape and bewitches the local beaux while appearing to disclaim any such calculated intention. The two apparently loving sisters set each other off with striking effect: and the best part of all is "that both the fair creatures were so utterly unconscious of all this! . . . Nature played them off against each other: *they* had no hand in it, the two Miss Pecksniffs" (2).

The fantasy these girls are dramatizing—and proving false at every point, Dickens keeps insisting, by their peevish unkindliness and sneaking dedication to the main chance—begins with a fundamental assertion that original human nature is unqualifiedly good, without guilt or depravity, malice or pretense, without pride, ambition, calculation, or contrivance. If we find men wicked, it is because they have lost their natural innocence in and through their social life, which has made them competitive, emulous, envious, covetous, mendacious, hypocritical, flaunting, hostile and even violent to their fellows, anxious, ill, gluttonous, jaded, and depraved. Thus human wickedness is of man's invention, and if everything natural in man is to be cherished, everything artificial is to be shunned. The more developed and elaborate and complex—and therefore artificial—social life becomes, the further men will be estranged from their original innocence and the more corrupt they will become.

Simplicity is to be preserved above all things; and Pecksniff, giving young Martin Chuzzlewit a tour of his house, draws the appropriate, fatuous moral from the potted plants and caged sparrow in his daughters' room—or "bower," as he calls it: "Such trifles as girls love, are here. Nothing more. Those who seek heartless splendour, would seek here in vain" (5). The unspoken claim of this version of the pastoral is that the splendid *is* the heartless, for splendor is the offspring of pride and ambition, and the degenerate lust for preeminence it entails seeks to make one's fellow men into envious admirers or overmatched competitors rather than friendly, equal companions. To achieve splendor requires us to distort and coarsen the primal human sympathy and spontaneity which constitute the ground of all human virtue; to admire splendor betokens a heart that has already turned to stone. Thus, those accomplishments— those transformations worked on the world and on the self—which from one point of view appear to be humanity's highest realization actually attest to its lamentable debasement. A taste for ceremonious dress and manners, for magnificence in architecture and decoration, for complicated cookery and elaborate entertainments, for trained virtuosity in performance and polished technique and sustained thought in art—in short, all taste for high civilization, for the artful and premeditated instead of the simple and "natural," indicates that one's essential humanity has been subjected to the same denaturing contortions as a ballet dancer's body or a skilled musician's hands.

These notions belong to an ancient intellectual tradition, but in fact the Misses Pecksniffs' version of the pastoral belongs to a tradition not so much of thought as of taste or style. This is a tradition which includes (for example) Marie Antoinette masquerading as a shepherdess at the Petit Trianon, and it includes also the porcelain shepherds and shepherdesses so beautifully made throughout the eighteenth century from Chelsea to Capodimonte to Meissen. It is a tradition Dickens parodies not only in *Chuzzlewit* but also in *Dombey and Son*, where he makes its spokesman the shrivelled old coquette Mrs. Skewton, who read Wordsworth in her youth and who, with her false hair, false teeth, false eyelashes, and so on, "had as much that was false about her as could well go to the composition of anybody with a real individual existence." Society, as this utterly social-minded lady affects to believe, "is a false place: full of withering conventionalities: where Nature is but little regarded, and where the music of the heart, and the gushing of the soul, and all that sort of thing, which is so truly poetical, is seldom heard." As for herself, she simpers,

Nature intended me for an Arcadian. I am thrown away in society. Cows are my passion. What I have ever sighed for, has been to retreat to a Swiss farm, and live entirely surrounded by cows—and china. . . . What I want, is frankness, confidence, less conventionality, and freer play of soul. We are so dreadfully artificial. . . . I want Nature everywhere. It would be so extremely charming.[27]

Well, people will affect even a desire to renounce affection; and this pose of Mrs. Skewton's, like that of the Pecksniff girls, is mere fashionable attitudinizing. Indeed, all this is so conventional a sentimentality that an elaborately and rigidly artificial woman like *Little Dorrit*'s Mrs. Merdle has it ready to mind among her stock of notions for all occasions, and she uses it with a complexity of consciousness that dismisses creatures like the Pecksniff girls or Mrs. Skewton with a glittering wave of a jewelled hand. For in mocking the notion of pastoral innocence even while invoking it, Mrs. Merdle shows up its utter untenability by highlighting the fatally inescapable bad faith on which it must inevitably be based. Her frank cynicism in using it, in other words, calls attention to the irreducible quantum of hypocrisy in the pastoral pose which people who habitually affect it, like the Misses Pecksniff, are at pains to conceal. This "woman of snow," who lives her life entirely in the ever-vigilant eye of "some abstraction of Society," concedes in her blandly insincere way that Society (with a capital S) is

hollow and conventional and worldly and very shocking, but unless we are Savages in the Tropical seas (I should have been charmed to be one myself—most delightful life and perfect climate I am told), we must consult it. It is the common lot. . . . [W]e are not in a natural state. Much to be lamented, no doubt, particularly by myself, who am a child of nature if I could but show it; but so it is. Society suppresses us and dominates us. . . . If we could only come to a Millennium, or something of that sort. . . . A more primitive state of society would be delicious to me.

"There used to be a poem when I learnt lessons," continues Mrs. Merdle, putting her finger on the passage from Pope's *Essay on Man* that is one of English primitivism's central texts, "something about Lo the poor Indian whose something mind! If a few thousand persons moving in Society, could only go and be Indians, I would put my name down directly; but as, moving in Society, we can't be Indians, unfortunately—Good morning!"[28] Moving in Society (and also in society), one's heart can indeed turn to stone, as the example of this marmoreal lady testifies, raising a host of additional questions beyond the scope of the matter presently at hand. To this condition of petrifaction, however, Dickens's antidote is not to be a poor Indian or an Arcadian but rather a fully human citizen of the European nineteenth century.

Mere fashion, this pastoral simplicity of the Pecksniffs: but this personal style, as often happens with fashionable sentimentalities, has had political ramifications as well, which, though they would certainly scandalize the Pecksniff girls no less than Mrs. Skewton or Mrs. Merdle, are nevertheless the real center of *Martin Chuzzlewit's* interest in the pastoral notion of human nature. From the high-waisted white "grecian" dresses and thin sandals, appropriate to the Golden Age, worn by the uncorseted maidens of French Revolutionary times, down through the embroidered peasant skirts and blouses worn by 1930s radicals to match their taste for folk singing and folk dancing in preference to anything laboriously trained and polished, this artful pretension to artless simplicity and authenticity, based on an assertion of the natural virtuousness of man, has regularly tended toward a radical politics, opposed not only to the culture of what Mr. Pecksniff windily calls "heartless splendour" but also to the whole social structure that goes along with it. For the dominant class which sponsors so degenerate a culture, according to this political viewpoint, is itself notoriously artificial, unfeeling, and corrupt, and it has no right to rule classes that, preserving much of man's natural simplicity, have largely retained man's original, natural virtue, too. More important still, the wholesale inequality and oppression and exploitation which have always been the social and economic concomitants of high culture—and not accidental concomitants but premeditated and intended ones, for the unequal social structure springs from precisely the same emulous furor for preeminence which generates high culture and which finds its satisfaction in devaluing others—are so flagrantly indefensible that we must condemn the whole civilization of "heartless splendour," from the palace to the stock exchange to the opera house, and sweep it away.

"What are the Great United States for, sir," crows one of *Chuzzlewit's* most odious Americans, "if not for the regeneration of man?" (21). Here is the very heart of the prevailing American ideology, which Dickens views as the most egregious example of the pastoral fantasy at work in politics that he has ever seen or imagined; and here his satire of the pastoral takes on a special ferocity. The United States, its citizens claim, is engaged in restoring men to their original virtue and innocence. Having indeed swept away the "artificial barriers set up between man and man," they have taken care that there should be no "arbitrary distinctions in that enlightened land, where there were no noblemen but nature's noblemen, and all society was based on one broad level of brotherly love and natural equality" (17). Here "man is bound to man in one vast bond of equal love and truth" (21). Very different, Americans claim, is this happy situation from the deplorable state of affairs in Europe's decadent nations. How unlike England, for example,

. . . a country, sir, that had piled up golden calves as high as Babel, and worshipped 'em for ages. We are a new country, sir; man is in a more primeval state here, sir; we have not the excuse of having lapsed in the slow course of time into degenerate practices; we have no false gods; man, sir, here, is man in all his dignity. (21)

Primitive, Mr. Pecksniff would say approvingly, all very primitive; and what this brand of pastoral primitivism, rampant in the America of the 1830s and 1840s, piously asserts is that here men live the kind of life wise nature intended us to live, uncorrupted by the host of artificial needs and desires engendered in men by an emulous society, undistorted by age-old structures of authority and deference, undepraved by effete *over*-civilization, leading to a taste for heartless splendor, for overspiced sauces, for the sexual inventiveness that so offended the Genevan soul of Jean-Jacques Rousseau, and for the whole array of perfumes, call-girls, confectionary, and theater-going that Plato reprehended in Book Two of *The Republic* and which, as he went on to remark, could only be had at the cost of ceaseless expansionist aggression and (worse) unending recourse to doctors and lawyers. Man in America has not "lapsed" or "degenerated" from his "primeval" natural excellence. Here he is not a quack or phantasm; he is not a lackey or a valet, forced by dependence and degraded desires to grovel before his fellows. For here man is truly *man*, with all that we mean by his *virtue* intact and in full vigor.

What has regenerated man here, restoring him to his natural virtue? His emancipation from an ancient double enslavement, an enslavement both external and internal, political and moral. And therefore, as their cardinal article of faith, the liberated citizens of this redeemed nation are quite understandably "[d]evoted, mind and body, heart and soul, to Freedom, sir," as General Choke's typically American prose phrases it, "—to Freedom, blessed solace to the snail upon the cellar-door, the oyster in his pearly bed, the still mite in his home of cheese, the very winkle . . . in his shelly lair" (21). Americans, according to Dickens, really do sound like this; but he is deriding more in this absurd credo than its inflated language. For General Choke's illustrations are symptomatic of how grotesquely distorted the American conception of freedom is, imagining it to be an isolation so total as to enclose each atomistic individual in his own adamantine shell. "We are independent here, sir," Mr. Jefferson Brick boasts; which means simply that "We do as we like" (16).

And so the golden rule here is the principle that the whole of *Martin Chuzzlewit* opposes—"Every man for himself, and God for us all" (39). No emancipated individual in the Land of the Free has any responsibility to his fellows or to the community. As a result, Dickens believed, the communal life was in process of drying up and blowing away in America. Or, to put it another way, these regenerate men, in relieving themselves of oppression, had thrown out the baby with the bath water. Hostility to oppression had insensibly metamorphosed into hostility to society itself.

So Mark Tapley wryly insinuates when informing the detestable Mr. Chollop that he does *not* feel at home in Eden, where, Dickens believes, the central tendencies of American life have reached their logical consummation:

"You miss the imposts of your country. You miss the house dues?" observed Chollop.

"And the houses—rather," said Mark.

"No window dues here Sir," observed Chollop.

"And no windows to put 'em on," said Mark.

"No stakes, no dungeons, no blocks, no racks, no scaffolds, no thumbscrews, no pikes, no pillories," said Chollop.

"Nothing but rewolvers and bowie knives," returned Mark. "And what are they? Not worth mentioning!" (33)

Mark agrees with Chollop that there is no excessive or despotic interference with the individual by the community here, but that is only because there is *no* communal interference, however legitimate, in the individual's affairs. As a result, the essential achievements of the collective life of man are not much in evidence in America. True, there is no irksome taxation, but can one really believe, as Mark quips, that, the "soil being very fruitful, public buildings grows spontaneous, perhaps" (21)? And if, as Mark finds, there is no excessive social authority in America only because there is virtually no social authority whatever, men are bound to be, as he also finds, ferocious prodigies of "murderous violence" (21), whose only "Institutions" are "pistols with revolving barrels, swordsticks, bowie-knives, . . . bloody duels, brutal combats, savage assaults, [and] shooting down and stabbing in the street" (34). Which is to say that there are tending to be no social institutions at all in this society that can hardly be called a society.

It is not surprising that some early travellers, like Bishop Las Casas (who accompanied Columbus on one of his New World voyages), viewed the American natives not as Edenic innocents but rather as natural men living "still in that first rude state which all other nations were in, before there was anyone to teach them," a state sixteenth-century French writers on America formulaically described as being *"sans roi, sans loi, sans foi"*— without kings, laws, or religion.[29] But it comes as a shock to find that centuries later, when by "Americans" was not meant aboriginal Indians but the free and independent citizens of the United States, European visitors were still making such a judgment. The Girondist Jacques Pierre Brissot observed that "freedom in that country is carried to so high a degree as to border upon a state of nature," and the poet Tom Moore (whom *Chuzzlewit* both quotes and paraphrases) endorsed this view, going on to remark that "there certainly is a close approximation to savage life" among the Americans, "not only in the liberty which they enjoy" but also in the unspeakable "violence" and "animosity" of their perpetual factional strife.[30] To this tradition Dickens belongs, too: the state of nature is what the new republic often seemed to him; and so when Martin sees all the diners at a New York boardinghouse ravenously eating their utmost, apparently "in self-defence," Dickens cannot help resorting to the language of political philosophy and concluding that they no doubt were all "asserting the first law of nature" (16). In the same vein, Mrs. Lupin of the Blue Dragon bewails Mark's decision to go to America, wondering why he did not "go to some of those countries where the savages eat each other fairly, and give an equal chance to every one!" (43).

"Man is in a more primeval state here," crows one American. Primeval indeed. Consider the monitory example of Mr. Chollop, as one of his brother Aristocrats of Nature describes him:

> Our fellow-countryman is a model of a man, quite fresh from Natur's mould! . . . He is a true-born child of this free hemisphere! Verdant as the mountains of our country; bright and flowing as our mineral Licks; unspiled by withering conventionalities as air our broad and boundless Prerarers! Rough he may be. So air our Barrs. Wild he may be. So air our Buffalers. But he is a child of Natur', and a child of Freedom; and his boastful answer to the Despot and the Tyrant is, that his bright home is in the Settin Sun. (34)

Here is a character who really is free from "withering conventionalities," as Mrs. Skewton says she wishes to be, and who really is the "child of nature" Mrs. Merdle professes herself, if she "could but show it." Here is an example of "man in all his dignity," stripped of the artificial, distorting accretions of social life and intact in his original—virtue? innocence? Well, what does this "model of a man quite fresh from Natur's mould" reveal about our "primeval" character?

> He was usually described by his friends, in the South and West, as "a splendid sample of our na-tive raw material, Sir," and was much esteemed for his devotion to rational Liberty; for the better propagation whereof he usually carried a brace of revolving-pistols in his coat pocket, with seven barrels apiece. He also carried, amongst other trinkets, a sword-stick, which he called his "Tickler;" and a great knife, which (for he was a man of a pleasant turn of humour) he called "Ripper," in allusion to its usefulness as a means of ventilating the stomach of any adversary in a close contest. He had used these weapons with distinguished effect in several instances; all duly chronicled in the newspapers; and was greatly beloved for the gallant manner in which he had "jobbed out" the eye of one gentlemen, as he was in the act of knocking at his own street-door. (33)

Raw material indeed: it is Hugh the Centaur with a Yankee accent. For clearly Dickens believed that America, in showing him the Mr. Chollops its ideology was proudly and abundantly producing, had provided him with a good look at the natural state of *man* as well as nature—a look which confirmed his theories about human nature's essential aggressiveness more conclusively than such other of his glimpses into uncivilized human nature as (for example) the outcast children of the London slums had afforded him. In the baby savage or the grim figures of Want and Ignorance, the potential for eruptions of primal human aggression remains just that. If the crimes against property, the general insolence described by Dickens in his article on "the Ruffian," the verbal and sometimes physical assaults committed regularly in the public streets by this class in England are the smoke and vapor that attest to the volcanic forces bubbling beneath the surface, the full-scale eruption into savage murder or into the wholesale anarchy that characterized the Gordon Riots happens relatively infrequently in English life. England has, after all, laws and policemen—not without their effect. But by contrast American life converts this potential into blood-curdling actuality over and over again, and in doing so it extinguishes in Dickens's mind all doubts about whether a man "quite fresh from Natur's mould" would be as "rough" and "wild" and "raw" as he had always imagined.

Equipped with a magic ring conveying the power of invisibility, hypothesized Glaucon in the *Republic*, the just man would behave exactly like the unjust man, rioting in wrongdoing of every kind: for "no man is just of his own free will, but only under compulsion."[31] As most philosophers represent natural man, complains Rousseau, he is really only a modern-day civilized man provided with the impunity Glaucon's ring assures. He is no more than an ordinary man snatched off the streets of Paris—his breast seething with every bad passion engendered in man by long ages of corruption by life in society—and spirited in imagination to a state where all law is abolished.[32]

But though it is true that Dickens believes America to be a country largely without law, he does not believe that the general license by itself accounts for the existence there of such children of Natur' as Mr. Chollop. It is his opinion—sharply focused and coolly assured in this novel after having been so deeply meditated in *Barnaby* and so completely corroborated in America—that being a civilized man is more than a matter of responding to the external coercion of social authority. For him, at last fully comfortable with his answers to the questions at the intellectual center of this stage in his career, civilization is an inner, personal condition as well, the civilized self having undergone a transformation that makes it very different from the self as it comes quite fresh from Natur's mould. And thus Dickens's emphasis on Mr. Chollop's being "unspiled by withering conventionalities": for these really are what *Nick-*

leby, in a genial mood, called the "polite forms and ceremonies which must be observed in civilised life, or mankind relapse into their original barbarism." The withering conventionalities are in fact the very grain and tissue of that life of culture in and through which the raw material of man's nature acquires its full measure of humanity. They are, as *Martin Chuzzlewit's* only admirable American says in bewailing their conspicuous absence in his nation, the "humanising conventionalities" (17), the thickly significant social rituals, the value-laden codes of social interaction that provide human life with its density of worth and meaning and that signalize and nourish the working of that fully human soul that makes man something grander than a Barr or a Buffaler.

.   .   .

Thus America strengthened Dickens in his belief that man is man in all his dignity only in society, and he dramatizes that view in *Chuzzlewit* not only negatively, in that unit of savagery Mr. Chollop, but also positively, in his representation of Todgers's commercial boardinghouse, which is, as Steven Marcus has argued, the embodiment in little of society itself. It is "a city within a city, a kind of encapsulated citadel of human society."[33] Like society, too, "that noun of multitude or signifying many, called Todgers's" (9), is a collective whole different from and greater than the sum of its parts, more complex by far than anything Dickens was able to imagine in *Nickleby*. Its structure mirrors the illogical and mystified structure of society, full of disguised connections and obscure relationships. It stands in a "labryinth," and its "grand mystery" is its cellar

approachable only by a little back door and a rusty grating: which cellerage within the memory of man had had no connexion with the house, but had always been the freehold property of somebody else, and was reported to be full of wealth: though in what shape—whether in silver, brass, or gold, or butts of wine, or casks of gunpowder—was a matter of profound uncertainty and supreme indifference to Todgers's, and all its inmates. (9)

Here the social mysteries, as is not usually the case in the later Dickens, are reassuring rather than ominous, and moreover the social labyrinth opens itself to the practiced mastery of the initiate. "Congested, shabby, haphazard, impenetrable, and withal utterly humanized," Todgers's is, says Marcus, "the visible and palpable presence of a complex civilization and its history, eccentric, elaborate, thick, various, outlandish, absurd."[34]

As for the people who live at Todgers's: Dickens's point is not simply that they are wholly at home there, as is emphatically so. More important still is his wish to show that the medium of Todgers's is the medium in which human selfhood flourishes. Every boarder there is a well-defined individual, strongly marked by some notable and carefully cultivated idiosyncrasy, which his fellows recognize and honor. The company includes "a gentleman of a sporting turn, . . . a gentleman of a debating turn, . . . and a gentleman of a literary turn," not to mention those of vocal, smoking, and convivial turns, or those with turns for whist, billiards, and betting. Like most members of the great human family, too, they all have a turn for business and, "everyone in his own way, a decided turn for pleasure to boot" (9). How weightily significant a pronouncement is Dickens's exultant assertion that in this achieved community "every man comes out freely in his own character" (9). For only within society does man's full humanity flower—a process of course involving the attainment of that unique selfhood that distinguishes each of us.

If, by the time he had finished *Barnaby*, Dickens had well digested the lesson that it is essential to the nature of society to transform the self, in *Chuzzlewit* he came to focus more sharply on the magnitude of the transformation—on how radically far from being a pure production of nature the truly human being is. This consciousness pervades his description of Todgers's and accounts for the unsettling unnaturalness of nature as he imagines it to be found in Todgers's neighborhood, where it flourishes chiefly under the auspices of fruit-brokers and wholesale dealers in grocery-ware, and which it penetrates most notably in the startling form of a continual, slowly-pouring "stream of porters from the wharves beside the river, each bearing on his back a bursting chest of oranges." The beasts of the field represent nature from a profoundly unnatural vantage point here, for "deep among the very foundations" of the buildings around Todgers's "the ground was undermined and burrowed out into stables, where cart-horses, troubled by rats, might be heard on a quiet Sunday rattling their halters, as disturbed spirits in tales of haunted houses are said to clank their chains." Nor is this the only way men have undermined nature's very ground: "many a ghostly little churchyard," densely tenanted, is to be found here, "which bore much the same analogy to green churchyards, as the pots of earth for mignonette and wallflower in the windows overlooking them, did to rustic gardens" (9).

But, the prime exhibit of nature unnaturally transformed by men at Todgers's is man himself. Guiding the reader through the boardinghouse, Dickens ends the tour by pointing up to one last feature at the very top of the staircase—"an old, disjointed, rickety, ill-favoured skylight, patched and mended in all kinds of ways, which looked distrustfully down at everything that passed below, and covered Todgers's up as if it were a sort of human cucumber-frame, and only people of a peculiar growth were reared there" (8). A cucumber-frame is a miniature hothouse, about two feet high, which protects cucumber plants from the cold, unnaturally forcing them to bear fruit all year round—and fruit, moreover, of bigger than natural size. To fit in the cucumber-frame, vines have to be pruned sharply early in their growth, a deformation which improves them by making them exuberantly productive. What more apt image could Dickens choose to embody his notion of the primary function of society? Like the hothouse, society at once overcomes nature and enhances it, fostering for human purposes the growth of something valuable and healthy which is neither altogether natural nor altogether fabricated.

It is thus with a sure touch that Dickens brings to a close the novel's interlude at Todgers's: as the Pecksniff girls board the coach that momentarily will take them away from London, one of the admirers they have won at Todgers's tosses them "a flower, a hot-house flower that had cost money." No artless, simple daisy, this forced blossom is a product of nature transformed by culture, possessed of a human meaning not only in being cultivated as an object of commerce but also in being metamorphosed into a highly charged *symbol*, the ardent assertion of a human connection. But alas, the young lover missed his aim; the flower "reached, instead, the coachman on the box, who thanked him kindly, and stuck it in his button-hole" (11), as the coach rumbled away.

Dickens's consciousness of this highly paradoxical relationship, in which man is enmeshed in nature while at the same time transcending it, finds even more explicit registration later in the novel. One morning after breakfast, Tom and Ruth Pinch go off to the butcher's to buy the makings of a beefsteak pudding for dinner.

To see the butcher slap the steak, before he laid it on the block, and give his knife a sharpening, was to forget breakfast instantly. It was agreeable, too—it really was—to see him cut it off, so smooth and juicy. There was nothing savage in the act, although the knife was large and keen; it was a piece of art, high art; there was delicacy of touch, clearness of tone, skilful handling of the subject, fine shading. It was the triumph of mind over matter; quite.

Perhaps the greenest cabbage-leaf ever grown in a garden was wrapped about this steak, before it was delivered over to Tom. But the butcher had a sentiment for his business, and knew how to refine upon it. When he saw Tom putting the cabbage-leaf into his pocket awkwardly, he begged to be allowed to do it for him; "for meat," he said, with some emotion, "must be humoured, not drove." (39)

We are, to be sure, absorbed in nature, with sordid animal needs; the eating of other creatures forms the ground of our existence. But there *is* triumph of mind over matter; we *have* refined upon the inescapable given of nature by replacing savagery with high art. For it is precisely where man's needs most firmly hinge him to nature that he most zealously asserts and establishes his humanity, redeeming the natural fact by imbedding it in social convention, ceremony, artifice. Thus, having cooked, we eat off plates with forks; we give dinner parties; we conceive children in marriage; we commemorate our dead. And so we make of a natural reality a human reality, as we ourselves are animals transformed into men.

But this relation of man to nature is not the only such paradox that keenly fascinated Dickens in *Chuzzlewit*: he found even more intriguing here the paradoxical character of fully developed selfhood. *Barnaby Rudge* had clearly understood that the civilized self is a divided self, burdened with inner conflict; but in this novel the matter becomes still more highly problematical, for Dickens now perceives that if fully human selves can be manufactured only in society, they are to some extent artificial, and moreover they must inevitably be marked by traces of insincerity, hypocrisy, and play-acting. Authentic selfhood is inseparable from a certain measure of inauthenticity, and this is so both because the self is a production not just of nature but of culture too and because living in society where selves are nourished—living, as we do, in the eyes of our fellows— we are driven alike by vanity and by dependence to care deeply about what others think of us and thus self-consciously to try to gain their good opinion by presenting a creditable *appearance*.

The irrepressible Young Bailey exemplifies the first of these two cases. Introduced into the novel as Todgers's boy-of-all-work, he reappears later splendidly transformed into Tigg's smartly attired footboy or "tiger." No figure in the novel is more charged with self-dramatizing energy than this vivid urchin, who comes out freely in his own character with breathtaking assurance and disarming single-mindedness; and yet his vigorously achieved identity, his density of self, is almost wholly factitious even while it is wholly his own. Dressed in the showy livery of his new job, Bailey presents himself to his friend Mr. Sweedlepipe as a knowing veteran, seasoned in matters equine, amorous, and fashionable:

Mr. Bailey spoke as if he already had a leg and three-quarters in the grave, and this had happened twenty or thirty years ago. Paul Sweedlepipe . . . was so perfectly confounded by his precocious self-possession, and his patronising manner, as well as by his boots, cockade, and livery, that a mist swam before his eyes, and he saw—not the Bailey of acknowledged juvenility . . .—but a highly-condensed embodiment of all the sporting grooms in London; an abstract of all the stable-knowledge of the time; a something at a high-pressure that must have had existence many years, and was fraught with terrible experiences. And truly . . . Mr. Bailey's genius . . . eclipsed both time and space, cheated beholders of their senses, and worked on their belief in defiance of all natural laws. He walked along the tangible and real stones of Holborn-hill, an under-sized boy; and yet he winked the winks, and thought the thoughts, and did the deeds, and said the sayings, of an ancient man. There was an old principle within him, and a young surface without. He became an inexplicable creature: a breeched and booted Sphinx. There was no course open to [Sweedlepipe] but to go distracted himself, or to take Bailey for granted: and he wisely chose the latter. (26)

For society provides us with a vast array of ready-made roles, styles, and manners, defined by rich historical accumulations of convention, available for incorporation into our own identity, piecemeal or whole, singly or in combination, and (if need be) " in defiance of all natural laws." Our cultural inheritance includes, in other words, established, elaborately artificial forms of demeanor, by which we readily know how we are to behave in presenting ourselves plausibly as doctors, rug merchants, professors, men of the world, or honest men, or cultivated men, or Athenians or Spartans or what have you. There are even conventional ways of behaving as a rebel or a free spirit or a revolutionary.

From the "anxiety to display himself to advantage" in the heart of each man living in society springs the second great source of the inauthenticity inherent in every fully realized self (44). This motive impels us to dissemble our more unsavory designs—"we never knows wot's hidden in each others hearts," as Mrs. Gamp puts it, "and if we had glass winders there, we'd need keep the shetters up" (29)—and the same motive moves us to assume a virtue if we have it not and to express solicitude, admiration, and affection which we do not feel, like Mr. Mould, whom we catch "glancing at himself in the little shaving-glass, that he might be sure his face had the right expression on it" (19). The uses to which we social beings are obliged to put one another motivate many of the unavoidable hypocrisies of achieved selfhood. Thus, in order not to lose one of her much-needed boarders, Mrs. Todgers must somehow smother her contempt for the ridiculous Mr. Moddle and mollify his unreasonable pique by assenting with a show of warmth to his absurd view of the world and by flattering him with no less skill than labor and no less labor than insincerity. Watching the harried landlady abase herself by such obsequious falsehood, honest Mr. Pecksniff asks her what rent young Moddle pays and finds it to be but eighteen shillings a week.

> Mr. Pecksniff rose from his chair, folded his arms, looked at her, and shook his head.
> "And do you mean to say, ma'am . . . that for such a miserable consideration as eighteen shillings a week, a female of your understanding can so far demean herself as to wear a double face, even for an instant?"
> "I am forced to keep things on the square if I can, sir," faultered Mrs. Todgers. "I must preserve peace among them, and keep my connection together, if possible, Mr. Pecksniff. The profit is very small."
> "The profit!" cried that gentleman, laying great stress upon the word. "The profit, Mrs. Todgers! You amaze me! . . . The profit of dissimulation! To worship the golden calf of Baal, for eighteen shillings a week!"
> "Don't in your own goodness be too hard upon me, Mr. Pecksniff," cried Mrs. Todgers. . . .
> "Oh Calf, Calf!" cried Mr. Pecksniff mournfully. "Oh Baal, Baal! oh my friend Mrs. Todgers! To barter away that precious jewel, self-esteem, and cringe to any mortal creature—for eighteen shilling a week!" . . .
> Eighteen shillings a week! Just, most just, thy censure, upright Pecksniff! Had it been for the sake of a ribbon, star, or garter; sleeves of lawn, a great man's smile, a seat in parliament, a tap upon the shoulder from a courtly sword; a place, a party, or a thriving lie, or eighteen thousand pounds, or even eighteen hundred;—but to worship the golden calf for eighteen shillings a week! oh pitiful, pitiful! (10)

The great lesson that Martin Chuzzlewit had to go to America to learn is that the self is "a poor, dependent, miserable thing," requiring a whole range of support and help from others in all aspects of life, beginning with bare survival (33). And thus we are obliged to show consideration and even deference to our fellows, in part by observing those "humanising conventionalities of manner and social custom" that inevitably lead us into insincerity and play-acting, as happens in Mrs. Todgers's wholly sympathetic effort to earn, as we say, an honest living. In other words, it is not just the Lord Chesterfields of the world, hot in pursuit of prestige and fortune, who are sunk in duplicity: no one can escape being spotted with it, even the most modest and honorable among us.

Thus the followers of Lord Chesterfield, Dickens had discovered by the time he came to write *Chuzzlewit*, are not different in kind from honest folk but only in degree. Seen in this light, such characters become of course at once more problematic and more interesting, for the villainy of figures like Mr. Pecksniff—that middle-class, truly Victorianized Chesterfield, who aims to advance his interest not by manners but by moral sentimentality—or like the entirely fabricated and indeed fraudulent Montague Tigg, does not come from a source completely foreign to the rest of us but is instead a grotesque exaggeration of impulses and habits lodged in every authentic self. Thus the fact that there is no depth of grovelling self-abasement to which Pecksniff will not stoop to gain his purposes is interesting to Dickens and to us not because we have never insincerely appeased or danced attendance but because we are constantly having to decide just where to draw the line. Nor does his overbearing, self-serving, hypocritical sanctimoniousness exist in a moral realm alien to the rest of us. Nor is Tigg's great insight—that spectacular advancement in the world can be gained by lying self-advertisement, by making a show, by fraudulently disguising nullity behind a flaunting appearance of solidity and substance—this is not something that has never occurred to each of us. And how much more interesting a figure is Tigg when we see that, unlike Chesterfield, he is not the cold-bloodedly self-controlled, utterly self-conscious master dramatist of himself, but that rather, as Jonas Chuzzlewit rightly tells him, he has "acted the gentleman so seriously since, that you've taken in yourself" (41). The problem of identity, Dickens has come to see, cannot be formulated by easy references to "the mask" as distinguishable from "the face."

An American looking at the Pecksniffs of the Old World would accusingly point to them as prime examples of how mankind has "lapsed in the slow course of time into degenerate practices," losing in the process man's original innocence and authenticity. But Dickens makes abundantly clear in *Chuzzlewit* that he has little patience with any interpretation of history as a slow decline or degeneration, a progressive loss by humanity of its most valuable attributes. The reality, he believes, is quite the reverse, and indeed he comically blazons his own understanding of history on the signboard of the Blue Dragon Inn. Faded by age and weather from blue to dull grey, the Dragon hung, "rearing in a state of monstrous imbecility, on his hind legs":

He was a courteous and considerate dragon too; or had been in his distincter days; for in the midst of his rampant feebleness, he kept one of his fore paws near his nose, as though he would say, "Don't mind me—it's only my fun," while he held out the other, in polite and hospitable entreaty. Indeed it must be conceded to the whole brood of dragons of modern times, that they have made a great advance in civilization and refinement. They no longer demand a beautiful virgin for breakfast every morning, with as much regularity as any tame single gentleman expects his hot roll, but rest content with the society of idle bachelors and roving married men: and they are now remarkable rather for holding aloof from the softer sex and discouraging their visits . . . than for rudely insisting on their company without any reference to their inclination, as they are known to have done in days of yore. (3)

Like the Cheeryble's rusty sword and blunderbuss, or the "drowsy, tame and feeble" carnivore depicted on the sign of the Black Lion Inn in *Barnaby Rudge* (31), the Dragon is an emblem of aggression transcended; but here Dickens's whimsical fancy emphasizes that the passage from savagery to civility is an historical matter. The "great advance in civilization and refinement" made by mankind in the course of its progressive development is in his view history's principal trend. Men have become the "reclaimed animals" (3) they now are not without having had to pass through successive "ages of bloodshed and cruelty" (17); and indeed much of the novel's first chapter, its atmosphere reminiscent of the Baron of Grogzwig's world, struggles to underline that truth by taking us back through the Gunpowder Plot and the Norman Conquest to Cain's murder of his brother and in that way illustrating how so much of history has been the record of "divers slaughterous conspiracies and bloody frays." For long ages, conquest and violence were the governing principles of human affairs, and certainly the further back one goes, "the greater the amount of violence and vagabondism" one finds (1).

From such a panoramic perspective as this, embracing the whole of human history, it is startling to see how dramatically the dragon-like, firebreathing components of human nature have been refined into hospitality and politeness. But of course these impulses of aggression and cruelty, so urgently at the center of Dickens's novelistic imagination throughout this stage of his career, have, along with the anarchy and injustice they engender in the world, by no means been utterly outworn as yet—nor, in spite of the grand advances in "civilization and refinement" undoubtedly still to be accomplished, are they ever likely to be, unless history itself comes to an end. For (as Marley's ghost pronounces in the *Carol*[35]) "ages of incessant labour by immortal creatures for this earth, must pass into eternity before the good of which it is susceptible is all developed."

Notes

INTRODUCTION

1. Humphry House, *The Dickens World*, 2d ed. (London and New York: Oxford University Press, 1942), p. 201.
2. Ibid.; G. A. Sala quoted in Philip Collins, *Dickens and Crime* (Bloomington: Indiana University Press, 1968), p. 196. The *Household Words* articles, republished in *Reprinted Pieces*, are "The Detective Police" (1850), "Three 'Detective' Anecdotes" (1850), and "On Duty with Inspector Field" (1851). See also "Down with the Tide" (1853), praising the Thames Police.
3. Collins, *Dickens and Crime*, p. 178; John Forster, *The Life of Charles Dickens*, 8th ed. (London: Chapman & Hall, 1872–74), 2:194–95.
4. Charles Dickens, "On an Amateur Beat" (1869), in *The Uncommercial Traveller* (London: Chapman & Hall, 1858).
5. Charles Dickens, "The Ruffian" (1868), in *The Uncommercial Traveller*.
6. Charles Dickens, "Murderous Extremes" (1857), in *Miscellaneous Papers* (London and New York: The Encyclopaedia Britannica Co., n.d.).
7. Dickens, "The Ruffian."
8. Charles Dickens, "The Begging-Letter Writer" (1850), in *Reprinted Pieces* (London: Chapman & Hall, 1868).
9. Charles Dickens, "Things That Cannot Be Done" (1853), in *Miscellaneous Papers*.
10. Charles Dickens, "Five New Points of Criminal Law" (1859), in *Miscellaneous Papers*.

11. Dickens, "The Ruffian."
12. Collins, *Dickens and Crime*, p. 170.
13. Charles Dickens, "Pet Prisoners" (1850), in *Miscellaneous Papers*.
14. Collins, *Dickens and Crime*, p. 46.
15. In *Reprinted Pieces*.
16. Edmund Burke, "Reflections on the Revolution in France," in *Reflections on the Revolution in France by Edmund Burke and The Rights of Man by Thomas Paine* (Garden City, N.Y.: Anchor Books, 1973), p. 91.
17. Angus Wilson, "Dickens on Children and Childhood," in *Dickens 1970*, ed. Michael Slater (New York: Stein & Day, 1970), p. 199.
18. *The Letters of Charles Dickens* (Pilgrim Edition), ed. Madeline House, Graham Storey, and Kathleen Tillotson (Oxford: Clarendon Press, 1965–), 2:198.
19. *Letters of Dickens*, 3:367.
20. Forster, *Life of Dickens*, 1:69.
21. Edgar Johnson, *Charles Dickens: His Tragedy and Triumph* (New York: Simon & Schuster, 1952), 1:58–59.
22. *Nicholas Nickleby*, ch. 16. Henceforward reference to Dickens novels under discussion will be given in the text, the numbers in parentheses indicating *chapters*, not pages. The Dickens text used in all cases is that of the first bound edition.
23. Burke, *Reflections*, pp. 145–46.

CHAPTER 1: The Problem of Aggression

1. "Victorian Readers and the Sense of the Present," *Midway* 10 (1970): 95–119.
2. Philip Collins, *Dickens and Education* (London: Macmillan, 1965), p. 104. For a useful account of the Yorkshire schools, see Michael Slater, *The Composition and Monthly Publication of Nicholas Nickleby* (Menston, Yorkshire: Scolar, 1973).
3. Cf. William Shakespeare, *Macbeth*, III.iv.108.
4. John Browdie remarks the same impulse in Squeers: "The schoolmeasther agin all England" (39).
5. Jean-Jacques Rousseau, *Discourse on the Origin and Foundations of Inequality* [the *Second Discourse*, 1755], in *The First and Second Discourses*, trans. R. D. and J. R. Masters (New York: St. Martin's, 1964), pp. 146–50. See also Arthur O. Lovejoy, "The Supposed Primitivism of Rousseau's *Discourse on Inequality*," in his *Essays in the History of Ideas* (1948; reprint, New York: Capricorn Books, 1960).
6. William Wordsworth, "A slumber did my spirit seal. . . ."
7. *Letters of Dickens*, 1:459–60 and note.

CHAPTER 2: Polite Forms and Ceremonies

1. A. S. G. Canning, *Dickens and Thackeray Studied in Three Novels* (1911; reprint, Port Washington, N.Y.: Kennikat, 1967), pp. 68–71. But such was the general state of rural society in Yorkshire in the early part of the nineteenth century, at least as Mrs. Gaskell describes it in Chapter 2 of her *Life of Charlotte Brontë* (1857).

2. Jonathan Swift, *Polite Conversation* (London, 1738), pp. lvi–lviii; Charles Lamb, *The Essays of Elia* (London: Dent; New York: Dutton/Everyman, 1962), p. 42.

3. George Ford, *Dickens and His Readers* (1955; reprint, New York: Norton, 1965), p. 39.

4. William Hazlitt, "On Modern Comedy," in *The Round Table* (1817; reprint, London: Dent, New York: Dutton/Everyman, 1957), p. 12.

5. Thomas Carlyle, *Chartism* (1840), ch. 8, in *Works*, ed. H. D. Traill (London: Chapman & Hall, 1896–99), 29:171.

6. John Locke, *The Second Treatise*, in *Two Treatises of Government*, ed. Peter Laslett (New York: New American Library/Mentor; 1965), pp. 312–13.

7. "The walls were decorated with several hunting-whips, two or three bridles, a saddle, and an old rusty blunderbuss, with an inscription below it, intimating that it was 'Loaded'—as it had been, on the same authority, for half a century at least" (*Pickwick*, 5). The rusty blunderbuss and ancient sword reappear in the 'Prentice Knights' initiation ceremony in Chapter 8 of *Barnaby Rudge*, but to different effect.

8. House, *The Dickens World*, p. 65.

9. Max Weber, *Economy and Society*, Part 1; reprinted as *The Theory of Social and Economic Organization*, trans. A. M. Henderson and T. Parsons (New York: Free Press, 1964), pp. 275, 200. I am indebted to Steven Marcus for this point.

10. Ibid., p. 193.

11. J. Hillis Miller, *Charles Dickens: The World of His Novels* (Bloomington: Indiana University Press, 1958), p. 93.

12. Thomas Hobbes, *Leviathan*, ed. C. B. Macpherson (Baltimore: Penguin, 1968), p. 186.

13. Forster, *Life of Dickens*, 1:27.

14. Ibid., 1:33. This account of his time in the blacking factory is contained in a fragment of autobiography probably written in 1846 and printed for the first time in ibid., ch. 2.

15. Ibid., 1:35, 38.

16. Ibid., 1:35.

17. Ibid., 1:31.

18. Ibid., 1:49.

19. Edgar Johnson, *Charles Dickens: His Tragedy and Triumph* (New York: Simon & Schuster, 1952), 1:331–32.
20. Forster, *Life of Dickens*, 1:35.
21. Ibid., 1:49.

CHAPTER 3: The Civilized Condition

1. John Ruskin, *The Stones of Venice*, (1853), vol. 2, ch. 6, sec. 40.
2. Louis Cazamian, *The Social Novel in England 1830–1850*, ed. and trans. M. Fido (London and Boston: Routledge & Kegan Paul, 1973), ch. 4.
3. *American Notes*, ch. 12.
4. Sigmund Freud, *Civilization and Its Discontents*, trans. James Strachey (New York: Norton, 1962), pp. 40–41.
5. Siegfried Giedion, *Mechanization Takes Command: A Contribution to Anonymous History* (1954; reprint, New York: Norton, 1969), pp. 51–52.
6. Ibid., p. 52.
7. Peter Laslett, *The World We Have Lost*, 2d ed. (London: Methuen, 1971), pp. 2, 14, 4, 5.
8. Steven Marcus, *Dickens: From Pickwick to Dombey* (New York: Basic Books, 1965), p. 184.
9. See *The World We Have Lost*, ch. 1.
10. Ibid., p. 5.
11. Johnson, *Dickens*, 1:303–4.
12. Ibid., 2:1102–10.
13. Mary Cowden Clarke, *Recollections of Writers* (1878), quoted in Charles Dickens, *Sikes and Nancy and Other Public Readings*, ed. Philip Collins (London and New York: Oxford University Press, 1983), p. vii.
14. *Letters of Dickens*, 2:377, 385.
15. *Nicholas Nickleby*, ch. 18.
16. *Martin Chuzzlewit*, ch. 7.
17. *Letters of Dickens*, 2:186.
18. He avoids the whole problem by never explicitly indicating what war Joe is fighting in. The British defense of Savannah in 1778, in which Joe lost his arm, was successful. In Joe's part of the war, paternal authority was vindicated.

CHAPTER 4. Natural Man

1. If it was all but explicit when *Barnaby* was first published that Dickens was thinking of Hugh in particular as Orson—Mr. Chester calls his rude son

"Bruin," for example (40)—it was made entirely explicit in three of the running titles Dickens added to the Charles Dickens Edition of 1867, which refer to Hugh as "Orson" (23, 40).

2. Richard Bernheimer, *Wild Men in the Middle Ages: A Study in Art, Sentiment, and Demonology* (1952; reprint, New York: Octagon, 1970).

3. Ibid., pp. 9–11.

4. Ibid., pp. 2, 4, 93–99. For example, two pictures by Piero de Cosimo in New York's Metropolitan Museum—pictures made especially well known by Erwin Panofsky in *Studies in Iconology* (New York: Harper & Row, 1962)— show how man, in his harsh, primeval existence, had not yet been fully differentiated from the beasts, for cavemen, satyrs, and centaurs are all represented as varieties of the same savage species. In a later period, Rousseau too connects satyrs with savage men and also (as in late antiquity and in the seventeenth century) with the anthropoid apes: the creatures we call *pongos*, *mandrills*, and *orangutans* are, he says, identical to the *satyrs*, *fauns*, and *sylvans* of the ancients, and it is quite possible that these creatures may be in fact "true savage men whose race, dispersed in the woods in ancient times, had not had an opportunity to develop any of its potential faculties, had not acquired any degree of perfection, and was still found in the primitive state of nature" (Rousseau, *Second Discourse*, pp. 203–13; Bernheimer, *Wild Men*, p. 87; Maximillian E. Novak, "The Wild Man Comes to Tea," in *The Wild Man Within: An Image in Western Thought from the Renaissance to Romanticism*, ed. E. Dudley and M. E. Novak [Pittsburgh: University of Pittsburgh Press, 1972], p. 189).

5. *A Most Pleasant Comedy of Mucedorus*, IV.iii.72–78, in C. F. Tucker Brooke, *The Shakespeare Apocrypha* (Oxford: Clarendon Press, 1908).

6. Hobbes, *Leviathan*, p. 186. See also the essay of Richard Ashcraft, "Leviathan Triumphant: Thomas Hobbes and the Politics of Wild Men," in *The Wild Man Within*. For an admirable account of the early anthropological descriptions, theories, and myths about the Indians in the New World—descriptions that Hobbes clearly has very much in mind in his description of man's natural condition (as he intimates in *Leviathan*, ch. 13)—see Hugh Honour, *The New Golden Land: European Images of America from the Discoveries to the Present Time* (New York: Pantheon, 1975), chs. 3, 5.

7. *Oxford English Dictionary*, s.v. "savage."

8. Bernheimer, *Wild Men*, p. 9.

9. Barnaby, Dickens's other representative natural man, has precisely the opposite defect. In his primitive animism, *everything* is haunted (10).

10. James Burnett, Lord Monboddo, *Of the Origin and Progress of Language*, 2d ed. (Edinburgh: J. Balfour; London: T. Cadell, 1774), 1:222–23. This criticism of Hobbes is still being made in modern times, most notably by C. B. Macpherson, *The Political Theory of Possessive Individualism: Hobbes to Locke*

(London and New York: Oxford University Press, 1962), pp. 45–46. See also Arthur O. Lovejoy, "Monboddo and Rousseau," in his *Essays in the History of Ideas*, pp. 38–61.

11. Arthur O. Lovejoy, "The Supposed Primitivism of Rousseau's *Discourse on Inequality*," in *Essays in the History of Ideas*, p. 21.

12. Arthur O. Lovejoy and George Boas, *Primitivism and Related Ideas in Antiquity* (1935; reprint, New York: Octagon, 1973), p. 13.

13. Forster, *Life of Dickens*, 1:223.

14. Rousseau, *Second Discourse*, p. 117.

15. Lovejoy, *Essays in the History of Ideas*, p. 22.

16. Henry John Stephen, *New Commentaries on the Laws of England* (London, 1841–45), 2:62.

17. Michel Foucault, *Madness and Civilization: A History of Insanity in the Age of Reason*, trans. R. Howard (London: Tavistock, 1967), p. 74.

18. Rousseau, *Second Discourse*, p. 115.

19. Hobbes, *Leviathan*, p. 317.

20. Rousseau, *The Social Contract*, trans. Maurice Cranston (Harmondsworth: Penguin, 1968), p. 65.

21. Arthur Lovejoy, "The Supposed Primitivism of Rousseau's *Discourse on Inequality*" and "Monboddo and Rousseau," in *Essays in the History of Ideas*, pp. 26–27, 55.

22. *Letters of Dickens*, 2:196.

23. Dickens, who had three ravens at various times, expressed a similar thought in a letter to Mrs. Hall, written a week or so after *Barnaby Rudge* was finished and about nine months after the demise of his first (and favorite) bird. "Be careful in your choice of a Raven. Have an undeniable character with him from his last place. I have one, now, whose intelligence is scarcely beyond a fowl's. I have another, whose infancy and early youth were passed at a village alehouse in Yorkshire, who is a wonder—a paragon. I could tell you such things of him, as would make your hair stand on end. Nothing delights him so much as a drunken man—he loves to see human Nature in a state of degradation, and to have the superiority of Ravens asserted. At such time he is *fearful* in his Mephistophelean humour" (ibid., 2:438). Barnaby's Grip, of course, always sees in his master "human Nature in a state of degradation," for Barnaby, unlike the drunken man, suffers a loss of reason that is not temporary but permanent.

24. Enid Welsford, *The Fool: His Literary and Social History* (1935; reprint, Garden City, N.Y.: Doubleday/Anchor, 1961), pp. 71, 205, 201. Compare also the account of a related figure, the Lord of Misrule, in C. L. Barber, *Shakespeare's Festive Comedy: A Study of Dramatic Form and Its Relation to Social Custom* (Cleveland and New York: World, 1963), p. 29. There is still one more way in which Barnaby's costume links him with a *playful* version of man's precivilized nature. For Barnaby's feathers and his carrying around a bird in a

basket strapped on his back associate him with Papageno, the feathered bird-catcher in *The Magic Flute.* And who is Papageno but a watered-down version of the medieval wild man? See Ehrhard Bahr, "Papageno: The Unenlightened Wild Man in Eighteenth-Century Germany," in Dudley and Novak, *The Wild Man Within.*

25. George Orwell, "Charles Dickens," in *The Collected Essays, Journalism and Letters of George Orwell,* ed. Sonia Orwell and Ian Angus (New York: Harcourt Brace Jovanovich, 1968), 1:419.

26. *Letters of Dickens,* 2:86–89. His comments on the execution appear as the second part of "Capital Punishment" in *Miscellaneous Papers.*

27. *Letters of Dickens,* 2:88.

CHAPTER 5: Lord Chesterfield's Conscience

1. James Boswell, *The Life of Samuel Johnson,* ed. A. Birrell (New York: H. W. Knight, n.d.), 1:216. For a more comprehensive discussion of Chesterfield's thought, see my "Lord Chesterfield, *Barnaby Rudge,* and the History of Conscience," *Bulletin of the New York Public Library* 80 (Summer 1977): 474–502.

2. Boswell, *Life of Johnson,* 4:59.

3. Plato, *Republic,* Book II (362d–367e). The theory was hardly lost between antiquity and the eighteenth century of course: it is of central concern to Augustine in *City of God* (Book V, chs. 12–20).

4. Arthur C. Lovejoy, *Reflections on Human Nature* (Baltimore: Johns Hopkins University Press, 1961), pp. 157, 179, 218–19.

5. Ibid., pp. 228, 236.

6. 27 May Old Style 1753.

7. 6 May O.S. 1751.

8. 19 November O.S. 1750.

9. 11 February O.S. 1751.

10. 2 January O.S. 1748.

11. 19 December O.S. 1749.

12. 5 September O.S. 1748; 5 June O.S. 1750.

13. 19 October O.S. 1748; 29 February O.S. 1751.

14. 22 May O.S. 1749.

15. 19 October O.S. 1748.

16. 22 May O.S. 1749.

17. 6 May O.S. 1751.

18. 4 October O.S. 1746; 6 July O.S. 1749.

19. It has been argued that the *Letters* are best understood as a descendant of the courtesy book tradition which flourished in the Renaissance, but it seems that there is a more accurate analogy between Chesterfield and Polonius, who is in fact a satire on precisely that tradition, insofar as he exemplifies its almost

inevitable vulgarization in practice. These two men belong to the same character type, and they resemble each other remarkably as statesmen, moralists,
politicians, and fathers.

20. 4 October O.S. 1746.
21. 22 September O.S. 1749.
22. 2 December O.S. 1746.
23. Even "poor brutish Hugh," according to Forster, "with a storm of passions
    in him raging to be let loose" and "with all the worst instincts of the savage,
    [is] yet not without also some of the best" (Forster, *Life of Dickens*, 1:223).
24. *The Old Curiosity Shop*, ch. 27.
25. Mr. Rudge is, from the opposite end of the social scale, in agreement with
    this position. In his view, we have all sold ourselves to the devil, and, as
    Rudge remarks with classic Malthusian sense, "If we were fewer in number,
    perhaps he would give better wages" (16).
26. 29 March O.S. 1750.
27. William Hazlitt, "On Vulgarity and Affection," *Table Talk* (1821–22; Lon-
    don: Dent; New York: Dutton/Everyman, 1959), p. 163. The analogy this
    essay makes between Chesterfieldian unscrupulousness and mob violence
    may have exerted an influence on *Barnaby Rudge*.
28. Monboddo, *Origin and Progress of Language*, 1:437, 438.
29. Friedrich Nietzsche, *The Genealogy of Morals: An Attack*, ch. 16, in *The Birth
    of Tragedy and the Genealogy of Morals*, trans. F. Golffing (Garden City, N.Y.:
    Doubleday/Anchor, 1956), p. 217.
30. Freud, *Civilization and Its Discontents*, pp. 71, 69.
31. Ibid., pp. 76–77.
32. Ibid., pp. 89–90, 97.
33. *City of God*, Book XIX, ch. 8.

CHAPTER 6. The Riots 1: Down with Everything!

1. Jack Lindsay, *Barnaby Rudge*, in *Dickens and the Twentieth Century*, ed. John
   Gross and Gabriel Pearson (London: Routledge & Kegan Paul, 1962), pp. 94,
   99, 101. Used with permission of the publisher.
2. G. A. Sala, quoted in Collins, *Dickens and Crime*, p. 310.
3. A. E. Dyson recognizes this uncomfortable feature of the novel in a very sensible essay on *Barnaby Rudge* in *The Inimitable Dickens* (London: Macmillan,
   1970). In this novel, he observes, "[t]he liberal myth of political stability as
   the fruit of long progress and constitutional development is not allowed us.
   We are shown, rather, a rootless and drifting society, where civilization is at
   best a very thin ice" (ibid., p. 51).
4. Avrom Fleishman, *The English Historical Novel* (Baltimore and London: Johns
   Hopkins University Press, 1971), p. 105.
5. Freud, *Civilization and Its Discontents*, p. 43.

6. Dickens's contemporary, George Lillie Craik—whose account of the Gordon Riots Dickens almost certainly read—had a similar view of the events of 1780. The object of the rioters, it seemed to him, was to "tear society, as it were, in pieces—that brute strength may carry all before it." In the 1834 insurrection of the Lyons silk-weavers, which Craik believed to belong to the same class of "popular tumults" as the Gordon Riots, that aim (he argued) really was achieved in "the complete overthrow, for a time, of the social system that binds man to man in mutual support, and mutual charity" (*Sketches of Popular Tumults; Illustrative of the Evils of Social Ignorance* [London: Charles Knight, 1837], pp. 24, 266). Craik's work appeared as a volume in Knight's "Contributions to Political Knowledge" series.

7. The Gordon Riots began as a demonstration of support for a bill to repeal the Catholic Relief Act of 1778—an act which itself repealed the main portion of a particularly misbegotten Act of 1699–1700, condemning Catholics who kept schools to *perpetual* imprisonment, and preventing Catholics from inheriting or buying land. But in spite of the Act of 1778 (as the Government found necessary to assure "many well-disposed Protestants" during the Gordon Riots), "Catholics were still liable to severe penalties for keeping schools, saying mass, etc." (George Rudé, *Paris and London in the Eighteenth Century* [New York: Viking, 1971], pp. 270n. and 290n.). See also Craik, *Sketches of Popular Tumults*, pp. 27–31. But, as Gordon Spence points out in his Penguin edition of *Barnaby Rudge* (p. 753), "Dickens assumes that the Act [of 1778] had not yet been passed in 1780. In chapter 37 the author writes of 'petitioning Parliament not to pass an act for abolishing the penal laws . . .' and Gashford speaks of 'next month, or May, when this Papist relief bill comes before the house'; and in chapter 43 Haredale and the others talk as if the Roman Catholics were still under the penalties and disabilities removed by the Act."

8. But Lindsay's invocation of Carlyle's great and complex *History* does remind us that a mob outbreak like the Gordon Riots invites comparison with the French Revolution, that transcendent "elemental upsurge of the oppressed," which became, in Carlyle's opinion, "the most remarkable transaction in these last thousand years" (Carlyle, *Works*, 4:205), and which for the modern period is virtually the archtypal radical political event. We are justified in asking why Dickens does not examine the comparison in this novel—to which we may answer, in the first place, that the events of 1789–95 have no place in an historical novel whose action is confined to 1775–80; in the second place, that the meaning of these two events is so immensely different to Dickens's apprehension that it is absurd to discuss them in the same breath; and, third, that Dickens is so uncomfortable with this mad and destructive uprising of 1780 that he would just as soon leave out of account the whole question of *justifiable* revolt, so as not to becloud the already vexed issue at hand. To this diffidence is also attributable his extreme reticence about the American War of Independence in *Barnaby Rudge*.

But of course the comparison of the Gordon Riots with the French Revolution was certainly in Dickens's mind in the writing of this novel, and he at least implicitly differentiates the riots from the Revolution in the second paragraph of Chapter 63, where he describes the mob's misreading of the intentions and feelings of the soldiers who were dispatched to confront the rioters. The passivity of the soldiers, which was due to the failure of the timid, indecisive civil authorities to issue orders, was interpreted by the crowd as evidence both of the magistrates' unwillingness to "molest" them and of the soldiers' secret sympathy with their grievances, an impression which was strengthened by the troops "answering, when they were asked if they desired to fire on their countrymen, 'No they would be damned if they did.' . . ." As a result, "[t]he feeling that the military were No Popery men, and were rife for disobeying orders and joining the mob soon became very prevalent. . . . Rumours of their disaffection, and of their leaning towards the popular cause, spread from mouth to mouth with astonishing rapidity." But the kindness and affability of the troops proceeded from their "honest simplicity and good-nature" and their being "naturally loath to quarrel with the people," not from their sympathy with "the popular cause." When called upon to fire, the soldiers resolutely do their duty.

What Dickens is thinking of here, I would suggest, is the celebrated behavior of the French Guards in the opening months of the Revolution of 1789. These troops, who shared entirely the grievances of the Paris mob they were sent out to quell, put their duty as French men before their duty as French Guards, and, unable to bring themselves to fire on an assemblage of the Paris citizenry whose sentiments were identical with their own, they not only refused to obey their orders but went so far as to throw in their lot with "the people," a body to which, as they recognized, they also belonged. One of the essential prerequisites for the success of the Revolution—and, moreover, a crucial ingredient in history's largely favorable judgment of its general aims and accomplishments—is its immense popular support: the fact that the shared discontents and aspirations of disparate social groups amalgamated those groups, for a time, into a relatively unified "people" who agreed to a remarkable extent in their opposition to an oppressive and bankrupt regime, counted heavily for the Revolution's success and its legitimacy in the eyes of posterity.

In hinting at the contrast between the behavior of these English soldiers and their French counterparts of 1789, Dickens seems to be implying that one of the large differences that make the Gordon Riots not at all comparable to the French Revolution is that the rioters do *not* give voice to the universal hopes and grievances of "the people"; Dickens's soldiers, who have as just a claim to the title of "the people" as the mob against whom they are ranged, are not in agreement with whatever it is that the rioters are expressing; loyal to the government they serve, this segment of "the people" emphasizes its opposition to the rioters with gunfire.

9. Quoted in E. P. Thompson, *The Making of the English Working Class* (Harmondsworth: Penguin, 1968), p. 77.

10. Norman Cohn, in *Warrant for Genocide: The Myth of the Jewish World-Conspiracy and the Protocols of the Elders of Zion* (London: Eyre & Spottiswoode, 1967), pp. 251–68. Lord George Gordon tells Gashford he dreamt that both of them were "Jews with long beards"—"Heaven forbid, my lord!" Gashford gasps. "We might as well be Papists" (37). Gordon, as Dickens reports, eventually did become a convert to the Jewish religion.

11. Ibid., p. 257.

12. William Blake, "The Garden of Love," in *Songs of Experience*.

13. As he confesses in the preface to *Barnaby*.

14. The church to whose beauties Little Nell serves as a guide in *The Old Curiosity Shop* comes to mind in this context. Phiz's illustration of the burning of the "spoils" from the Catholic chapels (ch. 52) makes especially clear both the desecration and the assault upon art that is taking place here.

15. See, for instance, the last paragraph of Chapter 46.

16. Like the Maypole, as attractive an example as may be found of an English local pub. George Orwell (in "The English People") calls the pub "one of the basic institutions of English life"; and he remarks (in the "England Your England" section of "The Lion and the Unicorn"), "All the culture that is most truly native centres round things which even when they are communal are not official—the pub, the football match, the back garden, the fireside and the 'nice cup of tea'" (Orwell, *Collected Essays*, 3:11 and 2:58).

17. Of course the name of the blacking factory where Dickens worked as a boy was Warren's Blacking, and Dickens is ambivalent about the monument to blighted family life that he calls by this name in *Barnaby*. On the one hand, he represents it as sacred; on the other, he burns it down.

18. The other great agency of the state's coercive force in *Barnaby Rudge* is the military, as we saw when we considered Joe Willet's service in the American War and as we shall see further in discussing Gabriel Varden's role as a militia sergeant.

19. And certainly it was far more than an assault on *private* property, for of course of the eight major buildings attacked by the rioters in this novel, the House of Commons and Newgate are not private property at all, and the two chapels both are and are not private property.

20. It is an interesting circumstance that one of the sources for Dickens's description of the destruction of Lord Mansfield's house is almost certainly G. L. Craik's description, not of the gutting of Mansfield's house in the Gordon Riots, but of the burning of the house and laboratory of "the celebrated Dr. Priestley," the radical and scientist, during the Birmingham Church and King riots of 1791. See Craik, *Sketches of Popular Tumults*, p. 131.

CHAPTER 7: The Riots 2: As Wild and Merciless as the Elements Themselves

1. *Letters of Dickens*, 2:417–18.
2. The syntax of the first clause of this passage's final sentence is slightly ambiguous: the demonstrative pronoun "those" refers back to "demons." Dickens is here paraphrasing Addison's *The Campaign*, and it is interesting to observe that whereas Addison imagines that it is an "Angel," who, "pleased the Almighty's order to perform, / Rides in the whirlwind, and directs the storm," Dickens replaces the angel with a demon. (These lines from *The Campaign* also stuck in Alexander Pope's mind; he parodies them in the *Dunciad*, Book III, ll. 263–64.)

   While Dickens was writing *Barnaby Rudge*, Tennyson had recently finished those central sections (51–56) of *In Memoriam*, which depict an even fiercer nature. For Tennyson (in this mood), such an all-devouring nature renders human culture a pathetic and meaningless delusion; whereas such a view of nature makes Dickens value human culture even more highly, as a counter-principle to nature.
3. The meanings of the adjective "wild" are so apposite in this connection that it is worth listing some of the *Oxford English Dictionary*'s relevant ones: "I. 1. Of an animal: Living in a state of nature; not tame, not domesticated. . . . 5. Of persons (or their attributes): Uncivilized, savage, uncultured, rude; also, not accepting, or resisting, the constituted government; rebellious. . . . II.6. Not under, or not submitting to, control or restraint. . . . 7.b. Giving way to sexual passions. . . . 8. Fierce, savage, ferocious; furious, violent, destructive, cruel. . . . 12. Not having control of one's mental faculties, out of one's wits. . . . 14. Artless, free, unconventional, fanciful, or romantic in style; having a somewhat barbaric character (usually in a good sense, as a pleasing quality). . . . b. Of strange aspect; fantastic in appearance. . . ." The whole history of Romanticism's transformation of the Western imagination is contained in the history of this word. While savoring the rich and fascinating complexity of the word "wild," a complexity which *Barnaby Rudge* turns to advantage, notice also how the meanings of the word start by describing Hugh and shade off into descriptions of Barnaby.
4. Norman Cohn, *Europe's Inner Demons* (New York: Basic Books, 1975), p. 73. My remarks on the idea of the demonic are heavily indebted to this work.
5. Most readers of *Barnaby Rudge* will have noticed the strong operation in it of what seems to be what Freud called the "death instinct." But it is important to notice also that the "death instinct" is here simply the logical final step of the urge to destroy *everything*, whereas Freud's formulation reverses the terms and deems the aggressive instinct the "derivative" of the (presumably prior and more fundamental) "death instinct" (*Civilization and Its Discontents*, p. 69). Later psychoanalytic thought has been unhappy with the "death instinct" formulation and has tacitly allowed it to lapse. But having abandoned the Freudian death instinct, the psychoanalysts have provided no comprehen-

sive theoretical account of aggression to take its place; and modern culture as a result finds its primary systematic explanation of human behavior embarrassed and confused on this central human problem. Certainly Dickens's view that a primary aggressive urge can result in aggressive behavior against the self seems much more plausible than the inverted relationship Freud posits between these two terms.

6. *Oxford English Dictionary*, s.v. "fierce" 1. The Latin root, *ferus*, not only has the literal meaning of "wild," "untamed," or "uncultivated" but has also the figurative sense, which the word "fierce" in some contexts retains, of "savage" or "uncivilized" (*Cassell's New Latin Dictionary*, s.v. "ferus").

7. Christopher Hibbert, *King Mob: The Story of Lord George Gordon and the London Riots of 1780* (Cleveland and New York: World, 1958), p. 121.

8. "Maniac" is one of those words that sums up in itself a whole complex of the ideas that we have been dealing with, at least according to the classification of Andrew Boorde in *The Breviary of Healthe* (1547): "*Mania* is the greke. In latin it is named *Insania* or *Furor*. In Englishe it is named a madnes or wodnes like a wylde beaste" (*Oxford English Dictionary*, s.v. "mania").

9. John Milton, *Paradise Lost*, Book I, ll. 210, 229, 46, and "Argument."

10. There are several explanations of why the rioters died from drinking this liquor. In *Barnaby*'s account, the rioters die because the gin they drink is scorching hot or actually flaming, and other writers give the same account (e.g., Rudé, *Paris and London in the Eighteenth Century*, pp. 273–74). But other accounts attribute the rioters' deaths at Langdale's to their drinking of (poisonous) unrectified spirits (e.g., Craik, *Sketches of Popular Tumults*, p. 83). Or they could have died from acute alcoholic poisoning.

11. *Measure for Measure*, I.ii.128–34.

12. *Troilus and Cressida*, I.iii.103–24.

13. And this does not exhaust the catalogue of resemblances between Ulysses' speech and the central propositions of *Barnaby*. For example, when Ulysses tells us that, without civilization, "Strength should be lord of imbecility," we are reminded of the relations between Dickens's representatives of the strength and imbecility of uncivilized man, Hugh and Barnaby. And Ulysses' belief that, if you abolished civilization, "the rude son should strike his father dead" reminds us that, in the first half of *Barnaby*, Dickens imagines such filial aggression as the specific antithetical counterprinciple to civilization: Mr. Rudge's murder of Reuben Haredale is a case in point, and the problem of such aggression and its repression are at the heart of Dickens's representation of the various father-son relationships which form the subject matter of Part I of the novel. Indeed, even Shakespeare's image of "the bounded waters . . . lift[ing] their bosoms higher than the shores" puts us in mind of how often Dickens describes the mob as a "human sea" engulfing this or that building. There is scarcely a major theme of Dickens's novel that is not to be found in these lines from *Troilus and Cressida*.

Before leaving the theme of the rioters' *self*-destruction, we should note that the casualty figures for the Gordon Riots are in sober fact shocking. Estimating "how many people in all lost their lives because of the riots," Christopher Hibbert concludes, "Allowing for the exaggeration in the accounts of eyewitnesses and journalists and taking into account the military reports in the Public Record Office the figure seems probably to have been not less than 850" (*King Mob*, p. 179n.).

CHAPTER 8: The Riots 3: Pirates and Patriots

1. Eric J. Hobsbawm, *Primitive Rebels* (New York: Norton, 1965), p. 125.
2. According to E. P. Thompson, who, however, in the same breath recognizes "the deficiencies in [Rudé's] analysis" (Thompson, *The Making of the English Working Class*, p. 76n.).
3. Rudé, *Paris and London in the Eighteenth Century*, p. 289.
4. Norman Cohn, *Pursuit of the Millennium*, revised and expanded edition (New York and London: Oxford University Press, 1970).
5. Ibid., pp. 172, 174, 175–76.
6. Thus, for example, the members of one sect "were often naked together, saying that one ought not to blush at anything that was natural. To be naked and unashamed, like Adam and Eve, they regarded as an essential part of the state of perfection on earth; and they called this 'the state of innocence'" (ibid., p. 180).
7. Ibid., pp. 150, 177, 158.
8. Ibid., p. 178, quoting John of Brünn.
9. Freud, *Civilization and Its Discontents*, p. 43.
10. Cohn, *The Pursuit of the Millennium*, p. 286.
11. Ibid., pp. 148, 151.
12. Thompson, *The Making of the English Working Class*, pp. 880–81.
13. Ibid., p. 881. We do not have to go as far back as the mid-nineteenth century to find millennial sects of the type Norman Cohn describes. A full-fledged example can be found in Charles Manson and his equally deranged followers, murderers of film actress Sharon Tate and six other victims in Hollywood in 1969. See Vincent Bugliosi and Curt Gentry, *Helter Skelter* (New York: Bantam Books, 1975).
14. Even the name of their society, which sounds like a modern youth gang, has reactionary overtones, conjuring up what Thomas Arnold identified as the radical individualism of the chivalric ethos, which he believed to be utterly opposed, in its "ideal of personal honor and personal glory," to "the collective principle embodied in the State" (Lionel Trilling, *Matthew Arnold* [London: Unwin, 1949], p. 54).
15. John Butt and Kathleen Tillotson, *Dickens at Work* (London: Methuen, 1957), p. 82.

16. See T. A. Jackson, *Dickens: The Progress of a Radical* (London, 1937), pp. 27–28; and Patrick Brantlinger, "The Case Against Trade Unions in Early Victorian Fiction," *Victorian Studies* 13 (1969): 38.
17. Butt and Tillotson, *Dickens at Work*, p. 82.
18. Christopher Hill, *Puritanism and Revolution* (New York: Schocken, 1964), p. 57.
19. Ibid., 118.
20. Ibid., pp. 117–18; George Rudé, *The Crowd in History, 1730–1848* (New York: Wiley, 1964), p. 179.
21. Thompson, *The Making of the English Working Class*, pp. 837, 836, 254–55.
22. Ibid., pp. 466, 557.
23. M. H. Abrams, "English Romanticism: The Spirit of the Age," in *Romanticism Reconsidered*, ed. Northrop Frye (New York: Columbia University Press, 1963), pp. 34–36.
24. Thompson, *The Making of the English Working Class*, chs. 2, 5, 11 (part 2); p. 882. See especially p. 54 on just what it means to say that political ideas were "clothed" in religious language.
25. Ibid., pp. 865, 867, 882–87.
26. Ibid., p. 865.
27. Ibid., pp. 921, 922n.
28. Carlyle, *Chartism*, ch. vi (*Works*, 19:156).
29. Ibid., p. 157.
30. Brantlinger, "The Case Against Trade Unions in Early Victorian Fiction," p. 38.

CHAPTER 9: The Authority Erected by Society for Its Own Preservation

1. Rousseau, *The Social Contract*, p. 78. Rousseau, *Second Discourse*, pp. 151–53, describes the process by which this happened.
2. Hobbes, *Leviathan*, pp. 223, 227; see also Rousseau, *Second Discourse*, pp. 158–60. In the *Second Discourse*, but not in the *Social Contract*, Rousseau is deeply ambivalent about this agreement, sensing that the social contract is in large measure a swindling contract, bringing into existence a society that in time will inevitably fall into such corruption as to be at last no better than the pure state of nature itself. How this corruption can be avoided or at least retarded is a central concern not just of the *Social Contract* but of the *Letter to D'Alembert*.
3. Hobbes, *Leviathan*, pp. 223, 185.
4. Rousseau, *Social Contract*, p. 64.
5. Hobbes, *Leviathan*, p. 188.
6. Rousseau, *Social Contract*, p. 83.
7. By the time *Barnaby Rudge* came to be written, Dickens had also changed the original spelling "Vardon" to the final form "Varden."

8. Hobbes, *Leviathan*, pp. 186–87.

9. Ibid., p. 699.

10. And indeed, our passage continues thus: "Tink, tink, tink. The locksmith paused at last, and wiped his brow. The silence roused the cat, who, jumping softly down, crept to the door, and watched with tiger eyes a bird-cage in an opposite window." This detail of the cat shows plainly enough the reservations in Dickens's mind as he describes his representative of public authority: the bird in the cage is powerless innocence in jail; the tiger-eyed cat suggests free aggression threatening it in its prison. In other words, while Dickens writes about Varden, he has in his mind also Mr. Dennis, the hangman, whose significance will be discussed shortly.

11. In H. H. Gerth and C. Wright Mills, eds. and trans., *From Max Weber: Essays in Sociology* (New York and London: Oxford University Press, 1958), pp. 77–128.

12. Ibid., pp. 77–78, 212, 119–20, 121, 123.

13. Ibid., p. 117.

14. Isaiah Berlin, "The Originality of Machiavelli," in *Studies on Machiavelli*, ed. Myron P. Gilmore (Firenze: Sansoni, 1972), pp. 177–79. What is the relation of this remarkable essay to Weber's "Politics as a Vocation"? Weber's greatest intellectual debt in these pages is of course to Machiavelli, whom he invokes throughout this speech and especially at its climactic moment (see Gerth and Mills, *From Max Weber*, p. 126). Weber has here made much more explicit what is only latent, though pervasive, in Machiavelli's thought. But even in "Politics as a Vocation," much remains unstated, and it is only in Isaiah Berlin's essay that all this becomes fully articulate—whether influenced by Weber or not, one can only speculate. But if there be such a thing as a hermeneutic circle, surely these three thinkers have joined hands in it.

15. Weber, "Politics as a Vocation," in Gerth and Mills, *From Max Weber*, p. 126.

16. Hobbes, *Leviathan*, p. 186; Freud, *Civilization and Its Discontents*, p. 58.

17. Thomas Holcroft, *A Plain and Succinct Narrative of the Late Riots and Disturbances . . .* , by William Vincent (London: Fielding & Walker, 1780; reprinted as *Thomas Holcroft's A Plain and Succinct Narrative of the Gordon Riots*, ed. Garland Garvey Smith [Atlanta: Emory University Press, 1944]), p. 28.

18. *Fanaticism and Treason: Or, a Dispassionate History of the . . . Rebellious Insurrections in June 1780*, by a Real Friend to Religion and to Britain (London: G. Kearsly, 1780), p. 42.

19. Craik, *Sketches of Popular Tumults*, p. 23.

20. Those assumptions are transparently clear in the language Dickens used at this time in a letter to an Edinburgh acquaintance who, in his capacity as sheriff, had unhesitatingly called in the military and stopped an incipient riot in its tracks: "I am delighted to hear the Orsons are at peace, and that you, Valentine, got home again undamaged" (*Letters of Dickens*, 2:338).

21. Craik, *Sketches of Popular Tumults*, pp. 66–68.

22. This copy of Holcroft's *Narrative* is now in the Emory University Library, Atlanta, Georgia.
23. Hobbes, *Leviathan*, p. 699.
24. This squib is reprinted in full in Chapter 17 of Forster, *Life of Dickens*, 1:253–54).
25. Ibid., 1:253–54.
26. William Smith, *Smaller Classical Dictionary* (New York: Dutton, 1958), p. 99.
27. Rousseau, *Social Contract*, p. 79.
28. Ibid., pp. 84–85.
29. Dennis's boast that, to preserve the gallows, he is willing to get hanged himself turns out to be an accurate prophecy of his fate in *Barnaby Rudge*. But the historical Edward Dennis, having indeed been sentenced to death for his part in the disturbances, was (as the editor of the Penguin *Barnaby Rudge* reminds us on p. 754) "reprieved and pardoned, 'so that he could hang his fellow rioters.'"
30. Charles Dickens, "Capital Punishment," in *Miscellaneous Papers*.
31. This is a true story, reported in a speech delivered by Sir William Meredith in 1777 in the House of Commons, as Dickens tells us in the preface. In the preface to the Charles Dickens Edition of 1867, he reprints the relevant portion of the speech.
32. Forster, *Life of Dickens*, 1:223.
33. Ibid., p. 220.
34. Letter of 16 March 1846 to the *Daily News*, reprinted along with Dickens's two earlier letters on this subject to the *Daily News* as "Capital Punishment" in *Miscellaneous Papers*. Yet by 1859, as Philip Collins points out, Dickens had changed his mind and had "withdrawn his opposition to hanging as such" (Collins, *Dickens and Crime*, pp. 245–46).
35. *Nicholas Nickleby*, ch. 53.

CHAPTER 10: *American Notes*

1. Forster, *Life of Dickens*, 1:252–53. Both the song and the statement date from 1841.
2. *Letters of Dickens*, 3:90, 156, 176.
3. Monboddo, *Origin and Progress of Language*, 1:190, 1. See also Daniel Defoe, *Mere Nature Delineated: or, A Body Without a Soul* (London: T. Warner, 1726), p. 68.
4. Aristotle, *Politics*, trans. Ernest Barker (London and New York: Oxford University Press, 1958), I.ii.1253a.
5. *Barnaby Rudge*, ch. 45.
6. Rousseau, *Second Discourse*, p. 155.
7. Defoe makes the same point about the deaf and dumb in *Mere Nature Deline-*

ated, p. 59, where he compares them to Peter the Wild Boy; see also p. 18.

8. Aristotle, *Politics*, I.ii.1253a.

9. *Letters of Dickens*, 3:111, 123–24.

10. Maximillian E. Novak, *Defoe and the Nature of Man* (London and New York: Oxford University Press, 1963), p. 33.

11. Cornelius de Pauw, *Recherches philosophiques sur les Américains ou Memoires intéréssants pour servir à l'histoire de l'espèce humaine* (Berlin, 1768–69), quoted in Antonello Gerbi, *The Dispute of the New World: The History of a Polemic, 1750–1900*, trans. J. Moyle (Pittsburgh: University of Pittsburgh Press, 1973), p. 53.

12. *Barnaby Rudge*, ch. 5.

13. *Letters of Dickens*, 3:124.

14. We can see even more clearly how profoundly impressed Dickens was by these prisoners when we remark that he drew on them seventeen years later as models for Dr. Manette in *A Tale of Two Cities*, as Collins observes in Chapter 5 of *Dickens and Crime*. The original title of that novel, Collins observes (p. 133), was *Recalled to Life*, and John Gross writes that Dickens had considered calling the novel *Buried Alive* (Gross and Pearson, *Dickens and the Twentieth Century*, p. 187).

15. Clifford Geertz, *The Interpretation of Cultures* (New York: Basic Books, 1973), p. 5.

16. Hobbes, *Leviathan*, p. 160.

17. *Letters of Dickens*, 3:158.

18. *Martin Chuzzlewit*, ch. 17.

19. See Quentin Anderson, "Property and Vision in 19th-Century America," *Virginia Quarterly Review* 54 (Summer 1978): 385–410; and Stephen Donadio, *Nietzsche, Henry James, and the Artistic Will* (New York and London: Oxford University Press, 1978).

20. John Stuart Mill, *On Liberty* (1859), ch. 3.

21. Carlyle, *Works*, 10:146.

22. Ibid., 4:247.

23. Rousseau, *Second Discourse*, p. 175.

24. As the editors of the Penguin edition of *American Notes* remind readers, Louise H. Johnson (in an article entitled "The Source of the Chapter on Slavery in Dickens' *American Notes*," *American Literature* 14 [January 1943]: 427–30) has demonstrated that Dickens drew these advertisements not directly from the newspapers themselves but rather from a pamphlet compiled by the American Anti-Slavery Society.

25. Thomas Moore, "Epistle VII: To Thomas Hume," in *Epistles, Odes and Other Poems* (1806). In the same volume, see also "Epistle VI: To Lord Viscount Forbes."

26. *Martin Chuzzlewit*, ch. 21.

27. *Letters of Dickens*, 3:141.

28. Ibid., p. 135.
29. *Nicholas Nickleby*, ch. 25.
30. Orwell, "Charles Dickens," in *The Collected Essays, Journalism, and Letters of George Orwell*, 1:460.
31. "Crime and Education," *Miscellaneous Papers*.
32. "Ignorance and Crime," *Miscellaneous Papers*.
33. Quoted in Trilling, *Matthew Arnold*, p. 381.

CHAPTER 11: *Martin Chuzzlewit* in Context

1. *Dictionary of National Biography*, s.v. "Burnett, James."
2. Monboddo, *Origin and Progress of Language*, 1:289, 189n.
3. Rousseau, *Second Discourse*, pp. 204–9.
4. Monboddo, *Origin and Progress of Language*, 1:381n., 144, 437, 24–25, 360–61.
5. Ibid., 1:188, 258–63 and note. Boswell's account of Johnson quoted in Lovejoy, *Essays in the History of Ideas*, p. 46. In discussing Monboddo, I follow a trail blazed by Lovejoy in his essay on "Monboddo and Rousseau."
6. *Letters of Dickens*, 3:23. Dickens also attended his mesmeric lectures and demonstrations.
7. *Dictionary of Scientific Biography* (New York: Scribner's, 1970), vol. 2; *The Encyclopedia of the Social Sciences* (New York: Macmillan, 1930), vol. 2; *Nouvelle Biographie Générale* (Paris: Firmin Didot Frères, 1853; reprint, Copenhagen: Rosenkilde and Bagger, 1964), vol. 5–6; *Encyclopaedia Britannica*, 11th ed., vol. 4; the *Times* (3 February 1840); *Morning Chronicle* (3 February 1840).
8. *On the Natural Varieties of Mankind: The Anthropological Treatises of Johann Friedrich Blumenbach* [etc.], trans. Thomas Bendyshe (1865; reprint, New York: Bergman, 1969), p. 296.
9. Johann Friedrich Blumenbach, "Über Menschen-Racen und Schweine-Racen," *Magazin für das neueste aus der Physik und Naturgeschichte* 6 (Gotha, 1789): 1–13.
10. Blumenbach, *Contributions to Natural History*, Part 1 (1806), reprinted in *On the Natural Varieties of Mankind* (etc.), pp. 290–96.
11. Ibid., Part 2 (1811), pp. 329–31; Novak, "The Wild Man Comes to Tea," in Dudley and Novak, *The Wild Man Within*, pp. 183–84; Defoe, *Mere Nature Delineated; or, A Body Without a Soul, Being Observations upon the Young Forester Lately Brought to Town from Germany*, pp. 4, 17, 5, 8, 16, 1, 61, 68, 63.
12. Lord Monboddo, *Antient Metaphysics: or, The Science of Universals* (London: Cadell; Edinburgh: Balfour, 1779–99), 3:62, 67, 68, 57, 65.
13. Blumenbach, *Contributions to Natural History*, Part 2, pp. 329–40.
14. *Measure for Measure*, II.ii.118–24.
15. Edward Tyson, *Orang-Outang sive Homo Sylvestris or, the Anatomy of a Pygmie*

(1699), quoted in Dudley and Novak, *The Wild Man Within*, p. 189.

16. Hobbes, *Leviathan*, ch. 13.

17. Locke, *Second Treatise*, p. 343.

18. J. H. Elliot, *The Old World and the New, 1492–1650* (Cambridge: Cambridge University Press, 1970), p. 24.

19. Peter Martyr, *Decades*, quoted in Elliot, *The Old World and the New*, p. 26. The Elizabethan translator is named—what else?—Eden.

20. Richard Hakluyt, *Voyages*, quoted in Harry Levin, *The Myth of the Golden Age in the Renaissance* (New York: Oxford University Press, 1969), p. 66.

21. Michael Drayton, "To the Virginian Voyage" (1606).

22. *The Tempest*, II.i.155–56; see Frank Kermode's introduction to the Arden edition (London: Methuen, 1962), pp. xxv–xliii.

23. *The Tempest*, I.ii.390–404. These lines from *The Tempest* are made to play a similar role in *The Waste Land*, where they serve to underscore by contrast the unmitigated sordidness of the antipastoral world T. S. Eliot excoriates. In this context, I cannot resist mentioning a pleasant reminder of the smallness of the world. When Dickens was in America, he was taken on an expedition to the Looking-Glass Prairie by "a very friendly companionable party" of gentlemen from St. Louis, as he recounts in *American Notes*. Among this party of a dozen or so, Dickens singles out for mention in a letter to Forster only one man, the Unitarian minister of St. Louis, "an intelligent, mild, well-informed gentleman of my own age," with whom he took a pleasant, friendly walk and shared a bedroom in the inn. This man, as the editors of the Pilgrim *Letters* note, was William Greenleaf Eliot (1811–87), who later founded Washington University in St. Louis (*Letters of Dickens*, 3:200–201). He was also, as they do not note, T. S. Eliot's grandfather.

24. Buffon is quoted in Gerbi, *The Dispute of the New World*, pp. 3–9. For one of Buffon's phrases, I use the translation of Hugh Honour in *The New Golden Land: European Images of America from the Discoveries to the Present Time*, p. 51. The inventory Dickens made of his books in 1844 is printed in the Pilgrim *Letters of Dickens*, 4:711–26.

25. Quoted in Gerbi, *The Dispute of the New World*, pp. 5–6. John Keats had used similar terms in his poem "To Fanny" to describe "that most hateful land" where "great unerring Nature once seems wrong." For in America the rivers are ungoverned by any "weedy-haired [river] gods," the winds have no zephyrs to direct them, the forests are untenanted by any Dryads: nature there is purely natural, undomesticated even by *this* kind of culture. Earlier still, Oliver Goldsmith, in *The Deserted Village* (ll. 345–58), had characterized America as a "horrid shore" with an intolerable, blazing sun, "matted woods," "poisonous fields with rank luxuriance crowned," scorpions, rattlesnakes, savages, tornados, and tigers.

26. Marcus, *Dickens: From Pickwick to Dombey*, p. 253.

27. *Dombey and Son*, chs. 27, 26, 21.

28. *Little Dorrit*, ch. 20.
29. Quoted in Honour, *The New Golden Land*, pp. 78, 56.
30. Thomas Moore, *Epistles, Odes, and Other Poems* (1806), preface.
31. Plato, *Republic*, trans. Desmond Lee, 2d ed. (Harmondsworth: Penguin, 1974), p. 106.
32. Rousseau, *Second Discourse*, p. 102.
33. Marcus, *Dickens: From Pickwick to Dombey*, p. 256.
34. Ibid., pp. 256, 257.
35. Stave One. I follow the punctuation of the manuscript: the comma was misplaced in the first edition and remains misplaced in most subsequent editions.

Index